SOCCER:
The Road to Crisis

SOCCER: The Road to Crisis

Anton Rippon

MOORLAND PUBLISHING

Illustrations have been provided by:
John Grainger: p 9, 12, 24, 27, 34-5, 37, 42,
92 (lower), 96 (both), 99, 112, 123, 127, 129,
132, 135, 140, 163, 167, 174, 180, 191, 193;
Coventry Evening Telegraph: p 8; Oxford
Mail and Times: p 17; Crewe Chronicle: p
18; Ashbourne News Telegraph: p 21; BBC
Hulton Picture Library: p 61, 79, 89, 92
(top); Bolton Evening News: p 64; Liver-
pool Daily Post and Echo: p 82; Steve
Bacon: p 109; Evening Gazette, Middles-
brough: p 117; Lincolnshire Echo: p 156;
Hull Daily Mail: p 159; London Weekend
Television: p 187; Wolverhampton Express
and Star: p 70; Evening Post-Echo (Hemel
Hempstead): p 83; Anthony Simms: p 194.

The author wishes to thank John Grainger
for compiling the index of this book.

For Nicola

Printed by Dotesios (Printers) Ltd
of Bradford-on-Avon, Wiltshire
for Moorland Publishing Co Ltd,
9-11 Station Street, Ashbourne,
Derbyshire, DE6 1DE England.
Telephone: (0335) 44486

British Library Cataloguing
in Publication Data

5331

Rippon, Anton
    Soccer: the road to crisis.

796.334

    1. Soccer — History
    I. Title
    796.33'09'04   GV943

Contents

1   A Game in Crisis   7
2   More Than Just A Game   15
3   The Game Nobody Invented   20
4   The People's Game   31
5   The Clubs   41
6   Tactics - 1   46
7   A National Industry   53
8   The Golden Years   59
9   Wider Horizons   66
10 Tactics - 2   74
11 The Players   88
12 The Managers   119
13 The Money and The
        Directors   147
14 The Union   165
15 The Violent Face of
        Football   169
16 Football and Television   180
17 The Future - Soccer in
        2000 AD?   190

A Game in Crisis

Three stories dominated the sports pages of the national newspapers on Saturday, 7 May 1983, adequately summing up the plight of Britain's national winter sport. It was the penultimate Saturday of the league season and that afternoon there were several matches vital to the outcome of promotion and relegation issues throughout the four divisions of the Football League. Liverpool already knew that they were league champions for the seventh time in eleven seasons, and Queen's Park Rangers and Wolverhampton Wanderers were already assured of First Division football. One or two other matters were also settled, but there was still much at stake and twenty years earlier the headlines would have concentrated on the afternoon's matches.

However in 1983, after a century of professional football, it was what happened off the field which took up more column-inches than what happened on it, and this particular Saturday was no exception. The three football stories which had prominence that day concerned two clubs, Coventry City and Stockport County, and also the subject of televised soccer. Coventry, the club which had shown football a brave new way twenty years earlier, was a club in crisis. Bent on changing the image which had served it well enough in the 'Swinging Sixties', Coventry City stood poised to scrap the Sky Blue theme which had been introduced by Jimmy Hill when he became manager in 1961. Hill had, that week, been deposed as chairman, the much-vaunted all-seater stadium of the future was to be returned to the traditional mix of seats and terraces, the axe hung over the club's luxurious £1.5 million training and leisure complex which had been hailed as the way in which football had to be run in the next century, and even the sky blue playing strip was to be abolished if supporters could come up with something better. The formula which had transformed Coventry City from a Fourth Division club with a ground which had all the atmosphere of a graveyard, into a busy, bright First Division club with big attendances was being swept away and nothing in the once-magic recipe was sacrosanct. The fact that Coventry had spent the past sixteen years in the First Division counted for nothing because they had won nothing. Attendances were down because the supporters wanted success.

At the other end of the scale Stockport County, the Fourth Division club, were reported to be just four days away from a High Court hearing to wind up the club. A reprieve had come in the unlikely form

Seating on what was at one time traditional terraced standing accommodation at Coventry's Highfield Road was hailed as the soccer stadium of the future. The experiment however, was unsuccesful.

of the Inland Revenue who had agreed to postpone half of the £120,000 which Stockport were reported to owe in PAYE payments. The secretary of the Professional Footballers' Association, Gordon Taylor, had negotiated an agreement which had saved, for the moment at least, the club's players from joining the ever-increasing ranks of the unemployed. Ironically, the previous evening Stockport had enjoyed one of their better attendances when over five and a half thousand people had watched them play Port Vale. But Port Vale were riding high towards promotion and the gate receipts had been swelled by their own supporters. Normally the figure at the regular Friday evening league matches at Edgeley Park was well below that number. A few minutes drive from Manchester, and United and City, Stockport had been forced to switch their home games away from the traditional Saturday afternoon and join the small band of Third and Fourth Division clubs who played on Fridays in the hope of increasing their support. A quarter of a century earlier Stockport County always played on Saturday afternoon. Even in the days of the Busby Babes of Old Trafford there were more than enough spectators to go round.

The third story on that May Saturday concerned the televising of league football in 1983-4. Twenty years earlier there were no televised league games, only cup finals, internationals and European matches. A plan to screen league games in 1960-1 had died a premature death after the first one resulted in a poor attendance and an equally poor

Although Fourth Division Stockport County offer a warm welcome to their spartan ground, the club was one of many threatened with closure in 1983. Life in the bottom reaches of the league is doubly difficult when glamorous Manchester United play just a few miles up the road.

match, and not until BBC switched its Match of the Day, begun in 1964 on BBC2, to BBC1 in 1966, did viewing figures soar and televised football become an accepted part of the game. But now, as football attendances dropped so did viewing figures (though not just for football, it should be said) and the recurring story throughout the 1982-3 season had been the renewal of contracts by BBC and ITV. There were many people in the game who claimed that the televising of too much football was a primary cause of the game's drop in popularity as a major spectator sport; but the real debate was about money. Many felt that television had been getting its soccer on the cheap. The question now was how much was television prepared to pay?; and would it allow shirt advertising which had previously been a subject both BBC and ITV had refused even to discuss.

The question of the correct balance was also held to be critical. Would it be better to reduce the number of recorded highlights, or would a live match, or matches, taken out of the weekly league programme and played on a Saturday evening or Sunday afternoon prove to be the answer? A counterbid by a company which offered football a considerably higher sum than television, in return for the right to screen video recordings in public houses on Monday evenings, had been withdrawn; there were many who felt that football's image was tarnished enough without forcing people into licensed premises to watch it, and the negotiations were now solely with BBC and ITV.

On the second Saturday of May 1983, football and television appeared to be as far from reaching an agreement as at any time during

9

the season, and John Bromley, the ITV head of sport, called the Football League's four-man television negotiating team *a bunch of amateurs*. Television had offered a 'final' deal of a £5.3 million package for the rights to screen live matches over a period of two years, a package which would also openly recognise the name of a sponsor who was prepared to give the Football League £3 million if agreement with television could be reached, and a limited amount of shirt advertising which had previously proved an insurmountable hurdle. But the ninety-two clubs which comprise the Football League rejected the offer unanimously. The sticking point was the number of live matches. Bromley and Jonathan Martin, BBC's head of sport, withdrew their offer. Said Bromley in a *Daily Mail* interview, *The tragedy with football is that it lacks leadership and authority. The sport is disintegrating in front of us . . . football is being run like it was in the 1920s. Major surgery is needed and if football cannot perform its own surgery, then from where I sit the game will continue on the decline, and that is very sad.*

So the football stories which dominated the sports pages at the end of 1982-3 were not about vital matches, talented players and great goals, and so it had been for some considerable time. The picture painted was one of a game in decline, a game with crippling debts and with some of its professional clubs on the verge of extinction. On the same day that Coventry, Stockport and television made the headlines for reasons unconnected with that day's league programme, it was announced that Chesterfield, already relegated to the Fourth Division, went to Oxford that afternoon with fears that mounting debts of more than £400,000 would engulf them. The following Saturday's final game of the season might well be the last in the club's 107-year history. Three weeks previously it had been announced that Third Division Wigan Athletic, the league's newest club and members for five years after a 40-year campaign to win such status, were £300,000 in debt and would go into liquidation at the end of the season. Hartlepool United were given a temporary stay of execution when a £52,000 tax claim against them was adjourned, a spokesman for an unnamed Fourth Division club said that his organisation was in a critical condition with no hope of clearing debts of more than £200,000, and Cardiff City's promotion to the Second Division saw only a modest amount of champagne uncorked because, at the last count, the Welsh club owed £1.5 million. Bristol City were operating only because a new company had been formed, and their neighbours Bristol Rovers now conducted their business from portable offices on the outskirts of the city and rented Eastville Stadium, their home for fifty years, only on match days.

It was not just the Third and Fourth Division clubs who were feeling the chill wind of poverty; some of the game's most famous names were in trouble. Wolverhampton Wanderers, founder-members of the Football League, had been only minutes from extinction that summer before being saved by a consortium engineered by a former player; Derby County, also founder-members, faced crippling debts and won time when a new board of directors took over; and Chelsea, another famous club, had twice been on the brink of disappearing under a mountain of unpaid bills. There was also the bizarre case of Crystal Palace who looked likely to be forced to sell a player, Kevin Mabbutt, to settle a debt with the creditors of the company which used to run Bristol City.

The London club had signed Mabbutt from Bristol City for a fee reported to be £100,000 and which was to be paid, as most transfer fees are today, by hire purchase. But they had fallen behind with the payments, thus preventing payments to the creditors of the old Bristol City company and delaying the legal winding-up process. One idea offered by a national newspaper was that the creditors of the old company could 'repossess' the footballer and sell him themselves. It was yet another example of how the problems facing football forced straightforward match reporting off the sports pages. The decline had reached even the topmost branch of the tree. Mighty clubs like Liverpool and Manchester United had reported recent big trading losses, and Manchester United, easily Britain's best-supported club, still had to face the fact that their average attendance in 1982-3 was their lowest for seventeen years and their season's total of 62,945 down on 1981-2.

Many reasons have been advanced for the decline in the fortunes of professional football. The financial plights of the clubs seems to have come about because of the apparent inability of football club directors to grasp the simple economics of Charles Dicken's Mr Micawber, and the result has been misery. But the game's problems are not simply the result of spending more than it has earned. Fewer people want to watch professional football. The emergence of players who were bought and sold for sums in excess of a million pounds, and who reportedly earned more than £1,000 per week, coincided with an alarming drop in weekly attendances. In 1950-1, when the Football League was enlarged to its present size, almost 40 million people watched league matches. Since then the crowds have fallen until, in 1982-3, the seasonal figure was less than 19 million, well over one million down in a single season. The decline has not been steady and there was a recovery immediately after England won the World Cup in 1966, but in 1972-3 there began another marked slump from which the game has not recovered.

The problem has been most acute, however, since 1979-80. In the twenty-one years from 1958-9 the drop in the number of people who passed through the turnstiles each season was nine million; between 1979-80 and 1982-3, a further six million had been lost. The fall of nine million between 1958-9 and 1979-80 had been more than offset by an increase of £27.5 million in gate receipts, due to proportionately higher admission charges; but in the early eighties, the dramatic fall in attendances, coming as it did during the worst economic recession in Britain for fifty years, left most clubs in a considerably weakened financial position. This has been compounded by big increases in expenditure. Wages, salaries and transfer fees have soared, clubs have spent more money than ever before on new stands and other ground improvements, some of it necessitated by the Safety of Sports Grounds Act, and much of the work has been financed by borrowing at unusually high interest rates. The dramatic decline in receipts over the three seasons following 1979-80 has therefore coincided with huge financial commitments and the result for many clubs has been massive overdrafts which have threatened the very existence of those clubs. The financial plight of soccer is causing grave concern, and the most worrying aspect of it all is the seasonal attendance figures which grow alarmingly smaller each season.

What are the reasons for the dwindling interest? Apart from the suggestion that television has done much to kill interest in football, there is the problem of hooliganism. The atmosphere of sheer joy and camaraderie which once flowed from league grounds has, it is claimed, been replaced by violence, obscentities, and the smell of fear. A Football League ground is no longer a place to take a wife and child. Then again, changing social habits, more sophisticated use of leisure time and a greater number of counter-attractions must also be valid

The unacceptable face of professional football in the eighties. A bloodied fan points out his assailant to a police officer. A national opinion poll showed that 10 per cent of 'lapsed' soccer fans cited fear of such violence as the main reason for their absence.

reasons why fewer people watch league football. The product, too, must take its share of the blame and it cannot be denied many people find the game itself much less entertaining than it was twenty years ago. It is better organised defensively, mistakes are eliminated and the game is too predictable, and therefore boring, to many supporters. They will ask where are the great individual stars who could bring perhaps 50,000 people to their feet, baying with delight at such inventive skill and absolute brilliance. The popular answer to the question of where are the Matthewses and Finneys, the Greaveses and Bests of today, is that coaches have stifled them, that young players have had fear put into their hearts, fear of doing anything other than the ultra-cautious. Coaches, it is alleged, have turned what was at one time a beautiful, simple, attacking game into a dour mix of sideways passing and defensive tactics which are geared to prevent the opposing side from playing before playing oneself. There is no doubt that the price put on success, and therefore the cost of failure, has resulted in crises like the one at Coventry where sixteen years of continuous First Division football (only four other clubs can boast that in recent times) have been insufficient to maintain the support of followers who demand, not just visits by the top clubs, but trophies.

Yet as a sport football is flourishing. At local amateur level more people play it than ever before, and more and more professional clubs have developed outside the Football League in recent times, many of them managing to make quite healthy profits. It is from the moment they join the Football League that their problems begin, so football is not so much a whole game in crisis, as a section of that game — the full-

Newcastle United made the bold decision to sign Kevin Keegan in 1982-3 and were rewarded with 150,000 extra spectators. But overall attendances were down yet again to 18.7 million, a loss of a further 1.25 million spectators on the previous season. Sixty-seven of the ninety-two clubs reported a fall and of the successful twenty-five, fourteen either won promotion or were already playing in a higher division. Swansea, relegated from Division One, lost over one-third of their total support in 1982-3.

time professional apex of a broad-based triangle. It seems that at the very time when soccer should be more attractive than ever before, to counter the new diversions and social habits which rob it of support, the game is in fact less entertaining than at any time since it became a major spectator sport in the last century. Coupled with that, the league clubs have indulged in reckless spending of money which they do not have, and they have thus compounded an already grave problem. Everything seems to have come together, or perhaps to be more precise, fallen apart at just the wrong time.

The above graph shows the attendances
of football matches since World War II.

Is there a quick and easy answer to these problems? Sixteen years ago the government of the day set up a committee of inquiry under the chairmanship of Sir Norman Chester. Its findings were largely ignored and in 1983 the more radical findings of a second Chester Committee, this time commissioned by the Football League itself, were also received with only lukewarm approval. The most radical change, the slimming-down of the First Division, was rejected and football once again showed itself to be a game resistent to major change. The structure of the Football League has remained largely unaltered for half a century and more. Yet a member of the Chester Committee, Cyril Townsend, who represented the Committee of London Clearing Banks, warned in a *Daily Express* interview immediately before the publication of the report in March 1983, *If clubs take the standpoint of staying together and protecting each other, they will go down the drain.* Speaking after it was revealed that the clubs were in debt to the banks to the tune of £40 million, he added, *I believe that there will no longer be a market for ninety-two full-time professional clubs.* Will football change, and if so, how? The reasons for the demise may be argued, so too may the possible solutions, but what is clear is that professional football has no divine right to exist come what may. The days of indulgent bank managers are over, so too, almost certainly, are the days of massive attendances. Football is indeed a game in crisis.

2

More Than Just a Game

To say that these men paid their shillings to watch twenty-two hirelings kick a ball is merely to say that a violin is wood and catgut, that Hamlet *is so much paper and ink. For a shilling the Bruddersford United AFC offered you Conflict and Art . . . .* So J B Priestley begins to describe the importance of a football club to a community. In *The Good Companions,* first published in 1929, Priestley tells the reader, *A man who had missed the last home match of 't' United' had to enter social life on tiptoe in Bruddersford.*

On the face of it the game of football is just that, a simple game with simple rules, but it would be naive in the extreme to dismiss it as 'just a game'. Football has many faces and is the one game which is played the world over; a game which has given us a universal language and which transcends colour and creed. In the dimly-lit bar of a small Mexican town in the autumn of 1980, the barman, on hearing my English voice, came across to our table, pumped me warmly by the hand and uttered just two words — 'Bobby Charlton'. He could speak no English, save the names of football stars, yet he wanted to communicate, and what better way to establish a common ground. Alas, I was unable to instantly recall the name of even one famous Mexican footballer and so the conversation was distinctly one-sided. Yet it did not matter. The feats of a man born in a small Northumberland mining town over forty years earlier had reached across the world. That Mexican barman might well have had difficulty in naming the British Prime Minister, but the name of the balding member of the 1966 World Cup-winning team caused him no problems. Football crosses barriers like no other medium.

What is the compelling attraction of association football? At its most obvious, football can be seen as warfare without weapons, a battle in which one team sets out to invade the other's territory. Yet this is only partly accurate, for, unlike real war, there is no intention to harm the opposing players. They are simply obstacles to be overcome on the way to planting the ball in the net. In that context football is a hunt with the goal as the prey and the ball used as the weapon. In his book *The Soccer Tribe* (Jonathan Cape, 1981), Desmond Morris explains the domination of soccer over all other sports by pointing out that for spectators, who can enjoy the event only by proxy, the more hunting elements there are on display, the more satisfying the sporting

15

Victory for the club means victory for the town or city. When Derby
County were revitalised by Brian Clough and Peter Taylor in the late sixties
and early seventies the town was alive with the phenomenon known as
football fever. Thousands thronged the streets to see the players bring
home their trophies after years of mediocrity.

ritual becomes, and association football retains more of the ancient
hunting elements than any other sport. Apart from the pseudo-
hunting quality of soccer, the sport offers several other faces,
according to Morris. Although it is misleading to look on a soccer
match as a kind of miniature war, because the teams are not, officially
at least, trying to destroy each other, it cannot be denied that there is a
warlike element in every game, and there is almost always a winner and
a loser, all of which adds to the excitement of the occasion. Soccer gives
us an emotional safety-valve and it is socially permissable for even the
most normally mild-mannered man to snarl and curse at a soccer
match, whereas such behaviour would probably lead to arrest if given
full rein in a supermarket on a Saturday morning.

Football also offers status to its followers and they readily identify
with the town team. Thus, a victory for that team is a victory for the
town, and it has been proved many times over that output in local
factories increases when the local team is doing well. In Derby, in the
late sixties and early seventies Brian Clough and Peter Taylor took the
local club into the First Division, after years of mediocre results, and
then steered it to the league title for the first time in the club's history.
That success came with the club's players on holiday in Majorca
having completed their programme and having to wait for other
results. I was dining in a local restaurant when news came through that
Derby County were champions. Suddenly, the pubs were full of people

who had heard the news on television, left their firesides, and poured into the streets. They wanted to share with each other the fact that their club was the best in England. To coin a journalistic cliche, Clough and Taylor 'had set the town alight'.

It is not simply success, however, that raises the temperature in a soccer town. When plans were announced in 1983 to merge Oxford United and Reading, two ailing clubs, to form a new side called Thames Valley Royals to play at a new stadium midway between the two, local passion ran high. Oxford supporters marched on the ground in protest, and at Reading the local *Evening Post* launched a campaign to keep league football in the town. More than one thousand letters and replies on the newspaper's own coupon were received, almost all against the takeover, and scores of people wanted to buy shares with one man offering £100,000 to help the club. Reading's mayor and the three major political parties on the council backed the campaign SOS — Save Our Soccer — and the High Court granted a temporary injunction to stop the merger. On the eve of the last match of the season the Reading chairman and two directors resigned and their shares reverted to the club. The editor of the *Evening Post,* Mr Peter Hiley, said, *We are delighted that Reading FC will now stay in the town.* So although neither club is well-supported, when there was a threat of extinction, public feeling ran high.

Football, then is also a social drug, and some political theorists have gone so far as to suggest that it has been used by capitalist bosses to keep the working class under control. The German political theorist, Gerhard Vinnai, wrote in *Football Mania* (Ocean Books, 1973) that the

When Robert Maxwell announced his idea of amalgamating Oxford United and Reading to form a new club playing at a new stadium midway between the two, the fans revolted. Poorly supported clubs under normal circumstances, both Oxford and Reading found plenty of emotion with the threat of their joint demise. This pre-match demonstration caused the delay of a Third Division game at Oxford in 1983.

disaffection caused by social conditions under advanced capitalism demands some form of emotional outlet. He said, *If this is not to lead to the overthrow of bourgeois society, it must be guided along 'safe' channels. Football provides an opportunity for emotional release of this kind . . . the pseudoactivity of football canalizes the engergies which could shatter the existing power structures.* He adds that in Victorian times *English entrepreneurs promoted the new sport, hoping that it would keep the workers away from political and trade union activity.* It is possible, if one stretches the imagination a good deal, to see football as a tool with which the ruling classes exploited the workers, at one and the same time finding something to occupy their new-found leisure time, and making them fitter for work in the cases of those who played rather than watched. In reality many enlightened employers were surely anxious about the well-being of their employees, and even if there was some self-interest in that, it could hardly have been to the extent of a sinister plot. It certainly did not stop the formation of trades unions and the labour movement. Nevertheless, perhaps, like religion, football was the 'opium of the masses'.

Religion is another way to view football. The great Liverpool manager, Bill Shankly, when asked if football was a matter of life and death, once answered, *Oh no, it is much more serious than that.* A big soccer match can resemble a religious ceremony. Although the lyrics

Football at Crewe is just as important to the club's small number of supporters as soccer at Anfield and Old Trafford is to the tens of thousands who support Liverpool and Manchester United. The Gresty Road ground is small and basic, but among the better-appointed of Fourth Division stadia and the fans of Crewe Alexandra are just as committed as those of the First Division giants. Even though they were forced to apply for re-election in 1983 Crewe's total attendance figure was 700 better than the previous season.

often offend, the songs of the terraces are like hymns, indeed, the tunes are often borrowed from the hymn book. Crowds come together and sing the praises of players who are sometimes referred to as 'gods'. The stadium is sometimes referred to as the 'shrine', Wembley Stadium is the 'mecca' of English football, the pitch is often the 'sacred turf'. The dressing room is a 'Holy of Holies' to many supporters, and they 'worship' the players. To draw the comparison between a big football match and a religious ceremony is not so far removed from reality. Certainly, for many people it is the one enriching experience of their week.

Football has often been called 'theatre'. Certainly it sets itself up, at the professional level, to be part of the entertainment industry. It has all the trappings of the world of show business: stars, fan clubs, even 'groupies', the young girls who attach themselves to star performers. Many of the incidents which happen during a football match are pure theatre. Relative to the match there are moments of high drama, tragedy and, on occasions, farce. There are great virtuoso performances, and there are performers who 'die'. The football pitch is a stage on which is enacted an unscripted play with a different ending for each performance, for no two football matches have ever followed exactly the same course, even if the final scoreline is sometimes the same.

Of course, show business is big business, and football is a big business too, though the restrictions on directors and shareholders, which will be explained more fully later, make it like no other business. The enormous amounts of money which have changed hands at the top level in recent years have made soccer into a multi-million pound sport, and yet many of its business deals are still conducted in a way which would seem amateurish in industry and commerce. Unlike some other countries, the United States for instance, soccer in Britain does not sell itself in the way in which one might expect such a business and an entertainment to do. In America, where they sell professional soccer as 'a kick in the grass', people are surely in it for the money. Perhaps it would be naive to suggest that in Britain, players see the cash as only a secondary consideration, and yet there is the overriding feeling, when talking to them, that they do love the game first and the money second.

Whatever the truth, there is no doubt that football is more than just a game. It occupies more space in the newspapers than any other single subject. Art and science compare badly by comparison with the number of column-inches swallowed up by soccer, and even politics does not manage to outscore the game. It is played in almost every country on earth, from giant stadia in capitals across the world, to windswept parks and sunscorched beaches, across widely differing cultures. No one who has ever been bitten by its bug — and there are tens of millions who have — can ever dismiss soccer as just twenty-two men kicking a ball.

3

The Game
Nobody Invented

Nobody invented football. The origins of the game which in the latter
half of the twentieth century has grown into a multi-million pound
part of the entertainment industry, albeit one which has reached a
crisis point, are lost in the mists of time. Exactly when and where the
first ball was kicked is a mystery which many of the game's historians
have tried to unravel. It is a task which has always eluded them, and it is
both unrewarding and pointless, for it is certain that ever since man
first learned the benefits of a curved surface, almost everywhere on
earth must have had some pastime which involved kicking or throwing
a spherical object. Football — and here the term has to be used to
encompass all such games and not simply the one we popularly know
as soccer — was a spontaneous pastime, often one which grew into
local tradition. Its appeal, as we have already seen, is both stunningly
simple and intricately weaved. At its most basic it was once warfare
without weapons and the early English ball games were violent affairs
in which severe injury, and even death, were not unknown. In the
Shrove Tuesday match at Derby, between the parishes of All Saints'
and St Peter's in 1796, one John Snape was killed, *an unfortunate victim
to this custom of playing football at Shrovetide.*

There are many examples of football being banned in England,
partly due to the often riotous nature of the games, partly due to the
fact that some monarchs and governments did not want large crowds
assembling for any purpose, lest the mob's wrath was turned on those
in authority. In the fourteenth and fifteenth century successive English
kings forbade football because they were worried that fit young men
might be injured and unable, or unwilling, to practise with the bow for
national defence. The Puritans banned football by ecclesiastical
decree, and the imminent end of the world was blamed upon *football
playing and other devilishe pastimes on the Sabbath.* Charles II
actually approved of the game but, later still, demonstrations against
enclosures of common ground grew out of crowds gathered to watch
football.

As towns and cities became busier, shopkeepers not unnaturally
objected to street football, and the 1835 Highways Act prohibited
football on the highway. This rough 'people's game' again came under
threat from the authorities. Yet it was increased urbanisation,
coupled, ironically, with a development in the English public schools,

The Shrovetide football game played annually at Ashbourne in Derbyshire is a relic of the old mob football of pre-industrial Britain. A similar game has survived at Kirkwall in the Orkneys where it is played at Christmas and New Year.

which gave birth to the game we know today. Football as played in towns and villages all over the country had, for centuries, known no uniformity. Where there were any rules they were so diverse as to render almost impossible a game between two different communities, so incompatible were their interpretations of football. The playing area might be anything from a field to the whole village; goals might be local landmarks, or they might be wooden posts, though even the posts could be of any dimension. Kicking was always allowed, handling the ball sometimes, and teams could number anything from a carefully regulated eleven to literally hundreds. All this was to change with the Industrial Revolution. The mines and dark satanic mills of Northern England and the Midlands meant that people with hitherto relatively generous leisure time were now working long hours, often in the most oppressive conditions. They had little inclination to organise or to participate in the hurly-burly of football on the few rest days that they enjoyed. The people's game was no longer theirs.

The salvation of football rested with the privileged classes who up until then had little to do with the rough, peasant games. Coincidental with the rise in industrialisation (and time-consuming factory life was only one reason why the old football had died out; there was a new middle-class philosophy that working people had no right to leisure time) came increased education for the children of the privileged and this brought a paradox where football was concerned. For years the public schools had drawn their pupils exclusively from the upper

21

classes. But in the 1830s-40s they underwent reform due to the new middle-class pressure to allow their offspring easier access to the public schools, and once there to be exposed to greater standards of discipline in work and behaviour.

Led by the reforms of Thomas Arnold, headmaster of Rugby from 1828-42, headmasters now looked towards *mens sana in corpore sano* and so there was the paradox of the rough game of football, so thoroughly condemned by the people who sent their sons to public schools, now being used as a means to organise and discipline the pupils there. It was agreed that outdoor pursuits were needed and football fitted the bill admirably. Hunting, shooting and fishing were expensive pastimes, beyond the reach of the sons of the new middle-class, but all that was needed for a game of football was a pitch and a ball. Suddenly the game of humble peasants and artisans assumed respectability, and so while the industrialisation of towns and cities, and the enclosures of much common land outside the main urban areas, had resulted in a drastic reduction in the old type of football, the need to curb indiscipline in the public schools had produced a new, tighter form, though again with little uniformity of rules. Though the development of football at the schools had resulted in a transformation of the old plebeian mob game into one which required discipline, teamwork and athleticism, there were still many different versions.

At Harrow, for instance, football was an eleven-a-side game, though it was played in a mudbath which was formed by the winter rains at the foot of the hill on which the school stands. A large, heavy ball was therefore needed and with a big pitch — about 150yd by 100yd — rules which allowed for movement were vital. High kicking and catching had to be allowed so that goals could be scored in such conditions. At Charterhouse the rules forbade handling, for here the game was played twenty-a-side on the stony cloisters, and this encouraged skilled dribblers, especially since no long kicks were allowed.

These variations were all very well so long as matches were confined to intra-school affairs; but when pupils left school and went on to university there were long debates over the rules before any game could be staged. Would carrying be permitted? How many players should there be in a team? How large should the goals be? What size pitch should be used? Clearly there was a need for a uniform set of rules and in 1848, fourteen students at Cambridge University sat down to draw up just that. Harrow, Eton, Winchester, Shrewsbury and Rugby were represented and each brought a copy of the rules of football played at their school. As might be expected the meeting was lengthy and debate continued from four o'clock in the afternoon until well after midnight. The 'Cambridge Rules' which emerged came down emphatically against carrying the ball, and the first die of the game we know as association football was cast.

22

Goals were scored by kicking the ball between two posts and under a length of rope which joined them; catching the ball was still permitted, but carrying it was not and the catcher had to kick it immediately; throw-ins and goal-kicks were given much as today, though the ball was thrown one-handed; and a man could pass the ball forward if the receiver had at least three opponents between him and the goal; tripping, hacking and pulling down an opponent were illegal. Football could now be played between any teams who agreed on these rules, without any of the previous lengthy arguments. The coming of the railways also meant that within the next few years, school teams would be able to travel much further afield in search of opposition, and the game of football would therefore gain a greater degree of uniformity. Loosely speaking, soccer, though the game was not yet called that, was the game played at Eton, Harrow, Westminster and Charterhouse; rugby was the game played at Rugby and their small but growing number of followers who allowed carrying.

Games under the Cambridge Rules were played at that university throughout the 1850s and taken further afield when graduates went out into the world. Given a common foundation, football benefited from the rapid industrialisation of the North and Midlands. Where the Industrial Revolution had all but killed off the old mob game, it now created a new breed of middle-class professional men who, unlike the workers, enjoyed considerable leisure time. They now aspired to football, the football of public school and university and not the plebeian game of earlier times. In the mid-1850s came the first football club of modern definition when former pupils of Sheffield Collegiate School, where they had presumably been taught by former public school men, put the Sheffield Club on a formal footing on 24 October 1857, though almost certainly matches had been played during the preceding two years. Sheffield is thus the oldest club in the world, still in existence today. In its infancy it was a fairly exclusive organisation and the occupations of the players' fathers were solidly middle-class. They wrote a set of rules based largely on the Cambridge Rules, though they were a trifle rougher and allowed pushing with the hands. The Sheffield committee decreed that 'the play day of the Club shall be Saturday from two o'clock until dark'. A second Sheffield club was formed the following year and a match between that club, Hallam, and Sheffield, on 12 February 1861 drew 600 spectators who saw Sheffield win 2-0 with the proceeds going to a local hospital. Other clubs were now springing up. Blackheath was founded in 1857, and two years later some Old Harrovians founded the Forest club (no relation to Nottingham Forest) to continue the dominance of public school football.

Sheffield, then, had its own set of football rules and still there was not complete uniformity, for the Sheffield Rules did not suit everyone. Still new variations were being discussed and published and in 1862 came *The Simplest Game* published by the Victorian educationalist J C

The Harrow School football team of 1867.

Thring, then an assistant master at Uppingham School, Rutland, where, incidentally, football was played with enormously wide goals. The rules themselves were unadventurous with no kicking the ball when it was off the ground, no physical contact, and no attacker being allowed in front of the ball. The wide goal made up for their unattractive nature and several schools adopted these new laws of football. In the autumn of 1862, a football match between Cambridge Old Etonians and Cambridge Old Harrovians closely paralleled Thring's rules. There was a neutral referee, as well as an umpire from each side, and the goals were twelve feet wide and up to twenty feet high. Play was to last for one and a quarter hours, there was to be the three-man offside law, and the teams were to be eleven-a-side.

The rules worked well and exactly one year later they formed the basis of a newly-revised set of Cambridge Rules when nine men from that university, representing Eton, Harrow, Shrewsbury, West-minster, Marlborough and Rugby, tightened up the original rules set down in 1848 and revised in subsequent years. Yet still there were variations, though the main division of opinion was whether or not the ball should be carried in the hands. In the early 1860s there were two definite kinds of football. It was either feet or hands which dominated the issue. The ball was either punted upfield from long scrimmages and then caught and carried under the arm; or else the player with the ball would dribble until he lost the ball. There was no passing and the star was the player who could run quickly with the ball at his feet, making as much ground as possible until he lost it in a ruck of opposing players who then set up a counter-attack. The differences were irreconcilable and the game of football was about to be divided forever.

On 26 October 1863, just a few days after the young men of Cambridge University issued their revised rules, a meeting of clubs took place at the Freemason's Tavern in Lincoln's Inn Field, London. Their purpose was nothing more than to codify the rules 'for the regulation of the game of football'. The clubs were not looking to spread the gospel of the game by forming an association, simply to establish one set of rules which would eliminate forever the often long and tedious debates which still seemed to precede almost every football match as the protaganists decided under which set of rules, or compromise, to play. The clubs represented were NN (No Names) from Kilburn, Barnes, War Office, The Crusaders, Forest (Leyton-stone), Perceval House (Blackheath), Crystal Palace, Blackheath, Kennington School, Surbiton, Blackheath School. Apart from an observer from Charterhouse there were no representatives from the public schools (as opposed to public school players with clubs), nor from Cambridge University, who had just drawn up their own rules, nor from the two principal football centres outside London, Sheffield and Nottingham.

The meeting was long and bitter, as indeed were the two which followed it in November and December. With the exception of Blackheath and the two Blackheath schools, everyone was committed to the dribbling game, and it was draft rules nine and ten which proved to be the stumbling blocks. The former allowed the player to run with the ball *if he makes a fair catch* and harked back to the days of Rugby School in the 1820s; the latter allowed a player to *charge, hold, trip or hack,* and that proved to be a point on which there was to be no agreement. The Blackheath man held that *hacking is the true football game and if it is done away with, then all the pluck and courage of the game will be at an end.* But the others, led by Barnes, claimed that if hacking was allowed *men of business would be unwilling to play football.* In short, the Rugby men felt it was both manly and desirable to kick the shins of opponents, and kick them hard. At that December meeting Blackheath left the Football Association (for that is what had been formed) and around its own brand of football was built up the rugby game, though the Rugby Union was not formed until 1871, when it immediately outlawed hacking. Strangely, out of all the clubs represented at that first meeting of the FA, only Blackheath, the rugby club, still exists at senior level.

But although great progress had been made by the formation of the FA, the control of the game passing out of the hands of the academics and into those of the clubs, there were still many local variations of the laws of the game. Well after the founding of the FA, any player was allowed to handle the ball. When he caught it he had to make a mark and win a free kick. In the first FA rules a 'touch down' was allowed, followed by a free kick at goal; the rugby try in fact. Offside still caused plenty of arguments with the first FA rules adopting the rugby-style of no one interfering with play in front of the ball. In fact the FA's first eight laws remain the basis of the laws of Rugby Union to this day.

There was a twenty-year delay before the laws were universally accepted, mainly due to the Football Association (in reality the London clubs) digging in their heels and largely ignoring the rest of the country. In 1862 there were fifteen football clubs in Sheffield and the following year the Sheffield Club wrote to the FA, enclosing its subscription and offering its opinion on certain points of the laws which Sheffield felt were *a very desirable code of laws.* Amongst Sheffield's proposals was the provision of a crossbar *without which it is sometimes difficult for an umpire to decide.* The FA did not respond immediately and for some time there was one set of rules for London and another for this part of Yorkshire, as well as others for different parts of the country. On 2 January 1865 for instance, Sheffield played their first out-of-town match when they visited Nottingham and played under 'Nottingham Rules'. The teams were eighteen-a-side and Sheffield won 1-0. Further defeats of Nottingham Forest and Lincoln established Sheffield as the major provincial club and on 31 March 1866, London and Sheffield met at last in Battersea Park. *The game,* wrote a newspaper reporter, *was a very hot one,* and London won by two goals and four touch-downs to nil.

Playing in that London-Sheffield match was an Old Harrovian named Charles W. Alcock. That year Alcock joined the Football Association committee and two years later he was responsible for inviting Yorkshire to send their first representative. This did not prevent the formation of a separate Sheffield Association which contributed much towards the game's development. The FA adopted the corner kick in 1872, but it was included in the Sheffield Rules four years earlier. The crossbar, as distinct from tape, was introduced into FA rules in 1875, but Sheffield had made bars compulsory well before that.

Most of the clubs which were founded around this time were still solidly middle and upper-class establishments and the formative years of the FA Cup competition underlined that. From when it was founded in 1872, until the first Northern professional side won it eleven years later, the FA Cup was dominated by London amateur clubs. Before the FA Cup was founded, however, football had to undergo several more fundamental changes. In 1869 goal-kicks were introduced, and the following year eleven-a-side games were finally accepted as standard. That same year also saw the introduction of the rule which set what is now association football apart from every other form of football in the world: the abolition of handling for any player, save the goalkeeper, left that position unique in world football. Until 1870 the player nearest the goal assumed the responsibility; from then, however, the goalkeeper was the only man allowed to handle the ball, though the penalty kick for an outfield player handling the ball in the penalty area was still two decades distant. In 1867 the offside law had been standardised to the three-man interpretation and stayed unaltered until 1925.

Charles W. Alcock, by now FA secretary, was one of the game's greatest administrators and his far-sightedness saw the introduction of both the FA Cup and international football. The first official England-Scotland game in 1872 had been preceded by games between England and a team of London-based Scots made up of people like William Gladstone, himself an MP and son of the Prime Minister, and Quintin Hogg, grandfather of Mrs Thatcher's Lord Chancellor, further proof that football was still a distinctly upper-class pastime. In 1871 Alcock suggested a knock-out cup competition based on the 'cock house' system of his former school, and played for by all members of the Football Association. Fifteen clubs entered with Donington School, Lincolnshire, and the Glasgow club Queen's Park being the only ones from outside the Home Counties. When the school was drawn away in Scotland in the first round it not surprisingly scratched from the competition. Other clubs had already withdrawn,

The programme for a match between Wanderers and the great Scottish club Queen's Park in 1875. Note that the players were distinguished, not by numbers, but by the colour of their caps or stockings.

Harrow Chequers and Reigate Priory giving Wanderers and Royal Engineers, respectively, byes into the next round, and it was these two clubs which provided the first FA Cup finalists.

Who were these two sets of players, Wanderers and Royal Engineers? The Wanderers had evolved from the Essex club, Forest, who were original members of the Football Association, and their leading light was none other than Charles W. Alcock. Originally a team of Old Harrovians, the club began in 1859 by playing games against ad hoc teams on the edge of Epping Forest. The secretary was J. F. Alcock, but it was his brother Charles who widened the club's membership and who took them to grounds throughout London, changing their name to the more apt Wanderers. They played in red, black and purple hooped shirts, and wore white cricket trousers tucked into black and white stockings. They were the archetypal football club of the period.

The Royal Engineers, who were 7-4 favourites, also had public school backgrounds. They were products of the Royal School of Military Engineering, set up at Chatham sixty years earlier. Their leader was Major Francis Marindin, brigade major at Chatham, Marindin was a keen footballer and he soon built up a fine association tradition there. The club joined the FA in 1869 and for the first few seasons of the FA Cup they were without doubt the best team in England. In four seasons they played eighty-six matches, won seventy-four and lost only three, two of them being FA Cup finals. Their colours were equally splendid and the Royal Engineers took to the field in red and blue hooped jerseys with matching caps and stockings and *dark blue serge knickerbockers.*

The spectators for that first FA Cup final, held at Kennington Oval, on 16 March 1872, paid one shilling each. They arrived in carriages and cabs and the atmosphere was predominantly that of the public school. The Royal Engineers team was comprised entirely of officers and they lined up in the usual formation of the day: one goalkeeper, one back, two half-backs and seven forwards, three in the middle of the line and two on either wing. Association football was still a dribbling game and not until the slick Scots dominated England in the mid-1870s was the benefit of the passing game finally accepted by the English. The Royal Engineers, according to Lieutenant Ruck, had centres *selected for weight, strength and charging powers as well as for their talent as dribblers . . . .* Apparently many of the goals scored by the Engineers were obtained *by hustling goalkeepers through their own goal all ends up.* The RE's were in fact one of the first English teams to realise the needs for 'passing-on' and 'backing-up' and Lord Kinnaird, another great figure in Victorian football, was moved to comment, *The Sappers had discovered a new development of the game due to greater combination.* We do not know if this style would have beaten the pure dribbling game of the Wanderers, for after ten minutes of the first FA Cup final, Lieutenant Cresswell broke his collar bone and the odds against Wanderers were cancelled. The Wanderers had the Reverend R. W. S. Vidal, the 'Prince of Dribblers', of Westminster, in their team and before half-time he had set up the only goal of the game for Betts, who was playing under the pseudonym of 'A. H. Chequer' (A Harrow Chequer).

The *Sporting Life* of 23 March 1872 reported the goal thus: *At once the Wanderers set to work with the greatest determination, and at the outset their play forward displayed more co-operation than is their custom, the backing up being vastly superior to anything they have shown during the present season. By this means, and with the aid of faultless kicking on the part of their backs, they were able, during the first quarter of an hour, to besiege the Sappers closely, to the surprise of many of the spectators. Thus consistently they maintained the attack till at length, after some judicious 'middling', by R. W. S. Vidal, the goal of the Engineers fell to a well-directed kick by A. H. Chequer.* Two thousand people saw Charles Alcock have a goal disallowed when another player handled, and the *Sporting Life* summed up the game: *Thus ended one of the most pleasant contests in which the Wanderers have ever been engaged.*

The Wanderers were to win the FA Cup on four more occasions, including three in succession from 1876-8. The Royal Engineers appeared in three more finals, winning the Cup in 1875, and impressing clubs around the country with their passing style. The Sheffield Association in particular enjoyed several fine matches with the Engineers and paid tribute to the Sappers' ability to be up in attack one minute and then back in defence the next. Fitness and speed were their hallmarks which enabled them to counter-attack quickly, and in those days of long, mazy dribbles, their short passing made them a particularly effective team. They were still good enough to win the FA Amateur Cup in 1908. Major Marindin went on to referee no less than eight FA Cup Finals and was president of the Football Association from 1874-90.

For the first eleven years of the FA Cup, the only major prize against which to measure success for seventeen years from 1872, the Southern amateur clubs reigned supreme. Oxford University reached the second FA Cup Final, when they lost to Wanderers, and then won the trophy themselves the following season. Oxford appeared in the final again in 1880, losing this time to Clapham Rovers, and the old boys' clubs, Old Etonians and Old Carthusians, also wrote their name on what was to become probably the most famous sporting trophy in the world. Once the Wanderers had bowed out, it was the Old Etonians who took over as the country's leading team and their true amateur spirit is best illustrated in the two finals in which they finished up on the losing side. Despite being a man short through injury they readily agreed to extra-time against Royal Engineers, though it was not compulsory, and in their final against Blackburn Olympic they again agreed to play on with ten men, and two more injured, to save the

Lancashire team from another trip to London. Such was the spirit which dominated first-class football in the twenty years following the formation of the FA.

The last FA Cup final in which the Old Etonians played signalled the end of one age and the beginning of another. Though the amateur clubs would play on with some success for a number of years after 1883, none would again reach the FA Cup final, much less win the trophy. By the late 1870s the newly-formed clubs of the Lancashire mill towns were beginning to flex their muscles and in 1879 one of them, Darwen, reached the quarter-finals of the FA Cup and were drawn against Old Etonians. It was the first time that a Northern club had seriously challenged the supremacy of the amateur South, and local subscription had to be raised to send the team of working-class lads up to London. At half-time the Old Etonians led 4-0 and early in the second half they added a fifth. The elite amateur side eased off, but they had reckoned without the skills of two Scottish players, Fergie Suter and Jimmy Love. Their combination of skilful ball play and short-passing brought first one goal, then another, and the Old Etonians collapsed. Darwen pressed home their shock advantage and scored three more times to leave the old boys stunned by the fact that they had been held to a 5-5 draw after leading so emphatically. The game had to be replayed, once more at the Oval, and again money had to be raised to send the Darwen team back to London, though on this occasion the Old Etonians donated £5 and the FA £10. The second match also ended in a draw, 2-2, and only when the sides met for a third time did the Old Etonians confirm their mastery with a 6-2 victory. But the die was cast and the cup-tie signalled the beginning of the end of the amateur era. Darwen's magnificent challenge was the beginning of a transitional period when the power in English soccer changed hands from the public schools, universities and army, back to the working class through the professional clubs. The people's game was about to become theirs once again.

The People's Game

The threat to the amateur game was coming from the North. In the same round of the FA Cup in which Darwen shocked the Old Etonians, Nottingham Forest beat Oxford University 2-1, but Forest were still a wholly amateur side in the southern tradition and were not to join the professional ranks until a decade later. In the late 1870s it was the emergence of the clubs from industrial Lancashire which spelled the end of the public school, varsity and army as the major forces in football, and the arrival of these clubs as the new power in the game was due in no small way to the coming of footballers from North of the Border. They were Scotsmen who had learned the more open version of football as played by Queen's Park and their followers.

Today, Queen's Park, the club founded in 1867 by young men who had come from beautiful Speyside, is still an all-amateur club and in 1983 they were relegated to the Second Division of the Scottish League, their cavernous Hampden Park ground swallowing up the bare handful of their spectators. A century ago the club was the dominant force in Scottish football and it was the more open Queen's Park style of play with the emphasis on passing the ball which gave the Scots the edge in the early internationals between the two countries. Their teamwork triumphed again and again over the individual game of the English and a report of the first official international, played at the West of Scotland cricket ground, Partick, on 30 November 1872, commented on the goalless draw: *Individual skill was generally on England's side . . . . The Southrons, however, did not play to each other so well as their opponents who seem to be adept at passing the ball.*

Darwen's Fergus Suter and James Love were probably the first professional footballers to be seen in the South of England when they came down to play against the Old Etonians in 1879, but they were certainly not the first in England. As soon as the game spread to the industrial North, professionalism was inevitable. The FA Cup was becoming a bigger attraction each season and as crowds grew larger it was not long before clubs saw the possibilities of taking gate money to pay for travelling, kit and other expenses. When the clubs realised that the more successful they were, the bigger gates they encouraged, and the greater amount of money they took, the leading sides began to look outside their immediate localities for better players. Players who had the skill to strengthen a club obviously needed some greater inducement to uproot from job and home than the mere love of football, and the competition for skilled players became intense. The clever Scottish players attracted most attention and the first professional footballer, so far as anyone can be reasonably certain, was just such a Scot, James J. Lang, who signed for Sheffield Wednesday in 1876 after playing for Clydesdale and Glasgow Eastern.

The previous year Lang had played for Glasgow against Sheffield and his skills were obvious. He came to 'work' for a Mr Walter Fernehough at his steel goods manufacturing business in Garden Street. Lang had in fact come to England solely to play football for money, and he admitted as much many years later when he was a steward at Ibrox Park, home of Glasgow Rangers. Not all of the Scots who found themselves with English clubs came to play football alone. At first they were part of a wider migration from North of the Border and they came looking for work in the textile industry which was booming at the time. The Scots impressed and soon the hunt was on for those footballers who had stayed at home. The trickle turned into a flood and at the beginning of the 1880s the football authorities took action. Bolton Wanderers, for instance, had only one Englishman in their team and in 1881 the Lancashire FA banned the signing of any more Scottish 'professors'.

The Birmingham FA followed suit and in 1883 the FA set up a sub-committee to look into allegations of professionalism. The committee could find no hard evidence that clubs were paying players. Nonetheless, there was a growing wave of resentment amongst the amateur clubs and open talk that they would withdraw from the FA Cup if forced to play against professionals. It was naive to ignore the tide which was sweeping football towards professionalism. The ideals on which the FA had been based may have been fine for the amateur players who had been to public school and university; they had little meaning for working-class footballers who had no leisure time in which to indulge themselves in playing the game for fun, at least not at the highest level with its demands on men's time for training and travelling. The wages of working men were not high and without some form of financial backing, no worker could find the time to hone his raw football skills until he was good enough to play in the top drawer.

There was another significant development which affected football. Between 1830 and 1870 the only guaranteed national holidays were at Christmas and Easter. But throughout the 1850s industrial workers in various towns and cities were granted free Saturday afternoons, with Liverpool the last to fall in line in the early 1870s. Shop assistants, clerks and the like were excluded from this half-holiday, and so when football came to dominate Saturday afternoons, along with other sports, it was from the workforce of the heavier industries that the supporters were drawn. Football became an 'industrial' game simply because the people in those industries were the only ones with enough spare time to play and watch. The potential support for football clubs was now much greater and club finances began to benefit. If a club wanted success it had to pay better players, and success with those better players meant more support and more money. Once started, professional football could not fail to grow in this environment.

At the beginning of the 1880s football reached a crossroads and decisions had to be made to accommodate the growing trend of professionalism. For some time after Darwen shocked Old Etonians in 1879, amateur clubs managed to retain their hold on the FA Cup. Darwen reached the semi-final in 1881,and in that year's quarter-final the Lancashire club defeated Romford 15-0. The FA Cup was now a much coveted prize and civic pride entered into the fray. In 1882 Blackburn Rovers carried the hopes of all Lancashire when they became the first Northern club to appear in the final. They lost 1-0 to Old Etonians, but it was the last time that an amateur club would win the cup. Blackburn's losing side that year included Fergus Suter, transferred from Darwen, and three other Scots. The goal, scored by Old Etonian W. J. Anderson, was the last gesture of the men who had founded the Football Association and held it in their grip for twenty years. It was not only the last time that an amateur club would win the FA Cup, but also the last Southern victory that century. At the end of the game Lord Kinnaird, a great figure in Victorian football whose flowing red beard had been seen in nine of the first twelve finals, stood on his head in front of the Kennington Oval pavilion. Kinnaird succeeded Major Marindin as president of the FA and he, Alcock and Marindin can be regarded as the fathers of English football.

One year after leading Old Etonians to victory over Blackburn Rovers Kinnaird was back at the Oval, this time captaining his team against Blackburn Olympic. There could hardly have been a greater contrast between the teams. Old Etonians were gentlemen of independent means; Olympic were spinners, plumbers, weavers and metal workers from one of the world's most industrialised areas. Even the names showed the gulf between the teams. Old Etonians boasted the Hon A. F. Kinnaird, P. J. de Paravicini and J. T. B. Chevallier; Olympic fielded Wilson, Dewhurst, Yates and Matthews. The Lancashire side even had a player-manager in Jack Hunter, who captained England and who had joined Olympic, along with George Wilson, from a Sheffield team called Zulus who played in theatrical costume. Hunter was dropped from a North versus South fixture in January 1881 because he had allegedly been paid to play. The following year Hunter moved to Lancashire where professionalism was not viewed with such horror, and the following year he found himself in the FA Cup final.

Blackburn Olympic were not officially a professional side, but there is little doubt that their players were paid. A raffle was held to finance a short stay in Blackpool immediately before the final, and employers gave the players Saturday morning off, totally out of keeping with the industrial traditions of the time. The Eton Chronicle said darkly, It may

There was no sports photography when the FA Cup was wrested from the hands of the southern amateur clubs in 1883. A newspaper artist gives his impression of the events in what was a watershed in the history of the game.

seem strange that a football eleven composed of mill-hands and working men should be able to sacrifice three weeks to train for one match, and to find the means to do so. Olympic had reached the final in emphatic style and perhaps their most significant victory was a 4-0 defeat of amateurs Old Carthusians in the semi-final. One writer called the final *Aristocrats versus Artisans . . . between teams from the historical playing fields of Eton and a nondescript eleven of working men from Blackburn.* The Old Etonians were *southern amateur cracks,* and yet their colours were lowered by what the writer described as *players of humble origin.* Up to half time it was Old Etonians who led, scoring on the half-hour. But while the amateurs stuck to their traditional dribbling game in the second half, Olympic made intelligent use of long and telling passes and they scored through Matthews, the ball finding its way into a section of the 8,000 crowd, for there were no goalnets in those days. Then the Old Etonians best forward, Arthur Dunn, was injured and had to leave the field. The game went into extra time, though there was no obligation on the part of Old Etonians to agree, especially since they had only ten men and were missing two other regular players.

It was a magnanimous gesture and one which saved the Lancashire club from an expensive return journey to London at a later date. But if Olympic were grateful, they were in no mood to be charitable and in the second period of extra time Dewhurst floated over a centre and Costley (some papers called him Crossley) ran in to score the winning goal. Blackburn Olympic took the cup back to Lancashire, where it

34

Though subsequently touched-up, this is the earliest known 'action' photograph of a soccer match. It is the 1887 FA Cup final between Aston Villa and West Brom and shows Bayliss heading towards the Villa goal. Some 15,000 people watched the game at The Oval. Note the lack of goalnets and the fact that the Villa goalkeeper wears the same strip as his team mates.

was to remain for four years because Blackburn Rovers then won it three times in succession, and the 1883 FA Cup final is seen as a watershed in the game's history. By 1886 there were only four amateur teams in the fifth round. Old Westminsters reached the sixth round before being beaten 6-0 by West Bromwich Albion, and only Swifts won through to the semi-final where they were beaten 2-1 by Blackburn Rovers at Derby. The following season Old Carthusians and Old Westminster reached the last eight, and Old Carthusians got as far as the quarter finals again in 1888. But they were the last amateur side to have a reasonable chance of winning the FA Cup.

By then professional football was legal, though there had been a desperate struggle by its opponents before the inevitable was accepted. Through the late 1870s and early 1880s the authorities had turned a blind eye to the activities of the Northern clubs, and indeed, the rise in professionalism meant that the standard of the game had increased with every season. But in 1883, the FA, urged on by outposts like Sheffield and Nottingham who feared that Lancashire and their professionals would have the monopoly on success, reacted by suspending Accrington for paying their players. The result was to widen still further the gulf between North and South. The professional clubs directed much bad feeling towards the FA, while the Scottish FA was deeply worried about the drain of its best players to England and fully supported the FA's action.

It was Preston North End who brought matters to a head after their FA Cup match against Upton Park in London in January 1884 which ended in a draw. Twelve thousand people saw the game and when it was over Upton Park complained that Preston had fielded professional players. An FA committee of inquiry was astounded to hear Preston admit the offences. What was more, the Preston president, Major William Sudell, offered to produce evidence that most clubs in Lancashire practised professionalism. The FA disqualified Preston who went away and, with twenty-five other Lancashire clubs and Sunderland and Aston Villa, formed a breakaway British Football Association. Had it been allowed to continue, then soccer would have seen the same kind of divide as that which split rugby into the Union and League games. Urged on by the enlightened Charles W. Alcock, the FA began to realise that such a move would break its hold as the ruling body and they eased their opposition, though not before, in June 1884, they had restricted payment for 'lost time' to one day per week and, more significantly, banned all but Englishmen from playing in the FA Cup. Most professionals were Scottish.

This harsh measure led to the projected British FA and a further threat from the Northern clubs that they would leave the FA Cup competition rather than submit to investigation. The FA now saw that their stance was futile and a sub-committee was formed to look anew at professional football. After sifting the evidence the committee this time came down firmly on the side of open professionalism and on 20 July 1885 professional football was legalised, though with strict controls. In the FA Cup, only those professionals qualified by birth or residence — they had to have lived within six miles of their club's headquarters for at least two years — were allowed and the rule was not relaxed until four years later. In 1887-8 Sunderland, despite winning an FA Cup replay against Middlesbrough, were disqualified after being found guilty of playing three Scottish professionals in violation of the residential qualifications. The effects on the Sunderland club were profound enough to lead to a split when some disgruntled members led by the club's founder, James Allan, formed a rival club called Sunderland Albion which lasted until 1892.

There were still many pockets of resistance to professional football, notably in the South and for quite some time there were no professional clubs south of Birmingham. But gradually others came into the fold and Luton (in 1890), Woolwich Arsenal (1891), Southampton (1892), Millwall (1893) and Tottenham Hotspur (1894) were among the first to pay their players, although the London FA held out until 1906 before falling reluctantly into line. The spread of professionalism brought with it the need for more competitive matches and the FA Cup was not sufficient to keep clubs fully occupied, while the hitherto prestigious friendly matches lost much of their impetus. There was little point in paying players to win matches with nothing more than pride at stake and when professional football was legalised in England (the Scots did not bow to the inevitable until 1893) the development of a more complex competition was a certainty. When it came it was the vital step towards the multi-million pound entertainment which is football today.

Before 1888 football was carried on in a haphazard manner. There was always the possibility that opponents would not turn up and it was far from uncommon for supporters to arrive at a ground to discover that the game had been cancelled. Matches often kicked off so late that spectators had drifted home, and many games lacked a competitive edge, for friendly matches, even those between the top clubs, lacked the excitement of cup ties. With professionalism spreading rapidly through the Midlands and the North it was vital for the clubs to find a regular source of income. One such club was Aston Villa who, with West Bromwich, Preston and Blackburn, was one of the country's leading sides. Villa's William McGregor, fearing that his club would die a slow natural death, suggested a league competition based on that used in American baseball. McGregor enlisted the support of West Bromwich, Wolves, Stoke and Derby, overcame the initial reluctance of Preston and Bolton, and on 17 April 1888, the Football League was officially formed at the Royal Hotel, Manchester, following an initial meeting at Anderton's Hotel in London's Fleet Street.

The enduring nature of the Football League's twelve original members is emphasised by the fact that in 1983-4, eleven were still members, six of them in the First Division.

In 1892 a Second Division was formed and although the league headquarters was inundated with protests and complaints (one referee was so vague that he filed two different scores for the same match) the idea of league football spread rapidly. The Scottish and Irish Leagues were both formed in 1890, the Southern League in 1894, and local and schoolboy leagues started up across the country. William McGregor's

Football supporters pictured outside St Paul's Cathedral before the 1906 FA Cup final between Everton and Newcastle United. For many from the North and Midland it was their first visit to the capital, so football was beginning to widen many people's horizons.

idea to provide what he called 'a fixity of fixtures' would become the basis of competitive football wherever the game was played.

By the end of the 1890s the pattern of the big city clubs as the dominant forces had emerged. The 'instant death' of the FA Cup meant that smaller clubs could still win through and between 1888-9 and 1914-5, eighteen different clubs won the cup; in the same period the Football League championship was won by ten different clubs and after Preston won the first two titles, Sunderland and Aston Villa dominated the scene. Between 1892 and 1902 one or the other of these clubs took the championship on all but two occasions. Throughout the decade professional football grew in stature and the game became a major commercial undertaking. A new breed of self-made business-men found themselves drawn to club directorships as a way of increasing their stature in the community. In 1893 one newspaper

Football programmes began to take on a more familiar format by the late 1900s. This one was for the Barnsley versus Swindon FA Cup semi-final at Stamford Bridge in 1912. The Yorkshire club did manage to beat Swindon and went on to win the cup for the only time in their history.

commented of the FA Cup final played between Wolves and Everton at Fallowfield, Manchester, before 45,000 people: *The vast crowd was good proof of the absorbing interest which a first-class football match now arouses in almost any of our great centres of population, but especially in the Northern and Midlands counties .*

In 1898 automatic promotion and relegation replaced the old 'test' matches where bottom clubs in the First Division played off against the top Second Division sides, and the pattern of football on the threshold of World War I was one which we would recognise today. When war came the FA and the Football League decided to carry on as normal through 1914-5, much to the anger of many people. The historian A. F. Pollard wrote to *The Times* in November 1914: *...Every club that employs a professional football player is bribing a much-needed recruit from enlistment and every spectator who pays his gate money is contributing so much towards a German victory.*

Such a reaction was perhaps inevitable when it became obvious that the war would not, as promised, be over by Christmas. Yet football was a necessary entertainment for both weary war workers and troops

Both national and local soccer associations encouraged players, officials and supporters to join the forces during World War I and football even had its own battalion.

at home on leave. The FA were, however, sensitive to criticism and it was agreed to encourage spectators to enlist. League matches were to be used as recruiting bases and military bands and speakers would rouse young men to the colours. The bands were received with great enthusiasm, the speakers less so, and the flow of recruits was minimal. The clubs, too, had problems. They had signed players on contract. How would they be able to pay them if there was no football? To compound the problem, attendances and receipts were down on 1913-14 and the league decided to stop 15 per cent of the wages of the highest-paid players down to 5 per cent of the lowest and put the money into a special fund to assist clubs in difficulties. Each club would also pay 10 per cent of its match receipts to the visitors. The FA, meanwhile, hit back at its critics, pointing out in a letter to *The Times* in November 1914, that 10,000 recruits had already been raised from soccer and that of 5,000 professionals, some 2,000 were already in the services. Only 600 unmarried professional footballers had failed to answer the call. By Christmas the public debate had subsided and football carried on to the end of the season before reforming into regional competitions for the duration. Lord Derby, who presented the FA Cup to Sheffield United in April 1915, said later, *The clubs and their supporters had seen the cup played for, and now it was the duty of everyone to join with each other and play a sterner game for England.*

The Clubs

Until the current crisis threatened the existence of some of even the most famous English league clubs, perhaps the most surprising aspect of the game had been the enduring nature of those clubs, most of which sprang up from obscure origins a century ago, and which grew quickly to become some of the most celebrated names in football. Their emergence is an integral part of the story of soccer and they came from four broad aspects of nineteenth-century English society: church, works, schools, and middle-class organisations.

The first clubs, like Forest (later Wanderers) were from public school backgrounds and they ultimately faded into oblivion in the face of growing competition from other clubs whose origins were less deeply-rooted in tradition and who adopted profressionalism. Some of the earlier clubs were born out of county cricket clubs, notably Notts County and Derby County, Midland rivals whose origins go back to the summer game. Notts County are the only Football League club whose formation pre-dates that of the Football Association. The club was formed at a meeting at the Lion Hotel in 1862 and in its earlier days was known simply as 'Nottingham'. The 'County' indicates the association with the Nottinghamshire County Cricket Club which dominated the county game in the 1870s and 1880s, and many of Notts famous cricketers, such as Richard Daft, George Parr, and later, William Gunn played for the football club too. Notts County's development was such that when the first official international match was played in 1872, just ten years after the club came into being, one of their players, Ernest Greenhalgh, was selected for England. From 1881 until 1910 Notts played at Trent Bridge.

Nottingham Forest was founded three years after County by a group of shinty (a hockey-type game) players and the first recorded description of the club stated, *They are a bunch of harmless lunatics who amuse themselves by kicking one another's shins.* There are several imaginative versions of how the players were converted to football and, although there was some stout resistance from the die-hard shinty players, the football club was put on an official footing at the Clinton Arms. They took their name from the clearing north of the city where they played. Forest first owned a set of red flannel caps and that has remained their main colour to this day. In 1866 they met Notts County at the Forest recreation ground in a game which was a mixture of soccer and rugby. Forest won when their player, Revis, won a thrilling dash with Browne of Notts and 'touched down'. The ball was then brought back rugby-fashion and the place kick sailed between the posts (no crossbar in those days) to give the younger club victory. Forest joined the Sheffield Association and played a mixture of Sheffield, Rugby and London rules with a few of their own interpretations included for good measure. Nottingham Forest's Sam Widdowson gave shin-guards (worn outside the stockings) to the game; and the first match in which a referee's whistle is known to have been used was the Forest versus Sheffield Norfolk match in 1878. Nottingham Forest have the unique distinction of having played FA Cup matches against teams from Scotland, Wales, and Ireland.

Derby County was another club to emerge from a cricket club. The club was founded in 1884 by players from Derbyshire County Cricket Club and originally the colours were the cricket club's gold, amber and chocolate. The club wanted to be called the Derbyshire County Football Club, but the local FA objected to the name 'since only the county football association can field a truly representative side' and the name had to be amended to the present one. Old Etonians and Old Reptonians were among the first Derby players, but the club was a professional one in its first year and by 1903 had played in three FA Cup finals, though losing them all.

The two Sheffield clubs were also formed from cricket clubs. Sheffield Wednesday came into being in 1867, in the smoke-room of a Sheffield public house, to provide cricketers from the club from which Wednesday took its name, with some winter activity. They played

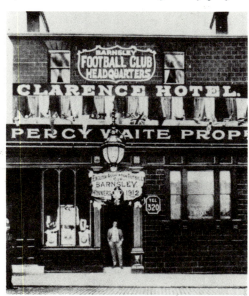

Barnsley's early headquarters was a local pub where board meetings were held.

42

some early games at Bramall Lane before settling in the Owlerton district, which gave rise to the nickname of the Owls. Sheffield United was formed for a similar reason, in 1889, and the club's ground at Bramall Lane was used for county cricket until 1971 when it finally lost its curious three-sided look.

As working class people, particularly those in the heavy industries, found more time, money and inclination for organised leisure after 1870, more football clubs were formed. The modern recreation was much more disciplined and regulated than that of pre-industrial times, and the church in particular gave football its main introduction to the working class communities of the great industrial centres. There was strong belief, especially amongst young clergymen, in a brand of 'muscular christianity' where athleticism was next to godliness, and the laws of physical well-being went hand-in-hand with the laws of God. From this philosophy grew many of today's league clubs.

Aston Villa, formed in 1874, was started by young men connected with the Wesleyan Chapel in Lozells, Birmingham. Bolton Wanderers assumed that title in 1877, previously they had been Christ Church FC. Everton began as St Domingo's Church Sunday School, and an offshoot of that club became today's mighty Liverpool. St Andrew's Sunday School, West Kensington, started a football team which grew into Fulham FC; and boys from St Luke's Church, Blakenhall, formed their team in 1877 which became Wolverhampton Wanderers. St Mary's Church, Southampton, had a team which became Southampton FC; and Small Heath Alliance was organised by boys from Trinity Church. Today the same club is called Birmingham City.

Church teams were only an element in the rise in working-class football and many more sprang from factory life. In 1886 men at London's Woolwich Arsenal formed a club called Dial Square FC from the area of that mighty munitions factory in which they worked. They quickly realised that this was too narrow a title and renamed their club Royal Arsenal, later Woolwich Arsenal, and now just plain Arsenal, perhaps the world's most famous club. Thames Ironworks side became West Ham United, and both Stoke City and Crewe Alexandra were formed by railway workers. Stoke, who claim to be the second-oldest league club, formed in 1863, was started by Old Carthusians who took engineering jobs with the North Staffordshire Railway Company; Crewe Alexandra were named after a public house where railway workers met in 1876. Though often the butt of jokes about their lowly status, Crewe were at one time a team good enough to play in the semi-final of the FA Cup, when they lost 4-0 to Preston in 1888. Their Gresty Road ground staged two semi-finals in the 1880s, mainly because of its accessibility. Newton Heath was founded by the dining room committee of the Lancashire and Yorkshire Railway's carriage and wagon works and became Manchester United. Singer's cycle factory in Coventry had a side which is now Coventry City, and Millwall was formed by workers at Morton's factory in London. Not all works teams survived. Derby Midland were the leading club in that town for many years after being formed by workers of the Midland Railway Company. The club appeared in the FA Cup before Derby County was formed, but in 1891 the railway company withdrew its support and Midland quickly folded.

The 1870 Education Act also encouraged working-class football. The infant state education system gave public schools and university men the opportunity to impose their educational ideals on the children of working-class people and within a decade there were schools football teams throughout the country, though it would be another ten years before the new elementary school code recognised the need to care for the physical welfare of children. Physical education became an integral part of school life and teams were formed from the grammar schools downwards, some of which became professional clubs.

At first it was inevitable that the older grammar schools would copy the public schools and in 1874 old boys from Blackburn Grammar School formed the club which is today Blackburn Rovers. A decade later, the team from Wyggeston School, Leicester, was established and eventually became Leicester Fosse, changing its name to Leicester City in 1919. King's School, Chester, had a hand in forming Chester FC, and the boys of Droop Street School, London, formed a team in 1885 and two years later changed its name to Queen's Park Rangers. Teachers at Northampton began the club which is now Northampton Town; and Sunderland started life as the Sunderland and District Teachers' Association AFC. The beginnings of schools football did more than simply give us some of today's clubs, and these clubs are merely the survivors of a much more significant social phenomenon. By the 1890s schools football, particularly inter-town matches and local cup finals, was drawing thousands of spectators to league

Middlesbrough FC were formed at a tripe supper and were a famous amateur club before turning professional. This team won the FA Amateur Cup in 1895.

grounds where the top games were staged. Schools football was educating the boys of the country to take up the game at an early age, and it provided them with the first step towards the works, church and other clubs which were fast multiplying. The game at the English school was a vital part of the overall pattern of football. Many sociologists claim that the great emphasis on football in state schools at the turn of the century was the most important reason for football's mass appeal, and a determining factor in it becoming the national sport.

Finally, some clubs were formed by no particular institution. Middlesbrough started life in 1876 at a tripe supper held specifically for the purpose of forming a club; and although Portsmouth is a naval town, it was the Royal Artillery team, from a pub named after that regiment, which gave the football followers their fare. When that club disbanded, after allegations that it had contravened the amateur code, a group of supporters got together, bought a field near Fratton station, and formed Portsmouth FC in 1898. Preston North End began as a rugby club and switched codes in 1881, though there was the cricket connection with North End CC. Tottenham Hotspur began under a Victorian gas lamp in Northumberland Park, again, the boys belonged to a local cricket club; and Manchester City can trace themselves back to when two minor clubs joined to form Gorton FC, and a further amalgamation with West Gorton produced Ardwick FC, the forerunner of the present club. In 1882 a group of football enthusiasts formed Newcastle West End. Their dressing room was a tiny hut. By amalgamation with Newcastle East End in 1892, a club was formed called Newcastle United, and although East End are held to be the true ancestors of the present club, the famous St James's Park ground is on the site of that where that humble dressing room first stood and where the first gate-money collected amounted to less than eight shillings. Thus like all today's mighty teams, Newcastle grew from small beginnings, and each one of today's Football League clubs reflects some aspect of past society.

Tottenham Hotspur were formed under a street lamp by boys from a local cricket club. In 1901 this Spurs team became the only non-Football League club to win the FA Cup since the league was founded. Spurs then played in the Southern League.

Tactics-1

Were it possible to journey back in time to a football match being played in England in the middle of the nineteenth century, the tactics adopted by the teams would cause a great deal of bewilderment to the modern spectator. The first thing he would notice would be that no player deliberately passed the ball. <u>Individuality was the key word to the footballers of that era and although the art of passing is the very essence of modern football, it had still to be invented in the 1850s</u>. A player who found himself with the ball would simply set off on a long dribble towards the opposing goal. He would go as far as he could

In the earliest organised football the player with the ball simply dribbled until he lost it. There was no passing and the ball acted as a magnet. The game was rather like that played today by young beginners.

before he either over-ran the ball, or lost it to an opponent who would then set off on his own lone progress in the opposite direction. When a player attacked in this way, he received the support of his team mates who backed him up in the hope of retrieving the ball when he lost it, but at no time would he deliberately pass it to one of them. Team formation consisted of a goalkeeper, one defender to assist him, and nine forwards in a game of eleven-side.

By the time the Football Association was formed in 1863, there had been a slight modification, and one of the forwards dropped back to play in what can be described as a half-back position to give a 1-1-8 formation. The development of attackers' individual technique led to the need for a better balance between attack and defence. The need to prevent the other side from scoring assumed more importance, though the game was still based emphatically on attack. Thus, a second forward came back into what we would know as the midfield and teams now fielded a 1-2-7 line up. That seven-man forward line comprised three central attackers and two men on either wing.

The reason for this highly individual style of football was the old offside law, which is still the rugby offside law today, that a man could

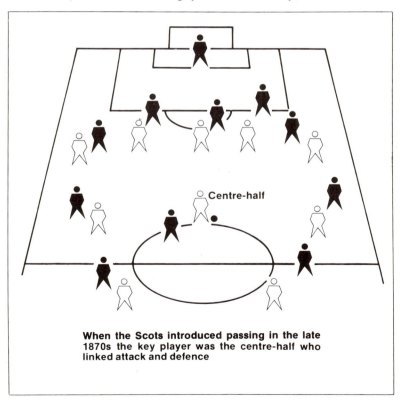

When the Scots introduced passing in the late 1870s the key player was the centre-half who linked attack and defence

only be onside if he was behind the ball. This meant that a player with the ball could only pass it behind him, therefore he considered it better to put his head down and go for the goal. Passing the ball was an art which was never developed. Yet in Scotland there were footballers who did not operate under this law and theirs was a more open style of play. Even after the uniform adoption of the three-man offside law, English footballers found it extremely difficult to relearn the game.

A team committed to the dribbling game faced grave problems when confronted by a team which played the passing game. The dribblers found themselves in total disarray when faced with teams which adopted the style developed by the Scottish giants of the day, Queen's Park. When they went to tackle an opponent who had the ball, they found that it had been transferred to another opponent before they could put in their tackle. They rushed about the field and used up a considerable amount of energy chasing the ball which had become altogether too elusive. Again there was the need to become more defensively organised and in the 1870s, as Scotland dominated the international scene, another player was brought back to join the original full-back to give teams a 2-2-6 formation. The Scots adopted this formation first, and their passing game meant that football was now more open with players spread wider instead of rushing about in clusters. Still the English were reluctant to follow this style, but after winning only two of the first ten internationals against the Scots, English players began to realise the benefits of this unselfish brand of football.

Passing skills improved still further and yet another forward was taken out and brought back to help the increasingly beleaguered defences. He went into the half-back line, in the centre, and became the forerunner of the centre-half. For some time before this 2-3-5 formation came into general use in the 1880s, teams had experimented with three half-backs and Cambridge University was probably the first side to use a formula similar to today's when they played with three half-backs in 1877. A year later Wrexham won the Welsh Cup with the same line-up, but for some years after that most teams persisted with six forwards. England used three half-backs for the first time in 1884, though the Scots themselves resisted it until 1887, by which time it had become general practice for clubs to line up 2-3-5.

This was the 'pyramid system' on which later strategy was based. In the early 1880s, Preston North End, who had imported several talented Scottish footballers, developed this system and with it they won the first league championship and the FA Cup, in 1889; and took the league title again the following season. For over half a century this pyramid, with the goalkeeper at its apex and five forwards at its base, was the dominant formation throughout world football. There was now a perfect balance of five forwards being opposed by five outfield defenders. In those early days of 2-3-5, the full-backs marked the opposing inside-forwards: the men either side of the lone centre-forward who had been left to drive up the middle of the field after his partner reverted to centre-half. The full-backs were ready to deal with attacks which had pierced the first defensive wall of the half-back line. The half-backs who played either side of the centre-half became known as wing-halves and in the beginning they were primarily defensive players and had not developed the critical role of link-men between defence and attack which they would assume in later years.

The key man in the team was now the centre-half and he needed every ounce of stamina to cope with his new role. He was expected to fall back and defend when his team was under pressure, but primarily he had the freedom to circulate around the field and was expected to be up in support of his own attack when a move developed around the opposing goal. The centre-half was a man with the independence to go where he felt he would be of most use to his team, and he kept that role from the 1880s right through until the mid-1920s when a change in the offside law altered the face of football for ever.

It was the tactics of post-war defenders like Newcastle's Billy McCracken which led to the offside law being altered in 1925, and the

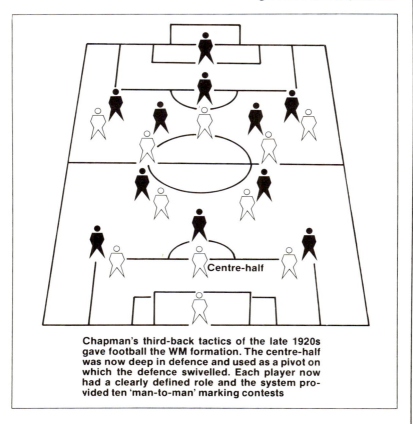

Centre-half

Chapman's third-back tactics of the late 1920s gave football the WM formation. The centre-half was now deep in defence and used as a pivot on which the defence swivelled. Each player now had a clearly defined role and the system provided ten 'man-to-man' marking contests

ultimate negation of the centre-half as an attacking player. The pattern of football until 1925 was based solidly on that which had evolved in the 1880s. The dribbling game of the public school, born at a time when anyone in front of the ball was offside, and the reason why spectators thrilled to the sight of players like W. N. Cobbold, the so-called 'Prince of the Dribblers', who weaved around opponents, dodging brutal tackles, his legs swathed in bandages, was long since dead. Cobbold belonged to another age, to a game as obsolete as the cricket caps which footballers once wore in matches.

The offside law which required three men to be between an attacker with the ball and the goal, at the moment the ball was played to him, had been in force since the 1860s and under that regulation the full-backs could afford to play much further upfield, although they had to ensure that they kept in a diagonal line. The forward had to be wary that he did not get behind the advanced full-back, otherwise he would be offside, and by the 1920s, full-backs had moved up almost to the halfway line with one playing slightly behind the other. This offside trap had been evolved to perfection and the game was becoming monotonous as stoppages for players caught offside increased enormously. One of the arch-exponents of the offside trap was the Irishman McCracken, and he and his kind made goals hard to come by. It was clear that if the game was not to suffer as a spectator sport, then some legislation had to be introduced to counter the trap.

In 1925, following a suggestion by the Scottish Football Association, the law was changed so that now only two men were needed between attacker and goal to play him onside. The result was a hatful of goals as defences failed to come to terms with this new-found freedom for forwards. In 1924-5, the last season under the old law, 4,700 goals were scored in the Football League; in the first season under the new legislation that total rose by almost one-third to 6,373. The crucial area of vulnerability for defences lay in the centre of the field. The centre-half was still an attacking player and if full backs continued to push forward in the old way, a forward could position himself between them so that he was still onside, and he had only one man to beat before having the goalkeeper at his mercy. The full backs were faced with a dilemma. If they played wide on the touchlines then they left a huge gap in the middle of the field; if they moved inside to close that gap, then the wingers enjoyed yards of space to move down the line and swing the ball over behind the defence.

Somehow the middle had to be closed up and the man given eternal credit for doing that was Herbert Chapman. Chapman had just steered Huddersfield to two consecutive League titles and left a side ready to do that a third time in succession when he moved to Arsenal. Chapman's reign at Highbury had hardly begun when the Gunners suffering a humiliating 7-0 defeat at Newcastle. The day was 3 October 1925 and it was a disaster which convinced Chapman that he had to shore up the middle of his defence. He decided to move centre-half Joe

Butler deep into defence and bring Andy Neil to link up in midfield. Two days after that reverse at Newcastle, Arsenal went to Upton Park to play West Ham with Butler operating deep between the full-backs. Arsenal won 4-0 and Chapman's theory was vindicated. From narrowly missing relegation in the previous two seasons Arsenal finished runners-up in 1925-6, just five points behind Chapman's old club, Huddersfield, who took their third successive title.

Butler was only a stop-gap for the new position of 'stopper' centre-half until Chapman could find the right man for the job. Eventually that man emerged in the shape of Herbie Roberts, a red-haired player from Oswestry who came to play 'third back' for the Gunners. Football was now in the 'Chapman Era', which lasted from 1925 to 1934, during which time Chapman built Arsenal into arguably the best football club in the world. They won the FA Cup in 1930, were beaten finalists in 1927, when Cardiff took the trophy out of England for the first and so far only time after Danny Lewis's famous slip, and 1932; and they took the First Division title in 1930-1, 1932-3, 1933-4, and 1934-5, the last occasion tinged with sadness when Chapman died before he could see his team complete the hat-trick. Arsenal were also runners up in 1931-2 (remember Chapman had already steered them

Arsenal captain Tom Parker clutches the FA Cup after the London club's triumph in 1930. It was the start of a remarkable run of success throughout the thirties and was the culmination of Herbert Chapman's 'third-back' game. Arsenal played this so well because they had exactly the right type of players to exploit the most fundamental change in tactics since professional soccer developed from the old amateur game. Arsenal's success as a London club shifted the game's power base from the Midlands and North, and did much to broaden its appeal.

to the number two position in his first season), and they went on winning trophies after his death. The 1936 FA Cup and the 1937-8 league championship were engineered by George Allison, but the base had been laid solidly by Chapman.

Arsenal were the team of the thirties. In addition to those honours they supplied many players for England and when Italy played at Highbury in 1934 no less than seven Arsenal players turned out for England, a club record if one discounts the Corinthians' feats of the last century which, though creditable, were hardly comparable. To put the seal on that match Tom Whittaker, the Arsenal trainer and later manager, was trainer to the international team. One man who did not play for his country that day was Herbie Roberts, whose only international appearance had been in 1931. Yet it was Roberts who personified Chapman's defensive theories, which the whole British game had taken up. Roberts was not a classy centre-half, but he won the ball in the air and as a pivot who effectively closed up the middle he had no peer. Arsenal had two international full backs in George Male and Eddie Hapgood and they revolved around Roberts. With the big centre-half staying in the middle of the defence instead of wandering upfield, the full backs looked after the thrust down the flank. When Hapgood, for instance, closed in on an attacker, Male moved around to cover Roberts and the interlocking final defensive wall was complete.

Arsenal had other pieces to find before the jigsaw was complete. They took two wing-halves, subsequently Jack Crayston and Wilf Copping, and gave them the job of playing in the middle of the field, linking with the inside-forwards, Alex James and David Jack, to form a parallelogram. The Arsenal plan was completed with two fast, direct wingers in Cliff Bastin and Joe Hulme, and a centre-forward, at first Jack Lambert and later Ted Drake, and there was now the classic 'WM' formation with the inside-forwards, or at least one of them, falling back to fill the former midfield role of the centre-half. It was, relatively speaking, the equivalent of a 3-4-3 or 3-3-4 formation. Every other club followed Chapman's formula, but it was Arsenal who dominated the game because they had exactly the right players to extract full value from the system. Alex James had the ability to make uncannily accurate long passes and this launched the counter-attacks upon which the fast, direct wingers and the centre-forward capitalised. Herbert Chapman was years ahead of his time and suggested, among other developments, floodlighting, the white ball, numbering of players, goal judges and independent timekeepers. But it was for this brilliant tactical innovation of the 'stopper' centre-half that he was best remembered. Chapman's strategy shaped the way football would be played until well after World War II. His elevation of Arsenal also meant that soccer was not now a game dominated by clubs from the industrial Midlands and North. Success for a London club gave the game a much broader audience.

7

A National Industry

When soccer picked up the threads after 1918 it found that there had been a significant shift in the game's position within society. Regional football, together with tens of thousands of men away in the services and thousands more working long hours on war work, meant that attendances had dwindled. When peace was restored, the myth that soccer had been an 'unpatriotic' game was perpetuated and in 1919 *The Times* reported: *There is much talk of making rugby the game in all our public schools.* Allegations of soccer's lack of patriotism masked the real reason why the public school establishment was turning away from the game. The ever-increasing moves towards professionalism meant that the amateurs could see little in the game with which to relate and rugby offered them an environment much nearer to their hearts and ideals. Soccer, to them, meant professionalism and the true-blue amateurs wanted none of it. Association football was not now the classless sport which it had once promised to become.

However, the game had no cause to fear, for although top-class amateur football (middle and upper class football) had received a setback, when the professional game resumed with the Football League and FA Cup, there was a tremendous boom in interest, just as there would be after World War II when men emerged from another conflict to find massive relief in Britain's national winter sport. Moreover, the economic climate in Britain between the wars greatly assisted professional soccer. First there was a brief expansion immediately after 1918 which helped clubs back on to their feet as people felt that life was returning to normal. Then the series of depressions, which carried on through the thirties, not only found young men looking towards football as a means of escaping the dole queue, but also brought about an environment in which the only bit of colour in an otherwise grey and cheerless world was to support the local team on Saturday. The prospect of that one afternoon of pleasure held thousands of unemployed men together for the remainder of the week.

Even those with jobs found great relief in Saturday football, and there is no better description of its meaning to those men than to quote once more from Priestley's *The Good Companions: . . . and what is more it turned you into a member of a new community, all brothers together for an hour and a half, for not only had you escaped from the clanking machinery of this lesser life, from work, wages, rent, doles, sick pay, insurance cards, nagging wives, ailing children, bad bosses, idle workmen, but you had escaped with most of your mates, and your neighbours, with half the town, and there you were, cheering together, thumping one another on the shoulders, swopping judgements like lords of the earth, having pushed your way through a turnstile into another and altogether more splendid kind of life, hurtling with Conflict and yet passionate and beautiful in its Art . . . .*

In Brazil, today, where life for the majority is bleak and unrewarding, attendances at football matches can sometimes be huge and capacity crowds for matches between the top clubs are common. Here again those lowest in the social order can find some escape in the game of football, and so it was in Britain in the twenties and thirties.

It was against this background that there was now an explosion in the growth of professional clubs. The First and Second Divisions each increased to the present twenty-two, and in 1920, a merger with the Southern League produced the Third Division which the following year became the Third Division South when a further twenty clubs were admitted to form a northern section. The First Division championship was still dominated by northern clubs and until Arsenal won in 1931 the title had never gone further south than Birmingham. In 1923 the FA Cup final was moved to the Empire Stadium, Wembley, after post-war seasons at the woefully inadequate Stamford Bridge. The official attendance for the first Wembley final was given as

David Jack who signed for Arsenal in 1928 for what was then a record transfer fee of nearly £11,000. Jack had already made himself a national folk hero by scoring the first goal in a Wembley cup final.

The annual England-Scotland match was also a great crowd puller and at Hampden Park in April 1929 another large attendance was recorded to see Scotland win 1-0. Here Dixie Dean (white shirt) watches the ball flash past the Scottish upright. Dean scored sixty league goals in thirty-nine games in 1927-8. It is a record which will never be broken under present tactical arrangements.

126,047 but it was thought that as many as a quarter of a million were present to see West Ham beat Bolton in the game made famous by the policeman on his white horse. It was yet another example that football was truly the national winter sport. Interest in the game increased throughout the twenties and soccer became more lucrative with each passing season. In 1928 Arsenal paid a record transfer fee of nearly £11,000 to sign David Jack, the man who scored the first Wembley goal. His fee was 50 per cent higher than the previous record, paid by Aston Villa for Partick Thistle's Jimmy Gibson a year earlier, and was yet another stage of the transfer trail begun when Alf Common moved from Sunderland to Middlesbrough for £1,000 in 1905. Arsenal broke the record again before World War II when they paid Wolves an estimated £14,000 for Bryn Jones, though his move was not a success (Jack repaid Arsenal with 112 goals) and proved that big fees were no guarantee of success.

Increased interest in football inevitably saw new 'industries' spin off from the game. There was a big demand for boys comics to include pictures of star players and just as these comics offered picture cards, so too did the cigarette companies. Cigarette smoking had increased

When cigarette firms included famous footballers on their picture cards, small boys who had never been to a professional match became familiar with the star players. There were many different interpretations of the players as these cards of Charlie Buchan, Don Welsh and Alex James show.

dramatically during the war, though the inclusion of cards in packets dated back to before 1914, and in the twenties and thirties the companies introduced more and more subjects. Sport was one such subject and boys who had never seen a professional match became familiar with star players through cards passed to them by adults.

By far the biggest ancillary industry connected with professional football was betting and gaming. There had always been betting on the results of football matches, even going back to the days when the gentry wagered on the old mob football, and before World War I several newspapers ran competitions. But all that was superseded in the twenties by the invention of the football pools. A competition similar to the pools had been in operation before 1914, but that depended upon the sending of circulars through the post to private homes. The FA was determined to put a stop to soccer matches being used in that way and they took the matter to Parliament. Eventually, in 1920, a prohibitive bill went through the Commons and the football pools which we know today were invented as a way around the legislation.

Frederick Jervis of Birmingham is generally recognised as having invented the first pools coupon, but it was three young men employees of the Commercial Cable Company in County Kerry, who began in a Liverpool back street with a working capital of £150 and turned their operation into today's multi-million pound Littlewoods Pools. They began in February 1923 and by 1932 one of them, who had bought out the other two and introduced his family to the business, was a millionaire. The Moores family did all the early hard work of checking and distributing their coupons. The main attraction of the pre-war pools was the penny points and the penny results pools and five-figure dividends were not infrequent. For a working man to win a five-figure sum before 1939 was a sensation. The pools influence became so great that it was claimed that they were responsible for the boom in football in the twenties and thirties. By 1936 the X-1-2 habit was a national pastime and the Football League still fearing that this form of gambling was detrimental to the game, decided to sabotage the football pools. The fixture lists were scrapped and games were rearranged and kept secret to try and force the pools companies out of business, since they would not be able to print and distribute their coupons in time.

For three weeks the scheme worked and the pools companies were badly affected; but so was football and posters advertising 'Nottingham Forest v ?' were hardly designed to bring in the fans. Eventually the fixtures were leaked by a 'mole' somewhere in the workings of the Football League and the plan had to be scrapped. Today the fixtures are the copyright of the Football League and the Scottish League and each member club benefits from the cash sums paid over by the pools promoters in return for the use of the fixtures.

The football pools did something else besides make the promoters,

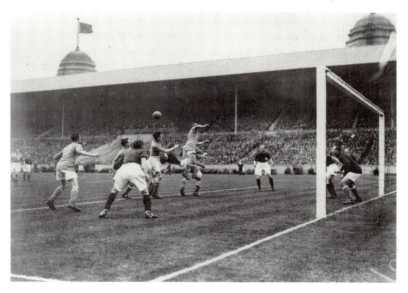

The FA Cup was now firmly fixed as a national event at Wembley. This is action from the 1927 game and although the famous twin towers are easily recognisable, note that the players did not wear numbers and that the goalnets were supported by ropes and poles.

and a few ordinary people, rich. They created still further industries when the pools companies found they had so much surplus profit that they could not put it back into their original business and so mail order firms and retail shopping outlets were started up. The pools also gave the man who had never been to a football match some identity with the game, and even housewives began to worry about the fortunes of Arsenal and Accrington Stanley, though admittedly purely for self-interest and not for concern over promotion or relegation, cup defeat or cup success. By the mid-thirties it was estimated that over sixteen times more people gambled on football than actually paid to go through the turnstiles and watch it. In 1937 *The Times* commented: *The pools, the transfer system and the amount of money involved in the gates have turned football into something like a national industry.* Indeed they had and the ultimate irony came, perhaps, when the raw winter of 1962-3 savaged the football season in Britain and a 'pools panel' was formed where experts decided the results of matches which had been postponed due to the bad weather. So the punters can now have their weekly flutter on the results of football matches, even when the matches are not played!

British domestic football expanded rapidly between the wars. The FA Cup final, now firmly established at Wembley, attracted regular 90,000-plus attendances and was now all-ticket to avoid a repeat of the potentially disastrous scenes of 1923, and league attendances, while not scaling the heights which would be reached in the forties, were nevertheless satisfactory. On the eve of war, British football was in a healthy state. More people played the game than ever before, more people watched it than at any time in its history, and on the few occasions when England did play abroad they reigned supreme, although that superiority had never been tested in the World Cup which began in 1930. Cocooned in its success on the international field, and with a bouyant domestic game, English football in particular had no apparent cause for concern.

The Golden Years

For over a million men there was only one place to be on Saturday, 31 August 1946, and that was on a Football League ground. It was the final sign that after a long and bitter war life was returning to normal. For the first time in seven weary years there was a full Football League programme. Not since 2 September 1939 had the eighty-eight clubs which then made up the league lined up under the customary headings of First, Second, Third South and Third North Divisions. After 1918 the game had boomed following a world war, but in 1946, football had emerged from a different kind of war, a war which had touched the life of every single inhabitant of the United Kingdom. Never in the nation's history had there been such a major upheaval and when peace dawned there was a universal need for relaxation as never before. Almost any kind of sport attracted large attendances, but professional

The importance of soccer to both servicemen and civilians was recognised during the war. RAF personnel sport leeks in their hats as they support Wales against England at Wembley in April 1940

football was watched by a staggering amount of people. Soccer filled the people's need for entertainment better than any other spectator sport, and it would do so for the next few years. By the late forties well over 41 million people in a season watched the league clubs.

The football of 1946 was essentially the child of the 1939 game, even the fixtures were a replica of the season interrupted by Hitler. Yet it was a game whose growth had been stunted by six years of war and a further year of regional matches and a strange two-legged FA Cup. Many of the pre-war stars were now ageing giants well past their best; players who would have reached their peak during the war would never do so in normal peacetime football, their time was sadly gone; and there were raw youngsters who had much still to learn. The standard of football was not good, but the people did not care. They wanted simply to see their teams in action once more. The players returned from their nomadic existence as 'guests', and the competitions now had a more familiar look to them. Who cared if the football was not as good as in 1939? Indeed, who even noticed?

At the end of the war football needed a season to sort itself out and in 1945-6, though the FA Cup was resumed, the league was still run on a regional structure. The cup was run on a two-legged basis up to and including the quarter-finals, and when Derby County beat Charlton 4-1 after extra-time on a beautiful late Spring day at Wembley, more than 98,000 people saw a thrilling classic which asured them that football was almost back to normal. It was called the 'Veterans' Final' because so many players were over thirty. They included Peter Doherty and Raich Carter, two of the pre-war game's greatest players, but the standard of this first peacetime final was not a sign of things to come in 1946, rather a glorious, golden reminder of how they used to be. Conscription and employment under the Essential Works Order robbed football of many young men and the game would take a year or two to settle down.

Yet grounds were hardly big enough to house the numbers of people who wanted to watch professional football in 1945-6. There was also the problem of the state of these grounds, some of which had altered hardly a jot since they were built in the nineteenth century. Some of them were downright dangerous and the clubs often courted disaster when tens of thousands packed into grounds not fit to hold such numbers. On 9 March 1946 the inevitable happened and thirty-three people were crushed to death and several hundred more were injured when a brick wall and crush barriers collapsed under the strain at Burnden Park, Bolton, where about 70,000 people had packed in to see Stanley Matthews and Stoke City in the second leg of an FA Cup-tie.

After this disaster the control of grounds was placed under the Home Office, with local authorities issuing licenses and police placing restrictions on numbers. The condition of the stadia remained largely the same, though it must be said that clubs were refused the necessary permission to improve their grounds in the forties. Earlier in that first

Stanley Matthews, later knighted for his services to football, was one of the great players who packed in crowds during the war. Here Matthews comes out to play for the RAF. Service teams were virtually full international sides during World War II.

post-war season, Moscow Dynamo had visited Britain and in their first match, against Chelsea at Stamford Bridge, had attracted 82,000 who saw a 3-3 draw. Thereafter they beat Cardiff City 10-1 in front of 45,000, enjoyed a farcical 4-3 win over Arsenal when most of the 54,000 crowd were unable to see the game because of fog, and rounded off their tour with a 2-2 draw against Rangers in front of 90,000 Glaswegians. The Russians surprised the British with their high-quality attacking football and it was the first sign that Continental European football had improved far more than the insular British had realised. When a Great Britain team beat the Rest of Europe 6-1 at Hampden Park in 1947, it only served to delay the realisation that the balance of power in world football was changing.

Still the crowds poured in to watch league matches and with the domestic game so healthy, who cared about the activities of the foreigners? By 1952 the annual attendances had averaged over 39 million each Football League season since the war. In the six seasons from 1946-7 to 1951-2, over 237 million people had passed through the turnstiles, with a peak in 1948-9 of 41,271,424. Some of the attendances at individual matches were equally staggering and on 17 January 1948, the First Division match between Manchester United and Arsenal at Maine Road attracted a record league gate of 83,260. Two months later there was a crowd of 143,570 to see Rangers play Hibernian at Hampden Park in the semi-final of the Scottish Cup. Even friendly matches attracted huge crowds and the Newcastle versus Liverpool friendly on 14 February 1948 was watched by 44,840 fans. Naturally the clubs' incomes were healthy and at the end of the first post-war season of league matches, all but six clubs made a profit with Stoke City out in front with an excess of £32,000. The players' wages were in no way related to their drawing power as entertainers (in 1947 the maximum winter wage was raised, reluctantly, to £12 per week), and with relatively small expenses the league clubs prospered from the large attendances.

Indeed, football was so popular that when vital matches were played, absenteeism was a major problem. As late as 1951 the docks authorities in Manchester ordered dockers not to attend a Manchester United FA Cup match because the men were wanted to clear a backlog of work caused by a strike. The men went to the match, and contingency plans to import Fleetwood dockers failed when men at that port preferred instead to watch Blackpool who were also playing in the cup. Midweek matches were a particular problem in the days before floodlighting. Replayed cup-ties on midweek afternoons often coincided with a spate of dear, departed grandmothers in urgent need of burial and the government considered banning midweek football in important industrial areas. But, mindful perhaps of a 1940 *Mass Observation* comment that 'one afternoon of League football could probably do more to affect people's spirits than the recent £50,000 Government poster campaign urging cheerfulness', the authorities opted instead for staggered working hours to accommodate the thousands who wanted to watch soccer.

Those thousands were fortunate in being able to see some of the greatest club sides ever produced by British football. Manchester United, despite being forced to play at neighbouring Maine Road until 1949 because the blitz had badly damaged Old Trafford, drew staggering attendances. Besides the 83,000-plus who saw them play Arsenal in 1948, there were 82,000 for the game between United, the cup holders, and Arsenal, the league champions, a year later, on New Year's Day 1949; while 81,000 watched giantkillers Yeovil humbled 8-0 a few weeks later. Matt Busby had inherited the shell of a club in 1945, but three years later his side, in company with Blackpool, gave soccer

The 1950 FA Cup final between Arsenal and Liverpool. Action here centres around the Liverpool goal and shows that the baggy shorts of the Alex James era were still very much in evidence.

one of its best ever FA Cup finals. Both sides threw caution to the Wembley breeze that warm April afternoon as United won 4-2, adding a new dimension to an occasion often made sterile by tension. Portsmouth were another fine side, champions in 1949 and 1950. Their style had none of the classy Manchester United game about it, but the uncomplicated Pompey way made the air at Fratton Park every bit as bracing as that of nearby Southsea. It was strong and vibrant football which was like a whiff of oxygen to those who made the fortnightly trip to see Portsmouth.

Arsenal, those great football aristocrats of pre-war days took the championship in its second post-war season, won the FA Cup in 1950, reached another final in 1952, and lifted the championship again the following year. Their immediate post-war fortunes dipped low until the signing of two ageing players, Joe Mercer, former captain of England, who came from Everton, and Ronnie Rooke who moved across London from Fulham. Between them Mercer and Rooke inspired the Arsenal revival. The 1953 title was won with only three of the 1948 side remaining — Mercer, winger Don Roper, and Jimmy Logie, a diminutive Scot and the cleverest of a clever side. Logie was both subtle and imaginative, a manipulator of the ball and the kind of Scottish player who had made English clubs look North of the Border

Bolton Wanderers's Nat Lofthouse, seen here flashing in a header against Aston Villa, was one of the great post-war centre-forwards who typified the British game at that time.

in the nineteenth century. Wolverhampton Wanderers, who were yet to enjoy their greatest post-war era, finished third, fifth, sixth and second in the First Division in the first four seasons of peace, and won the FA Cup in 1949. The seeds of the style which would make Wolves both vaunted and vilified in later years were sown.

Newcastle United, giants of an age long past, climbed back into the First Division in 1948 and for the first four seasons of their return they were never out of the title race, though they never looked like actually winning it. In 1951 and 1952 they won the FA Cup, the first side to win it twice in succession this century. One of the goals scored by Jackie Milburn at Wembley in 1951, thundered in from twenty yards after a delicate back-heel by Ernie Taylor, is a memory still imprinted on the minds of those who saw it, a memory which reflects the very essence of this golden age of English soccer. Then came Spurs, the push-and-run stylists of Arthur Rowe's Tottenham Hotspur. Second Division champions in 1951, Spurs went right through to take the First Division title the following year with brilliant precision football which eliminated defenders as though they did not exist. With Eddie Baily at inside-forward, Les Medley on his wing, and Ronnie Burgess prompting from wing-half, Spurs had the definitive left flank trio. Crowds in their ten of thousands poured into White Hart Lane for match after match to see such delights. Alas, Spurs' push-and-run side was already at its peak and when legs and wind ran out, this great side expired with them. Finally there was Stanley Matthews and Blackpool with three cup finals in six years and victory in an epic 1953 Wembley game.

This then was football's so-called golden age. The ad hoc football of the war had evolved, through that transitional period of early peacetime, into a domestic English game which produced great teams and great players. The crafty inside-forwards of the pre-war age like Carter, Doherty and Wilf Mannion of Middlesbrough were still around at one level or another. There were great players like Nat Lofthouse and Tom Finney who, while not members of the great club sides, were still the superstars of their day. For English fans the game was still about the Football League and the FA Cup. The nasty shock of being beaten by the United States in the 1950 World Cup had been buried, if not forgotten, and European competition was still some years distant, but 1953 was another watershed in the history of football in this country. There were still the great players to be seen every Saturday afternoon of the season, football was still an attacking game with the emphasis on scoring goals, not preventing them at all costs, and, in the North and Midlands at least, the working man's idea of Saturday was still to finish work at noon, have a couple of pints, and drift with his mates to the match. But the boom in attendances was slowly beginning to end. In 1952-3 the total was still a very healthy 37 million, but it would fall steadily each season and never again would the game see the regular 50-60,000 gates at league matches. Times were changing and already some of the men who flocked to football in the years immediately after the war had found something else on which to spend their leisure time. In the coming years the ranks of the absentees would swell until there would be less than half the number of people watching football compared with the absolute peak of 1948-9. Meanwhile, back in 1953, there were some Hungarians preparing to play at Wembley.

9

Wider Horizons

British football was totally unprepared for the shock it suffered on a grey November day in 1953 when the red-shirted Olympic champions from Hungary inflicted a humiliating defeat on the English national team. England's first defeat on her own soil by a foreign side was more than just a defeat, and the manner of that reverse, which left England dazed and demoralised in the wake of a 6-3 hammering, sent shock waves reverberating through the domestic game. Yet nothing happened. According to Billy Wright, England's captain that day, *We just carried on in our own sweet way. People still thought we had the best football in the world, despite the humiliation we had just suffered. The defeat came as a great shock to the public because our press did not report overseas football to any great length at that time. People just didn't realise how good the Hungarians were and, after all, they were the Olympic champions. A year later they won the World Cup, so undoubtedly the general public, through no fault of their own, underestimated them.*

Yet if the man who was happy to watch his football at Old Trafford or Molineux each week had stopped to analyse recent events, he would surely have realised that English colours would soon be lowered at home. The performance of the Austrian 'Wunderteam' at Stamford Bridge in 1932, when England won 4-3 but might easily have been held to a draw for the first time by a foreign team in England, would have probably been beyond his memory; and it was possible to dismiss the 1-0 defeat at the hands of the United States in the 1950 World Cup as a fluke. But what about the Yugoslavians' 2-2 draw at Highbury in November 1950? Or the French drawing 2-2 at the same stadium a year later? And had Austria, who had won 1-0 at Hampden Park in 1950, not held England, again 2-2, at Wembley in late November 1951? The draw with the Austrians might easily have turned into England's first home defeat by foreigners. The Austrians, with their great roving centre-half, Ernst Ockwirk, took the lead and England were happy to end the game on equal terms against a side of skilful ball-players who possessed a greater perception of the game than their hosts. Finally, there had been the 4-4 draw with the Rest of Europe team at Wembley in October 1953 when England's blushes were spared by a last-minute penalty from Alf Ramsey. The FIFA team, drawn from six nations, led 3-1 and gave a magnificent display of short passing, sometimes

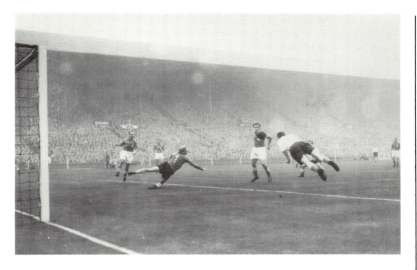

In October 1953 England drew 4-4 with a FIFA team and held on to their unbeaten home record against foreign sides only after a last-minute penalty. Here Blackpool's Stanley Mortensen makes a flying header.

building up moves of up to ten passes, despite their varied backgrounds.

Then came the Hungarians one month later, and the realisation that England were not the undisputed masters of world football should have dawned. The Hungarians' game was different to that of the close-passing FIFA team which had come within seconds of winning at Wembley. Their passing was both short and long, and their skills at killing the ball and evading the close attention of the English defenders brought gasps of admiration. But it was their shooting which made such a telling difference. Said Billy Wright, *They played fast, direct football and they got about eighty per cent of their shots on target, which is a phenomenal rate. They had placed great emphasis on attack in training, scored after only one minute, and with their deep-lying centre-forward Hidegkuti, we were never to establish a presence in the game.*

The Hidegkuti plan was devastatingly simple and effective. Hidegkuti was an inside-forward who wore the number nine shirt traditionally reserved for the centre-forward. He played deep, rather like the centre-half of pre-Chapman days, while the men in the shirts normally used by the inside-forwards, Puskas and Kocsis, pushed forward. They were both prolific goalscorers and the ruse worked perfectly. The tactics were perfected before the Hungarians came to Wembley where they baffled the English half-backs, who did not know whether to dog the players they were traditionally expected to mark, or remain where they were and trust that things would work out. Things did not work out for England and after conceding an early goal the home nation collapsed. Billy Wright can still roll the names of that Hungarian side off his tongue, and he delights in telling a story against himself concerning his attempted tackle on Ferenc Puskas as the Hungarian scored the third goal. Puskas's wizardry as he pulled back out of Wright's path before slamming the ball home, moved someone to comment that the England captain *looked like a fire engine heading at full speed towards the wrong fire.*

The sort of skill which enabled Puskas to pull that ball from the path of Billy Wright, and then swivel and crash home a brilliant goal, was almost unknown in English football. People may now talk enthusiastically about the skills of the great English footballers of the post-war era, and they are right to do so, but there was little or nothing to compare with the kind of genius displayed by individual Hungarians that wintry afternoon. Followed closely by a modest performance in the 1954 World Cup, England's defeat at the hands of Hungary at Wembley, and a 7-1 humiliation suffered in Budapest six months later, started a huge debate into what was wrong with the domestic game and what could be done to put it right. The inquest was conducted in the sports pages, on radio, in dressing rooms, and in public bars across the country. The Football Association set up a series of technical committees with such eminent men as Busby, Cullis, Rowe, Mercer, Winterbottom and others, offering their suggestions of how to rescue the English and the British game.

As Billy Wright said, there was no dramatic reappraisal of how England should play the game, simply a new desire to prepare for the game in a more sophisticated way. Slowly, out went the old training methods of lapping around a pitch and doing physical jerks in the old Army PT style. In came Continental training methods and the understanding that the ball had to be mastered at all costs. Until then it had been of secondary consideration in training and Danny Blanchflower tells the story of how he asked the manager at his first English club, Barnsley, for a ball: *He couldn't have looked more horrified if I'd asked for a transfer. He told me that they never used a ball at Barnsley. The theory was that we'd be hungry for it on Saturday if we didn't see it for the rest of the week. I told him that, come Saturday, I probably wouldn't even recognise it.* The myth of the short-passing Hungarians led to coaches examining that side of the English game, yet only one Hungarian goal at Wembley had come from a move originated in their own half. The shock of that defeat had led to the British game asking searching questions of itself; but the lessons had not been fully learnt and the answers to those questions were incomplete.

The period around 1952-4 was a watershed in the British game, highlighted by the defeats at the hands of the Hungarians. Attendances could not possibly maintain their absolute peak of the late forties and between 1949 and 1951 they began to decline, slowly at first, but then dropping alarmingly between 1952 and 1954 when the seasonal total was more than five million down on that for 1948-9. It was a slide which would never be checked.

The effect of the Hungarian victories was to bring about the final realisation that British football could learn from the Europeans. Until 1953 the domestic game had been an insular one with football in Britain proceeding along its well-worn and well-tested path, while the Continental game aspired to different avenues. From 1953 it had to be accepted that what had been good enough to give England supremacy before the war was not now sufficient to ensure continued domination of world football. British football had little to do with the rest of the world before World War II. Almost all the early European and South American clubs were started as a result of British influence, the earliest football missionaries being servicemen, diplomats and traders who took the uniquely British game of association football to the farthest corners of the globe. The home nations did not, however, rush to play foreign teams. The first England internationals played abroad were in 1908 when Austria were beaten 6-1 and 11-1, Hungary 7-0 and Bohemia 4-0. England returned the following summer and beat Hungary 4-2 and 8-2, Austria 8-1, and thereafter felt no further need to play against foreign opposition until after World War I, though there were plenty of international sides nearer home who would have relished the opportunity to host a match against football's mother country.

FIFA (Federation Internationale de Football Association) the world governing body, was formed in 1904, but the FA was not represented until two years later. Scotland, Ireland and Wales followed in 1910, but in 1919, when the FA decided that there should be no matches against recently vanquished Germany, Austria and Hungary, neutral countries, and later France, Belgium and Italy, decided to continue matches with those former enemies of Britain. The result was that in 1920 the UK associations withdrew from FIFA. In 1924 they rejoined, but the relationship was never easy and in 1928, following disagreement over payments for 'broken time', the home nations broke away once more and remained outside FIFA until 1946.

The British effectively turned their back on the rest and when the World Cup was introduced in 1930 there was no entry from the nation which had taken football to the world. As the England team was unbeaten by a foreign team until 1929 (when Spain won 4-3 after the England party had played in Paris, Brussels and Madrid within one week in the days before air travel) there seemed little reason for them to worry. The FA was much more interested in fostering the game in the Empire and there were many visits to Australia, Canada, New Zealand, South Africa and the West Indies, with trips lasting as long as modern cricket tours. The scores were often of cricketing proportions, too, and it is more likely that football in these areas was actually repressed by the clear examples of the wide gulf which existed between the footballers of the Empire and those of the mother country. Meanwhile, the Europeans and South Americans nurtured their own game largely unnoticed by the British. England's first appearance in the World Cup in 1950 resulted in a freak, though still humiliating defeat at the hands of the United States, and in 1954 they reached the quarter-finals of the World Cup in Switzerland before losing to the holders, Uruguay. Following hard on the heels of the two shattering defeats by Hungary, failure in the World Cup made the game's rulers in England start to take stock of its position.

European football was now seen to be advancing quickly and the movement towards European unification in the early fifties, which was seen as a means to end the national antagonisms responsible for two world wars within a single generation, carried football along in its tide. Well before the Treaty of Rome established the EEC in 1957, soccer was moving towards its own common market place. Competitive European football was about to be born, but first there was the example of an English club hailed as 'champions of the world' by the English press after some stirring and famous victories over Continental clubs, among them the Hungarian club side Honved who included five members of the 1954 World Cup winning team, and six of the side which had humiliated England at Wembley twelve months earlier. Of that now legendary forward line, only Hidegkuti was absent.

Wolves' three famous victories against Russian and Hungarian sides earned them the unofficial title of champions of the world with their successful long ball tactics. Billy Wright, Wolves and England captain, self-conciously clutching a bouquet of flowers, leads out the Midlands club for their match with the Russian side Moscow Dynamo in November 1955.

Wolves, most of all the English clubs, pioneered floodlit friendlies against foreign opposition and when they were televised they added a new dimension to the game in Britain. In front rooms throughout the country people gathered around small screens to watch Wolves and their long ball tactics defeat famous clubs. Among those beaten were Moscow Spartak, who went down 4-0 at Molineux in November 1954, and Moscow Dynamo, beaten 2-1 almost exactly a year later. Those were two of three famous victories for Wolves; but the most celebrated of all was the middle one of the three, a 3-2 win over Honved in December 1954. It was an epic match. Wolves, two goals down, snatched victory in the final fifteen minutes and the press celebrated this as proof that, no matter what had happened at Wembley and in Budapest, English football was still the best. Bob Ferrier, writing in the *Daily Mirror* claimed it was *one of the most glorious games I have ever seen,* and added, *What a golden double for Wolves. With these results Wolves have made English football once again a power in the world game.* David Wynne-Morgan in the *Daily Mail* also had no reservations and he wrote, *Immediately after the match, as Billy Wright led his team of mud-covered heroes into the dressing room, Stanley Cullis, their manager, said, 'There they are, the champions of the world'.*

Reaction from the foreign press was, naturally, somewhat more restrained. Gabriel Hanot, a former French international and then editor of the influential French sporting paper *L'Equipe,* wrote: *We must wait for Wolves to visit Moscow and Budapest before we proclaim their invincibility . . . there are other clubs of international prowess, Milan and Real Madrid to name but two. . . .* The following day *L'Equipe* published a plan for a European tournament to establish just who was the best European club team. Both FIFA and UEFA (the European governing body) were unenthusiastic, but when they saw that the clubs would go ahead anyway, they decided that they must give the new competition, which we know as the European Cup, their blessing. Sixteen clubs entered for the first season 1955-6, but there was no English entry. Chelsea were forbidden to take part as champions because the Football League feared a massive backlog of fixtures; had the runners-up, Wolves, finished one place higher things might have been different, for the Midlands club had captured public interest and there would have been a massive lobby for them to enter.

The history of the European Cup and its sister competitions, the European Cup-winners Cup and the UEFA Cup (formerly the Inter-Cities Fairs Cup) is deserving of a book on its own. Hanot's mention of Real Madrid was prophetic and for the first five seasons of the European Cup (full title European Champion Clubs' Cup) the Spaniards dominated the competition. Playing in all white they overran the defences of champion club after champion club. Their players — Di Stefano, Kopa, Gento, Rial, Alonso, Santamaria and company — became as well-known in England as the names of home

The 1960 European Cup final between Real Madrid and Eintracht Frankfurt was hailed as one of the greatest football matches ever played. Thousands of Scots remained on the terrace at the end of the game to cheer the teams. Here Di Stefano scores Real's second goal.

favourites. Their magnificent run of victories culminated in a 7-3 victory over Eintracht Frankfurt in front of 135,000 people at Hampden Park in 1960. It was one of the most glorious football matches ever played. Di Stefano scored three goals; and there were four goals for Ferenc Puskas, the former Honved star who now lined up in one of the greatest club sides of all time.

By the time Real won their fifth successive champion of champions trophy, European football had become accepted as part of the wider British game. In the European Cup's second season Machester United had incurred Football League displeasure by entering the competition. Busby's United reached the semi-final before losing to Real Madrid. That season the Old Trafford team won the First Division again and were back in the European Cup the following season. Returning from a tie in Belgrade, having once more reached the semi-final, Manchester United suffered the tragedy of Munich. The team which Busby had created would undoubtedly have dominated British, and perhaps European, football for a decade or more had it not been destroyed in the slush at the end of a Munich runway. Eight players died, among them the England trio of Roger Byrne, Tommy Taylor and the incomparable Duncan Edwards, a giant among men. The city of Manchester still bears the mental scar of that awful day in February 1958, while English football in general was set back by the death of the team. At a time when British football, through Manchester United, appeared to have come to terms with the challenge from the Continentals, the Munich tragedy severely checked the advance. Only slowly would it be resumed.

Centre spread from the programme for the Manchester United versus Real Madrid European Cup semi-final second leg played at Old Trafford on 25 April 1957. United were the first English club to make an assault on European competition and it took the might of Real Madrid to halt them. The teams show both the famous pre-Munich Busby Babes, notably the England trio of Byrne, Edwards and Taylor, and the famed names of the Spanish champions. The train fares to London for the following month's FA Cup final also make interesting reading over twenty-five years later.

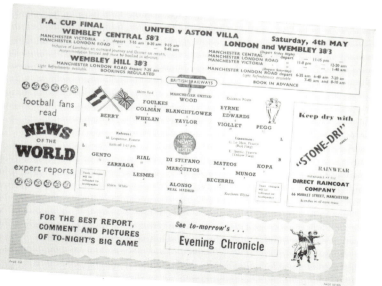

Tactics-2

When Nandor Hidegkuti came to Wembley in November 1953 and bemused the England defenders by wearing a number nine on his back, but playing much deeper than the traditional spearhead centre-forward, he showed just how stereotyped British football had become. The Hungarians had modified the game in a way which England's defenders found impossible to comprehend. Besides Hidegkuti's role

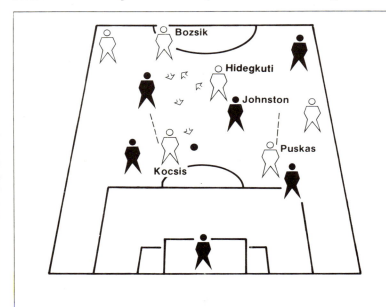

Hidegkuti, nominally the Hungarian centre-forward, came deep and Johnston, the England centre-half followed him and was pulled out of position. Kocsis and Puskas could move into space and still be onside because the England full-backs covered behind their centre-half. England's wing-halves were equally confused and did not know who to mark. The WM system foundered against this tactic

as a deep-lying centre-forward, and inside-forwards, Puskas and Kocsis, pushing up into what amounted to twin striking positions, the Hungarian wingers also came deep to add to England's confusion and misery. For decades British footballers had been indoctrinated with the same ideas: a centre-forward was a man who wore a number nine shirt and who led the forward line; wingers wore numbers seven and eleven shirts and stood wide on the touchlines waiting to receive the ball, upon which they would speed down the line and attempt to get around the full-back before sending over a high centre for the man wearing number nine to rise up and head for goal. When a team like the Hungarians decided that things need not always be so, England's best eleven had absolutely no answer.

The shackled minds of English footballers were also the reason why, when Don Revie played deep with Ken Barnes, as Hidegkuti had done with Bozsik, Manchester City were suddenly a major force. The numbers on players' backs had assumed such significance that when Revie went out wearing a number nine and then proceeded to play deep, opposing centre-halves, who had always marked the man with the number nine shirt, were at a total loss. The centre-half would wander upfield after Revie and leave a great hole in the middle of his defence. If footballers had stopped to think, and accepted that the number on a man's shirt meant nothing, then the deep-lying centre-forward plan would not have been nearly so effective. Revie would have been marked by someone else and the centre-half would have been in position to pick up whoever came through in the number nine's place. It was not surprising that hardly anyone knew what to do; the deployment of a deep-lying centre-forward was the first major development in the game since Chapman's 'third back' of thirty years earlier. Yet this new development was not so much about a man changing position as simply changing shirts.

Wherever revolutionary tactics evolved they would cause a ripple effect even in Britain, the country which had taught football to the world and which for years had been totally resistant to outside influences. When Brazil won the 1958 World Cup with their 4-2-4 system, it was very quickly copied in Britain, though without similar success since many managers and coaches failed to realise that a system alone could not bring success; the team had to include the players who were able to operate that system. Brazil's 4-2-4 was simple enough. A team with twin-strikers needed to move one wing-half upfield slightly, while the other had to come back to play alongside the centre-half, both to combat the twin-strikers and to maintain the cohesion of the team. The new partner for the centre-half was needed because, as more and more teams played with twin-strikers, teams with a back line of three men found themselves readily exposed. The new four-man back line rarely ventured over the halfway line, the two men in the midfield had the responsibility of building up attacks, and the wingers hugged the touchlines and found themselves tightly marked by a smaller, quicker breed of full-back who had replaced the old-style slow, beefy defender. The two central defenders pivoted on each other when danger threatened down the middle. Once a few teams adopted this style, every other team was forced to follow suit. Four defenders were needed to cope with four attackers; two central defenders were required to match two central attackers.

This was the style introduced by Brazil and yet, even in that 1958 World Cup final, the Brazilians modified it to what was the beginnings of the more defensive 4-3-3. When Sweden began to exert pressure on the South Americans, the Flamengo winger Mario Zagalo, who was to manage the Brazilians to World Cup triumph in 1970, dropped back to become a third man in midfield; in 1962 he was both a third midfielder and a fourth attacker in Brazil's World Cup team, but although the hint of the 4-3-3 system had showed itself in 1958, by the following year it was 4-2-4 which was slavishly being copied by Football League teams. There was much anguish, however, for it was still not understood that systems can only be of merit if the players who can work them are available. British football, with its emphasis on great strength and aggression, struggled to adapt and many teams found their central defenders caught square as they failed to work in unison.

The 4-2-4 system in its purest form never took a hold in British football and although there was a greater use of two central defenders and of tight-marking full-backs, many British teams were happy to retain the system which had served them so well for decades. Real Madrid had shown that with a team containing six or seven world-class players it was possible to dominate European football, but quite naturally every team could not be blessed with that number of truly great players. Coaches turned instead to searching for ways to compensate for the lack of top-class talent. Perhaps if it was not possible to outplay good teams, then it might well be possible to outfight them and outrun them; perhaps new techniques which put greater emphasis on defence, rather than looking towards attack, might be the answer. In 1961 the maximum wage for players was abolished and overnight professional footballers became much better paid. In return they were expected to be fitter and more organised, if not more skilful. The game of football, at the highest level at least, was about to become more difficult to play than at any time since the modern game was fashioned in the public schools. Under the old WM system, even under the Brazilians' 4-2-4, each player had a defined area of the pitch in which to work. There now came on the scene a manager whose philosophy was mobility. Eight years after the Brazilians excited the world in Sweden, England would win the World Cup with a system which produced just the opposite emotion, a system which would impose itself upon British football for more than a decade and which is alleged by many to be the main reason why hundreds of thousands of people decided that football was not the game they now wanted to watch.

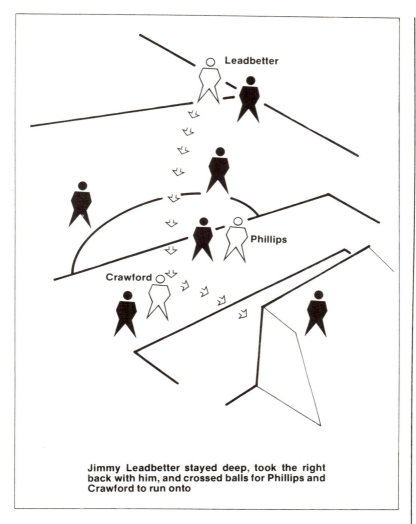

Jimmy Leadbetter stayed deep, took the right back with him, and crossed balls for Phillips and Crawford to run onto

The revolution began in the quiet footballing backwaters of Suffolk and reached its peak at Wembley Stadium where it proved itself capable of world conquest. In August 1955, Ipswich Town, newly-relegated after just one season in the Second Division, appointed the former England full-back Alf Ramsey as manager. Ramsey was the man who scored the last-minute face-saving penalty against the FIFA team at Wembley in 1953. He played against the Hungarians later that month, and so had felt the full blast of humiliation suffered by English soccer. Now, in one of the outposts of professional soccer, he began to unfold a revolution, refashioning the Ipswich team in a manner which was to herald the dawn of a new age in football.

77

In 1956-7 Ramsey returned Ipswich to the Second Division. Four years later they were promoted to the First Division for the first time in their comparatively brief professional history, and within twelve months they were champions. Ramsey's success lay, as had the success of the Hungarians, in the fact that he presented opponents with tactical problems of a kind which they had never before met. His main ploy was to take Jimmy Leadbetter, the best passer of a ball in the Ipswich team but a run-of-the-mill footballer for all that, give him the number eleven shirt and position him deep on the left touchline. His job was to accept passes coming out of defence and transfer them accurately to Ipswich's tall, eager strikers. The opposing right back, conditioned to marking the old-style left winger, was drawn forward while Leadbetter dropped the ball over his head and into the gap where Ray Crawford and Ted Phillips, and right winger Roy Stephenson were waiting. It was devastatingly simple and effective. As Ipswich won the title in 1962, Crawford and Phillips scored sixty-one goals between them and Ipswich had concealed their lack of real class with a tactical move. Two years before this, Tottenham had won the double with one of the most attractive club sides in history; now Ipswich won the league title with one of the least attractive. It was Spurs who finally exposed the flaw in Ramsey's plan. Right back Peter Baker ignored Leadbetter, who was picked up by a midfield man, and with Baker, and his full-back partner Ron Henry marking the two strikers, and centre-half Maurice Norman picking up anything they missed, Spurs beat Ipswich 5-1 in the 1962 Charity Shield match. Two years later Ipswich were back in the Second Division. Nevertheless, Alf Ramsey had started something which would fundamentally alter the face of football.

In October 1962 Ramsey was appointed England team manager. He replaced Walter Winterbottom and became the first real 'manager' of the national side, successfully doing away with the international selection committee which had hitherto presented the team manager with his team. Now Ramsey could name his own men and he set off on the path which would lead England to triumph. Ramsey's first match in charge saw England lose 5-2 in Paris and for a while he courted the 4-2-4 system. Ramsey knew, however, that systems need the players to make them work and he had no international-class wingers available. Equally he wanted players who would give him greater mobility in midfield and by the summer tour of 1965 England, while winning in West Germany and Sweden and drawing in Yugoslavia, was using more men in midfield. In December 1965 England played in Madrid and Ramsey's 4-3-3 style emerged from that game. The Brazilians had made 4-2-4 work because they possessed two world-class wingers. Ramsey's England now began to capitalise on its strength in midfield. From the first whistle in Madrid England completely bemused the Spaniards who were used to a tight-marking game. They could never hold on to the players they were expected to mark and the running,

West Germany have scored against England in the 1966 World Cup final at Wembley. But it was England who won the match, thanks to the revolutionary tactics of Sir Alf Ramsey.

switching England team left them helpless. The full-backs had no orthodox wingers to mark, and when they went in search of them, England's full-backs came forward and the Spaniards were beaten 2-0. Ramsey perfected the system, shuffled the midfield until he settled on the right combination, and in July 1966 his 'wingless wonders' won the World Cup by beating West Germany 4-2 after extra time in the final at Wembley.

Domestic football had already suffered from a taste of the dreary football imported by European competition. The Italians used the notorious *catenaccio* system of man-to-man marking backed up by a *libero* or sweeper, who moved behind the back four, sweeping up anything they missed. Though the system had first seen the light of day as the Swiss 'bolt' of Karl Rappan in the thirties, it was the Milanese teams, AC and Inter, who applied it so effectively in the sixties. It did not take long for managers to realise that what gained a draw in Athens and Belgrade could also net a point at Highbury and Old Trafford and here were the first signs of teams trying to stop the opposition playing before playing themselves. As negative football began to take hold, attendances slipped again; and when clubs began to emulate the 'wingless wonders' in the wake of England's World Cup triumph, football became even less attractive. The increase in attendances which followed immediately after 1966 would soon be reversed.

When English league clubs decided to copy the successful formula which had taken England to the world championship, there was an inevitable backlash. England's victory had been achieved by inter-

By the mid-seventies
players found little room
in which to work.
Arsenal's centre-half Jeff
Blockley finds his way
blocked by the
attentions of three Stoke
City players.

By the 1970s some teams were using only two, or
even a single attacker to try and break through
massed defences. Much of the football was
played in midfield and the old orthodox winger
was extinct

national footballers who had enough skill and knowledge to overcome the difficulties of performing in a confined midfield. When bread-and-butter footballers were faced with the same system, they did not possess the same degree of skill to escape close attention in a cluttered midfield. Players became fitter and better organised, but they could not become more skilful overnight, and the result was a dreadfully dreary league programme. The system spread down through to the lowest levels of the game and all the time the defensive arrangements grew more pronounced until there were matches where teams faced each other with five defenders, four in midfield, and only one man up front, a lone attacker smothered by defences who were now well organised. In 1960-1 seven league clubs scored more than 100 goals; by 1963-4, only Southampton, in the First and Second Divisions, reached three figures; and by 1970-1, Liverpool could finish fifth in Division One after scoring only forty-two goals, an average of one per game. They conceded only twenty-four and with one more point would have finished third.

The effects of European football, where away matches in two-legged ties made teams aware that they must defend at all costs, and Ramsey's World Cup success which had made wingers extinct, all brought about defensive soccer. In the absence of being able to do anything more constructive, teams packed their defences, for it is always easier to destroy than to create. Defenders, though they must have some skill, need far less to defend, especially if their organisation is good, than forwards need to attack, for attackers need skills for which no programme can be devised. When goals did come they were largely from set-pieces like corners and free-kicks. The Dutch reached the 1974 World Cup final with their so-called Total Football where every one of the outfield players was both attacker and defender, free from the constraints of fixed positions and rigid formations. They became known as the team without a centre-forward and when they lost the final to West Germany, it was Gerd Muller, the one type of player the Dutch did not possess, who scored the winning goal.

By 1979-80 the seasonal figure of Football League attendances had dropped to just over 24.5 million; the following season it had gone down to just under 22 million. Yet in European competition the English game dominated and the European Cup remained in England for six years from 1977. In 1980 the European Championship finals were played in Italy and they were a dreadful advertisement for soccer. Jack Rollin, in his editorial in *The Rothmans Football Year Book 1980-1* commented: . . . *Behind it lies the graver issue that the gap is widening between a fear-ridden negativity, thinly-veiled as a technical exercise to satisfy egoism of modern coaching methods, and providing first-class entertainment.* The championships were a disaster and following another mediocre British season, the televising of them could have done the domestic game no good whatsoever. Further examples of how sterile football had become must have been a major cause of

Liverpool's wonderful consistency was rewarded yet again in March 1983 when they won the Milk Cup final at Wembley. For Bob Paisley it was his last visit to the famous stadium as a manager. He retired at the end of the season, leaving a legacy of success upon which Joe Fagan, the latest in line of the famous 'boot room brigade' could build.

attendances in England dropping by a further 2.7 million in 1980-1.

Meanwhile the English season continued to be dominated by Liverpool. First under Bill Shankly, then Bob Paisley, Liverpool became the most consistent club side that the league had ever seen. Paisley's record alone saw him win the First Division title six times between 1976 and 1983, the European Cup three times, the UEFA Cup once and the Milk (League) Cup three times. Liverpool's secret lay in their remarkable 'boot-room brigade' where the managerial dynasty of Anfield is built upon solid tradition. Mistakes are logged and never repeated and in 1983-4, Paisley's successor Joe Fagan was able to draw on that same knowledge. The fount of football knowledge at Anfield never runs dry.

Throughout the seventies and into the eighties soccer was primarily a midfield game. Of course, in any game, one team was always on the attack; but much of the action took place in the middle third of the field and football was a teasing, testing game with players content to knock the ball sideways and backwards until the way was clear. Midfielders were content to wait, no matter how long it took. In 1983 there seemed to be a greater desire to move forward more quickly, and there were now players taking up positions wide on the flanks. It was not a return to the old-style wing play, but it was an encouraging sign to those who yearned for such days.

Beyond all that, however, one team appeared on the First Division scene whose tactics delighted those who wanted a return to the old-style football. Watford had spent almost all their time since joining the league, in 1920, in the Third and Fourth Divisions. Then millionaire pop star Elton John became their chairman, Graham Taylor, the former Grimsby and Lincoln player who had steered Lincoln to promotion, became their manager, and Watford's success was assured. In 1978 Taylor took Watford to the Fourth Division championship, and the following season they were promoted again. By the start of 1982-3 Watford were lining up for their first season in the First Division. It was a tremendous achievement and although Swansea City were promoted from the Fourth Division at the same time as Watford and made it to the First a season before them, the Welsh club achieved it with experienced players signed as short-term measures specifically to win promotion. Watford did it without a single household name of which to speak. Swansea, after finishing sixth in their first season, were relegated in their second after being handicapped by injuries and although at the time of writing Watford

Watford's 'long ball' approach took them to First Division runners-up spot in 1982-3; Graham Taylor's side had the right players to exploit the tactic and their black strikers Luther Blissett (right) and John Barnes excited crowds wherever they played. In the close season of 1983, Blissett moved into Italian football where he would find goals much harder to come by against the tight man-to-man marking *catenaccio* system employed there.

still have that traditionally more difficult season to face, they stormed away in their first and finished runners-up behind Liverpool.

It was the way in which Watford achieved their success which caught the imagination in 1982-3. Their system revolved around the long-ball tactics used so successfully by Wolves in the fifties. Under Stan Cullis, and with the help of research done by a wing-commander at RAF Bridgnorth, Wolves used fast, direct wingers Jimmy Mullen and Johnny Hancocks to capitalise on Wing Commander Reep's findings that the long pass was the most lethal. Mullen and Hancocks used their speed and cross-field passing, stylish Peter Broadbent fed the wingers, and central strikers Roy Swinburne and Dennis Wilshaw, and later Jimmy Murray, capitalised on the service. The Moscow teams and Honved were destroyed by this tactic, although when Wolves played in the European Cup in 1959 and 1960, they failed to make an impact and the long-ball tactic was found wanting in the face of more sophisticated European football, though it should be remembered that there were several notable absentees from the

Watford reintroduced the long ball, finding their front runners with passes of 70 or 80 yards and eliminating much midfield play

Wolves side of the mid-fifties, including Hancocks and Mullen.

The long-ball was abandoned and English clubs looked towards European ways which, coupled with Ramsey's approach, gave them notable successes in the European Cup from 1977 to 1982 (Manchester United became the first English club to win it in 1968), though more than one of those later finals were dreadfully boring affairs. Then, in 1982-3, the long-ball made a reappearance in the First Division. Graham Taylor had been to see Reep, by now living in retirement in Cornwall, and one year later Watford were Second Division runners-up. Watford had two central attackers in Luther Blissett and Ross Jenkins, and two fast, direct wingers in Nigel Callaghan and John Barnes. Callaghan and Barnes (who played alongside Blissett for the latter part of 1982-3) knew their job: to cross the ball and get in shots at goal. Watford played these four men in attack and got the ball to them at every opportunity, using long passes and eliminating much of the midfield work which had bored so many people. On some occasions it was not match-winning football, the infallible football team has yet to take the field, but it proved to be effective enough to take Watford to second place in the First Division. What is more, it proved popular with the supporters who had long yearned for a return to the 'good old-fashioned English game'.

On the reverse side of the coin Watford came in for more criticism than the infamous Leeds United team of the late sixties who achieved their success with so much negative, boring football. Watford, by playing just the opposite game, were accused of setting football in England back ten years. The argument against Watford's style was that they had simply exhumed a tactic which football had been thankful to bury twenty years before; that it was kick-and-rush football more suited to a public park than to the most competitive league in the world. The ability to kick a ball accurately over eighty yards might be thought of as a commendable skill, but this swift transference of the ball to the front runners, using one pass instead of half a dozen, offended football's 'thinkers'.

After Watford had beaten Spurs 1-0 at White Hart Lane in November 1982, Tottenham's manager, Keith Burkinshaw, told reporters: *We'll never use these tactics because if we did, we might as well get rid of Glenn Hoddle and company. You don't need sophistication in midfield to play like Watford. All they do is to help the ball along to their forwards... when you play them the ball is always going to be going forward and is always going to be in the penalty area....* There were those who now began to wonder if they had missed the point of football, that perhaps trying to move the ball towards the opposing goal was not, after all, the object of the game.

Undoubtedly there is room for both styles of football and teams will continue to play to their strengths, whether they be in midfield or at the vanguard. Many of Watford's critics were players when British football was trailing badly behind the rest of Europe. They saw the domestic game as badly organised and they set about changing it. Now they are afraid that Watford's success might result in football slipping back to the days of hopeful long balls and slipshod organisation. The point to dwell upon is that Watford do not play **hopeful** football and they play to the strengths of First Division footballers best equipped to work that kind of system, just as teams with the special midfield skills of Glenn Hoddle and Bryan Robson play to theirs. As long as a team has players of that calibre in midfield, it will continue to build up its attacks in that way, for what would be the point of bypassing such players?; but for the Watfords, who have wingers and tall strikers, then the long-ball game is a better bet. There is nothing to say that all football has to be the same and the fact that the midfield game has been practised by many teams with only humble artisans has been a major reason for much of the boring football of recent years.

Whichever way the English domestic game proceeds in the next few years, it cannot be denied that Graham Taylor's Watford have brought to it a blast of fresh air. It is unthinkable that Liverpool (who, though they do not use the long ball, still take only four or five passes to get into the opponents' penalty area) will suddenly begin to use aerial warfare on the Watford scale, or that Manchester United, with their brilliant midfielders, will abandon the possession game for what another critic described as *wham, bam, thankyou ma'am*. No one must forget that those golden days about which some people talk so enthusiastically, the days of 100 goals a season for some clubs, two wingers in every team and some fine individual strikers, were also the days when British football lagged far behind the top European clubs in the competitive arena. The answer to it all may lie somewhere between the two extremes of styles. The match analysis of Reep and Cullis has been used by Charles Hughes, the FA director of coaching, to show that, for instance, in 1982, seventy-five per cent of the 106 goals scored in the World Cup finals came from moves of fewer than four passes; and **intelligent** long passing increases the ratio of free-kicks and corners (and 50 per cent of goals come from such set-pieces). In November 1982 I saw Watford attack Nottingham Forest in a Milk Cup-tie which they lost 7-3 and which had both managers embracing on the touchline and the crowd applauding the teams off the field. The purists were, no doubt, upset: but as Graham Taylor said afterwards, *There is no rule to say that a game can't finish 9-9.* Taylor has never sought publicity. It is simply that his resurrection of the long-ball game has provided football with its biggest on-the-field talking point since Ramsey 'outlawed' wingers. Football is realising after all that it is better to attack than to defend. The game's place as an entertainment will depend on the degree to which this is achieved. What we should remember is that the long-ball suits Watford because they have good front runners and rather more ordinary midfielders and defenders. That must be kept in perspective for it would be wrong to assume that Watford offer a panacea for the game. What they do offer is an alternative which, in turn, makes the game more open and attacking. But it has to be accepted as a historical fact that all the truly great teams of the post-war era have played possession football. Once more the point to be made is that to be a great team, great players are needed.

If football's tacticians can evolve a balance between the creative midfield game and the 'Watford way', then football can satisfy both the purist and the man who likes his soccer served up with long-range passes and four-man raiding parties. Just as the midfield became clogged with too many footballers of less than modest ability, so any long-ball game which relies on footballers ill-equipped to work it, will be just as unattractive. The sight of conscientious but uninspired players chasing frantically after balls punted upfield by men who do not possess the skill to make the long-range pass will drive away just as many fans as do the midfields clogged by eight or ten mediocre footballers. However if teams play to their players' strengths, and Watford's tactics are executed by men of First Division calibre, then we should all be satisfied. In the final analysis it is not so much the tactics employed as the players employing them which may check the game's declining popularity. The creative arts of a Hoddle or a Robson, and the blitzkrieg strikes of Blisset and company each bring enjoyment. Employed properly they may also halt falling attendances.

The Players

The professional footballer is, to many people, the most revered man in Britain and, at the same time, the most maligned. On the one hand he is the superstar entertainer with the fast car, the attractive wife or girl friend, the luxury house, and the income of a highly successful businessman; most of all he is a hero. On the other hand he is the man who many people blame for the game's financial problems, the man who has taken out of football huge sums of money not commensurate with his ability or with the amount of money he can draw in through the turnstiles, and it is rare to find a club whose income from gate money exceeds its wage bill. Of course, one cannot base an argument on that alone. The professional footballer performs a greater function than simply making up a team. Each man, each team, each match supports the great football industry of pools, publishing, souvenir manufacturing and many other ancilliary businesses which depend on the weekly football programme for their existence. If there was no professional football then many more people than the players and managers would be out of work, not least those who are paid to build up the stars and then knock them down again.

The footballer was once the great working-class hero. He lived in the same street as his club's supporters, travelled on the same buses, and rarely moved far from the area where he was born and bred and where he first tasted the game. His earliest football was almost certainly played in the street, where the goals were the doorways of local factories, or perhaps railway arches. The ball may have been made of rag, or some boy, better off than the rest, might have had a tennis ball. The games were played until well after dusk under flickering street lamps and owed nothing to the playing fields of Eton or any similar establishment where hard knocks were taken with good grace. The street football of industrial England was a frantic affair which sometimes brought escape from the dole queue in areas of the highest unemployment. The clubs and their grounds flourished in such an environment where there was precious little hope. To be good at football was to be given hope, hope that the mine and the mill might be escaped. It offered possible work where there was none; and a brighter alternative to a routine existence.

Workmates and neighbours were cheered when a boy escaped and signed for his local club. They did not lose touch with him, nor he with

Wilf Mannion was the classic example of both the great inside-forward of the golden age, and the man who stayed close to his hometown and never lost touch with the people who regarded him as their hero. He was also a rebel and went without wages for six months in the fifties when Middlesbrough refused to transfer him and he refused to re-sign what he saw as a totally one-sided contract which favoured the club. Here he is in 1951 kicking a ball with small boys who must have revered him as a great England international. Mannion first played for Middlesbrough, his home town club, before the war, and he was one of the stars who drew tens of thousands to soccer in the late forties and early fifties.

them. He was their hero, the one who had escaped, but the one who remained. They could identify with him, and thus with their local club and with the game. The emancipation of the professional footballer changed all that and today the average working man, though he may well be more affluent than his father could ever have imagined, still cannot fully relate to the lifestyle of the new Saturday hero. Thus the supporter sets his hero higher standards. He knows that his income is high, that in many cases, simply by putting his signature to a signing-on form, he can pick up sums of money which the supporter can never dream of banking except, ironically, if he wins the football pools. Such knowledge inevitably breeds resentment if the star does not perform to the supporter's expectations. The picture is often painted of the footballer with the expensive car, gold jewellery and girl friend on his arm. He is sometimes held to have no real interest in the game, save in its ability to keep him in the manner to which he has become accustomed. So while the supporter still reveres his footballer, he now questions the star's place in society. Is it right that a footballer, or a pop star come to that, should earn far in excess of the Prime Minister? Of course, the pop star can only hold on to that income for so long as people buy his records and flock to his concerts. Footballers have been known to earn huge sums of money for playing before virtually empty houses.

The very lifestyle which makes the footballer appear larger than life to the supporter also brings him into contempt and there is one popular picture of the star soccer player as a dim-witted and inarticulate man whose own description of his emotions revolves around being either 'over the moon' or 'as sick as a parrot'; a man who is exceedingly well-paid for doing as little as possible and who is bleeding the game dry. In reality the majority of professional footballers are responsible members of the community, who care about the game which gives them their livelihood and who realise that they are fortunate to be paid for doing something they so thoroughly enjoy.

Naturally, as in any section of society, there are the unpleasant individuals; and there are, undoubtedly, those whose appreciation of the finer points of life is not as acute as it might be. I remember once interviewing a regular First Division player for a series of ghosted newspaper articles. He numbered two league championship medals among his souvenirs as well as a number of appearances in the European Cup and had travelled the world with his club. Within a very short space of time he had run out of anything to say, and by article number ten was confining his answers to yes and no. In desperation I asked him about a recent trip he had made to Egypt, thinking that here was one subject, at least, upon which he might venture an original opinion. His eyes lit up: *Great hotel in Cairo, swimming pool, the lot!* What about the country itself, I asked. Had he, for instance, visited the pyramids, one of the most awesome wonders of the ancient world? *Well,* he said, struggling to remember, *I think so. They took us on a bus trip and they reckoned that was where we were. But I'd seen them on the box so I stayed on the coach and we carried on playing cards.* At that point I gave up the interview.

Most footballers have led a cloistered life since they left school and joined their club. Unlike professional cricketers, who have to climb into cars and wrestle with road maps while moving themselves from Taunton to Middlesbrough, professional footballers are ferried almost everywhere. Their tickets and their passports are carried for them as they are shepherded from coach to airliner, to hotel, to ground and back, often without setting eyes on the outside world and forming absolutely no impression of the new city or country that they visit. Card schools in hotel rooms are likely to be their one source of intellectual stimulation; and anyone who has travelled the world will know that the inside of one Holiday Inn is very much the same as another, that one could be in Los Angeles or Birmingham for all the

90

difference there is.

However, all this does not mean that the professional footballer is just a muddied oaf. Most people would be pleasantly surprised if they were to get into conversation with a pro soccer player. He would have much more to say than they had been led to believe. The former Aberdeen, Tottenham, Arsenal and Nottingham Forest centre-half Willie Young is an example. To the person on the terrace, or in the stand, Young is a big, burly defender who is fed on raw meat and let out only on match days; to sit with him for an hour over a drink is to understand a quietly-spoken giant with a deep passion for the game and a great deal of sense to offer. Though hardly from the 'tanner ball' school of Scottish footballers who sharpened their skills on the cobbled streets of Glasgow half a century ago, Young can become quite nostalgic when recalling the street football of his native Edinburgh in the late fifties and early sixties. I spent an evening with Young on the day he had been given a free transfer by Forest in May 1983, due mainly to a personality clash with Brian Clough, in which he talked of the game's problems in a way which would have surprised his critics.

Of course, players from different eras will have different things to say. Those who played before the abolition of the maximum wage often feel that today's players are not so talented and creative as in their day. The only exceptions to that school of thought appear to be those who stayed in the game as managers and coaches and who have retained a close and constant association with soccer. Today's players mostly view yesterday's men as old reactionaries who would not know what had hit them if they had to contend with the tight, organised football of the eighties. Today's players claim that the old-time greats would not find it so easy now; that it was one thing, for instance, for a winger to waltz around a stiff, immobile full-back whose one job was to boot the ball upfield in the vague direction of the opposing goal, and quite another to cope with the fast, fit, all-purpose man of 1983-4. There appears to be far more logic on the side of today's players; yet the memory and the heartstrings lend enchantment to the others.

RAICH CARTER

Raich Carter can look back upon one of the most brilliant careers any footballer ever enjoyed. FA Cup winners' medals, First Division championship medal, England caps, they all came the way of the football genius who paraded his priceless talents on Wearside before the war. But through all the triumphs there is one abiding memory which Carter, the crafty, arrogant inside-forward of the thirties and forties, will carry painfully with him to the end of his days, a memory which literally brings him to tears.

Raich Carter has only to think of the ranks of unemployed men trudging to Roker Park, Sunderland, in the hungry thirties, anxious

Raich Carter leaves a London station in 1937, proudly showing the FA Cup which he has collected as captain of Sunderland.

Now in his seventies, Raich Carter still has his medals to remind him of his glory days as he sits in the conservatory of his Hull home.

for some relief from the grim realities of the dole queue and the means test, and the tears come rolling down his cheeks. He finds the words hard to say, but with difficulty he recalls the way in which Sunderland supporters scraped together their admission money and then banged their encouragement on the windows of the bus carrying Carter and the other Saturday heroes to do battle with Arsenal, Manchester City and the other giants of those days.

Fighting back the tears he said, *I used to take one look at those fans – heaven knows where they got their money from to come and support us – and I knew that I had to turn it on for them, to entertain them, to make that one day brighter than the rest of their miserable week.* Carter now lives in comfortable retirement on the outskirts of Hull, and the man who lorded the midfield in English football for nearly twenty years has another reason to be sad. Football, the game that he and his kind lit up for the massed ranks of the dole queue, is no longer the game he knew and loved. The new generation of unemployed, and everyone else for that matter, will find little to brighten up their Saturday afternoons in 1983, according to the man who was born to be a great footballer.

He says, *It is sad, but I no longer enjoy watching football today. Most of the time I find myself looking at my watch and wishing that the referee would blow his whistle and put us out of our misery.*

Carter was born at Hendon, the birthplace of soccer in Sunderland, in 1913, and as a youngster he hung on to the railings at the Roker end, watching Charlie Buchan, Albert McInroy and Bobby Marshall, his boyhood heroes and players from another great era in football's story. Young Carter went into one of the finest England schoolboy teams of all time, where his colleagues included Cliff Bastin and Len Goulden; and was then rejected by Leicester City, who must have long rued the day they sent him packing after a trial period. Carter signed for his hometown club where he stayed for the next fourteen years. He was soon in the first team, then into the full England side against Scotland in April 1934, and as one of the Football League's youngest captains he led the Wearsiders to glory. By the age of twenty-three Carter had achieved every honour then available to an English footballer: First Division championship medal, FA Cup winner's medal, and full international caps.

The Sunderland side which Carter steered to those honours was typical of the way professional footballers saw the game in the thirties. He said, *We attacked all the time. Even away from home we never thought about losing. It was win, win, win, all the time. We never went to an opposing ground and thought that, as we had started with a point, then we would hang on to it. Not like they do today. Our philosophy was to attack. Mind you, we had a great manager in Johnny Cochrane, a little man who'd come to us from St Mirren and who always wore a bowler hat. What a great character he was. The manager's job in those days was to assemble a good team. Once he had done that he just let them go out and play. There was none of this blackboard nonsense you hear about today. Team talk? Johnny used to stick his head around the dressing room door just before a match, smoking a cigar and smelling of whisky, and ask, 'Who are we playing today?' We'd reply, 'Arsenal, boss,' and he'd just say, 'Oh well, we'll piss that lot', before shutting the door and leaving us to it.*

Carter has a fund of stories about Cochrane which illustrate the apparently carefree way in which professional football was played before the last war. One such tale concerns a succession of missed penalties which the Sunderland team suffered on their way to the First Division title in 1935-6: *We came in at half-time in one particular match having missed a penalty and Johnny started to tell us how we ought to tackle the job. We knew he hadn't played much football himself and one or two of the lads started to rib him, asking him how he would have taken the kick which had just been missed. Johnny put his bowler hat on the dressing room floor, we cleared a space, and he ran up and kicked the hat high into the air. We all cheered and mobbed him, telling him, 'Great goal, boss!' to which he replied, 'Well, actually, I hit the bar!' That was Johnny Cochrane and that was football in those days, played first and foremost to be enjoyed.*

Carter also has a special memory about the time that Sunderland won the FA Cup in 1937. He said, *It made me smile when Sunderland won the Cup in 1973 and Bob Stokoe, who was then the manager, took the players away to Miami for a holiday. Do you know where we went when we won the Cup? We went to Seaham Harbour – and we only went there because Johnny knew a chap who owned a pub.*

But for all his apparent eccentricities, Cochrane was held in high regard by Carter who is unashamedly nostalgic about those days on Wearside. He said, *We had a great manager, a great board of directors who did not interfere, a great team – and, most important of all, no coaching. That is what is wrong with football today. The players are not allowed to go out and do their own thing. All their natural flair is coached out of them. The good player should be encouraged to be unorthodox, to invent.*

Carter's first FA Cup Final triumph came two years before the war when he inspired Sunderland to pull back from a goal down to Preston North End to win 3-1. That day he measured his passes with the perfection of a champion bowler sending a wood towards the jack, scored the goal which put Sunderland into the lead, and when war came was at the height of his powers as one of the world's best inside-forwards. Carter is still bitter about that war and it shows when he tells you, *I was twenty-five when war broke out and people don't often realise that I was still a young man when I left Sunderland. A player reaches his peak around twenty-eight and I lost my best years to the war.*

That war also cost Carter most of his international caps which were destroyed in an air-raid on Sunderland. Worse still, as far as he is concerned, the conflict cost him many more appearances. He still smarts at the thought of winning only thirteen full caps: *Imagine playing your first game for England in 1934 and your last in 1947 and only ending up with thirteen recognised appearances. I played in seventeen wartime and Victory internationals with some of the greatest players who ever kicked a ball. But the matches never counted towards full caps.*

It was the war which brought Carter's Sunderland career to an end. He joined the RAF, found himself at Loughborough, Leicestershire, helping to rehabilitate injured airmen, and joined Derby County as a guest player. It was here that he teamed up with another great pre-war inside-forward, Peter Doherty, who was also serving in the RAF at Loughborough. When the war ended both men found their respective clubs unwilling to guarantee their futures and a joint fee of £15,000 took them to Derby's Baseball Ground where Carter picked up another FA Cup winners' medal in 1946. From there he moved to Hull as player-manager and guided the Tigers to the Third Division North championship in 1948-9 in front of gates of 50,000. Then followed a spell in Ireland with Cork Athletic, and finally managerial spells with Leeds and Middlesbrough.

Raich Carter still has the meticulously-kept scrapbooks charting his career from schoolboy to international star. He needs no second bidding to produce them and will quickly point out an item, *Look at that for a headline,* which seems to underline the opinion that other people had of him as an arrogant inside-forward; but Carter's arrogance is not that of a know-it-all. It is just that he knows he was a world-class player and cannot see the harm in admitting it. Besides, he will tell you that it was good for football: *When I was at Derby I never wanted Peter Doherty to get a better press, a bigger headline, than me; Peter was the same, and that was good for the club and good for the game.*

Raich Carter strode the midfield, a silver-haired general, in the glorious days of Matthews, Finney, Hagan, Mannion and the rest. His arrogance showed in his game as he put his foot on the ball, changed the pace and direction of play, stroked inch-perfect passes, and hammered glorious goals from twenty yards *(I was never one for the goalmouth)*. It is that skill which he wants to see return to the game today.

Never mind about messing with the rules, giving three points for a win and all that nonsense. Let footballers be themselves. I am convinced that money is not the problem. If I had been a millionaire I would still have played in the same way. It makes me sick to hear players say that they need motivating. What a lot of rubbish. If a player needs motivating to take part in this beautiful game, then he shouldn't be allowed anywhere near it. Take off the shackles, don't stifle the players coming into football. Until that happens football grounds will remain half empty, people will look at their watches and pray for the final whistle. But if they see skill and invention . . . well, then there is still hope for the game.

PETER DOHERTY

They used to say that Peter Doherty, the flame-haired Irishman who danced his brilliant, erratic way through English football with Blackpool and Manchester City in the thirties, and with Derby, Huddersfield and Doncaster after the war, was a discontented footballer. Doherty was not pompous or bad-mannered, nor was he petulant or sulky in the way of some of the highly-paid stars of later years. Indeed, it would be difficult to meet a more courteous and gentle man. Doherty's discontent was with the system, and he was a trade unionist far ahead of his time, scornful of what he thought was an iniquitous professional game which held an unfair stranglehold on the rights of players. Peter Doherty's discontent manifested itself on the field, in the need to be a more innovative and skilful player. Many of his contemporaries described him as the greatest inside-forward they had even seen, a brilliant and inventive football genius.

In his seventy-first year, 'Peter the Great', as the press dubbed him, moved almost as spryly as the day he last pulled on the emerald green shirt of his country back in 1951. What saddened this son of Ireland who thrilled football audiences through the game's golden age either side of World War II with his unique brand of innovative soccer, is the fact that in 1983 he saw only footballers who were afraid to do even the simplest things with the ball. Sitting in the lounge of his Blackpool home surrounded by the caps and medals which bear witness to his achievements, the former Coleraine junior bus conductor who became an Irish national hero, despaired for the future of football.

A rare picture of Peter Doherty who danced his brilliant, erratic way through English soccer before the war.

Peter Doherty now lives in Blackpool where he has retained just one Irish international cap — the first he ever won.

What is more, he could not understand why he, and people like him, were rarely, if ever, asked for their opinions on how to save the game he loves from what he sees as a slow and lingering death. It is not that Doherty needs the work, for he has long since reached the age when most men reach for pipe and slippers. It is just that after a lifetime in football, as First Division champion and FA Cup winner, international player and team manager, he has one priceless commodity to offer — knowledge.

Peter Doherty was one of the most gifted footballers in the game's history. From the moment he signed for Blackpool in 1934, he lit up English soccer as a man who could shoot equally hard with either foot, tackle, head, dribble, and measure out the most inch-perfect passes. In addition he had the most brilliant football brain and the ability to invent. He won a League championship medal with Manchester City before the war, an FA Cup-winner's medal with Derby County in the first season of peace, was capped for Northern Ireland sixteen times although, like Carter's, his international appearances were meagre because of the war, and later steered Doncaster Rovers to the Third Division North title, and Northern Ireland to the last eight of the 1958 World Cup. They are all impeccable credentials, and yet no one has come knocking on his door in recent times to ask him what he would do to solve football's ills. If they did, they would be treated to tea and cakes, and one of the most fascinating discussions with one of football's master craftsmen.

He would tell them, *You know, a few years ago you would go past Bloomfield Road, Blackpool, where I started my English career, and you would hear the 'oohs' and the 'aahs' of the fans on the terraces and sitting on the edges of their seats. They were so involved in the game that they thought they were playing. If you watched the man next to you you'd probably see him flinching involuntarily, straining for a high cross or bracing himself for the tackle which was about to happen out there on the park.*

Today those fans are bored, they want the match to end. And that is not because Blackpool are having a bad time, it's the same almost everywhere you go. The reason the fans are bored is simple. Football sets itself up to be an entertainment and yet most of it is far from entertaining. The coaches have seen to that. They have frightened players to the point where they dare not be inventive. They pass the ball across the field, back to their goalkeeper, anywhere but up the field. The fans yawn and football takes a step nearer its grave. Coaches should put confidence into the minds of young players. Instead they put only fear. They make him afraid of doing anything other than the safe, predictable thing, playing the ultra-safe ball. He is inhibited and will never learn to experiment.

In Peter Doherty's day, no manager would have called instructions to an international player once he was on the pitch. Said Doherty, *He would not have dared to do so. After a game the manager could call me in and speak to me, tell me what he thought I might have done wrong. But out there on that park I was the sole judge of what I did. Today they have coached the skill out of the individuals. Maybe if I had been born later, then they would have shut me down too. If I was playing today – and I watch and sometimes think I still could – then I would not have been anywhere near as successful. In my day the managers let the players do their own thinking out on that park.*

Not surprisingly for a man who spurned the off-the-field system which he felt kept the players in subjugation, Doherty despises the coaching systems which he feels inhibit players of invention today: *These awful systems like the dreadful 4-3-3 and 4-4-2 are the bane of football. They have obliterated the wing forward from hitting the dead-ball line, they have narrowed the game down, and they have confined most of the play to a funnel up the middle of the pitch. The answer is to change the law so that there is no possibility of being offside except in the eighteen-yard box – and then only to protect the goalkeeper.*

But Peter Doherty's overriding worry is a lack of skill among today's players. It is a theme to which he continually returned, often jinking across the room to illustrate a point. He said, *Even the elementary things are not done properly. When I was playing I never took my eyes off that ball for the whole ninety minutes. I was always watching it, even when it was at the other end of the pitch. I was working out what I would do next. Today I see players walking about with their backs to the ball, even in the World Cup. I cannot believe what I am seeing. To take your eyes off the ball is the biggest crime in football and yet there are international players doing exactly that. The game of football is all about habits, good and bad, and too many of today's established stars have too many bad habits and too few good ones.*

Peter Doherty was not just a crafty inside-forward of the old school. Modern coaches who talk about 'work-rate' would have been open-mouthed at the amount of work which Doherty got through each match. People who saw him at his prime claim that there was not a pitch big enough for him, that one of those Saturdays they felt sure that he would drop down dead from sheer exhaustion. Besides a super-abundance of skill, Peter Doherty had more than his fair share of stamina and raw courage. Yet he is in no doubt about a footballer's most priceless asset: *The organ of success is the brain. Juggling with the ball is all very well if you want to go into a circus – but the game is played from here,* he said, jabbing his forehead with a finger.

What could you teach a player like Matthews or Finney, or Carter or Hagan? They all had this instinct born in them, and they knew the strengths and weaknesses of those around them and adapted their play accordingly. It is a sad indictment of coaching that we have developed football almost to an exact science and yet failed miserably to produce those kinds of players. In fact, there is exactly the reverse situation because, as I have already said, we have players who can't do even the basics.

Peter Doherty cannot understand why managers do not play more open, attacking football: *It began with England winning the World Cup and continued when Leeds were successful. People copied them. If someone would now come along and play total attacking football, and if they had success, people would follow them. If I were involved in football today, then I would guarantee results with attacking football, because it can be done. Perhaps the success that Watford have had will make people sit up and take notice that the best way to win is to attack. Better to play with the ball in front of your opponents' goal than in front of your own.*

Most people outside the Professional Footballers' Association now agree that the freedom of contract which the players won is one of the game's main problems, and Doherty is no exception: *It was the worst thing which every happened,* he says, a remark not without a touch of irony considering his fight for players' freedom. But as he says, *That great champion of players' rights, Derek Dougan, will see things rather differently now that he is on the other side of the fence.*

The Irishman who had so much vision as a player also has a far-reaching view of how he imagines the game will be in ten years time. *The day will surely come when we will have that super league, not just comprising the top English and Scottish clubs, but encompassing the best in Europe too. Air travel has cut down journey times, Western Europe is not that big compared with the distances which the North American clubs have to travel, and I feel it is a near-certainty. Third and Fourth Division football – perhaps even Second Division too – will be part-time and will be almost a nursery for the few rich clubs which will be left.*

Football is sick and I fear greatly for its future. It needs a tonic and it needs it urgently. People go to football out of habit and once they change their habits they may be lost to the game forever. There are so many more diversions. Look, even bingo gets bigger gates than football here in Blackpool.

DANNY BLANCHFLOWER

When Danny Blanchflower tells you that what happens to football's losers is more important to the future of the game than the fate of successful clubs and managers, it is difficult not to see a gentle irony in the fact that the speaker was himself rarely, if ever, a loser. Captain of Tottenham Hotspur when they won the double in 1961, the FA Cup again the following year, and the European Cup Winners' Cup the year after that, Danny Blanchflower is still a household name in Britain, well-known even to those who were not born when he played his last professional match in April 1964. He was voted the best attacking wing-half of all time in 1983 in a brewery-sponsored opinion poll on sporting greats, and so, even two decades after his last game, he is remembered and revered.

Blanchflower in reflective mood at his Virginia Water home twenty years after his retirement as a player.

The reasons for the endurance of the Blanchflower legend stretch far beyond his exceptional ability as a player, for he is one of the game's most original thinkers. When he played for Tottenham and Northern Ireland (he was capped fifty-six times) he did not confine himself to the nominal duties of a skipper. *Too many captains just carried the ball out and called 'heads',* he said, and it is doubtful whether any player has had a greater impact on the British game. Blanchflower played football with his head as well as his feet. He won the ball, not with the bone-jarring tackles which are the hallmark of so many of his trade, but with exquisite timing; he held it until precisely the right moment before releasing a pass which was both neat and beautiful. Danny Blanchflower was a neat, precise, cool artist of a footballer. He possessed the genius to alter the entire face of a game if it displeased him, and although he endured an occasional dark moment, like the time he was deposed of the Tottenham captaincy for a while when certain directors disapproved of his making tactical changes, he was a winner in every sense of the word.

So what does Blanchflower mean when he says that what happens to the losers is more important than the lot of the winners? *I mean that we must eliminate this terrible fear of losing. Each season only one team can win the First Division title, there can be only one winner of the FA Cup, and the Milk Cup can be lifted by only one side. But does that make all the others failures? We drive fear into the hearts of managers and players because we won't allow them to lose. They become cautious and unadventurous. A fellow becomes a better player only if he is extended. For too long we have been happy to see two attackers face eight defenders. This has left us with footballers who are unable to improve. So, unless we change our attitude to losers, nothing will improve.*

Blanchflower has always been entranced by football. Born in 1926, in a terraced house in the Bloomfield district of Belfast, the son of a shipyard worker tells the story of how his mother found him hanging precariously out of his bedroom window, captivated by the sight of boys playing football in the street below. Blanchflower does not remember the incident, for he was only two years old at the time, but he recalls how his mother retold the story in later years, recounting her horror at the thought of her baby son falling from that window and thus ending a brilliant career before it had begun.

It was the ball which fascinated me, said Blanchflower, his striking blue eyes emphasising every word, every syllable, for he thinks and talks about football as passionately and as articulately as he played it. *I was drawn to those streets where the game was played before and after school, often until late in the evening under the shadow of the gaslamps. I was about five when I was first allowed to take part, playing with boys who were years older than me. It was about a year before I actually touched the ball, but it was this game of chase which fascinated me. I knew nothing about winning and losing, the first demand was simply to play. That ball was my god and I soon learned that you could play football without any other players, but you could not play without the ball. I found that the more attention I gave it, the easier it was to control, the friendlier it became. Yet there were days when the more I chased it, the more it went its own way. I discovered that although you could master the ball, you could never master it enough. It is the elusive god of the game.*

RAF service was followed by football with Glentoran and then representative soccer with the Irish League team which brought him to the attention of English scouts and a move to Barnsley who paid £6,500 for Blanchflower's signature in 1949. Two years later he moved to Aston Villa, less than enamoured with a system which left him sitting in the kitchen of a Derby hotel while Villa and Barnsley officials discussed his transfer over lunch. Three years on, he moved, for the last time, to Tottenham. Arthur Rowe, of push-and-run fame, took the classy, free-thinking Irishman to White Hart Lane and under Rowe's successor Bill Nicholson, Blanchflower and Tottenham prospered together. Spurs became one of the most cultured club sides in history. His career lasted until he was thirty-eight, by which time he could no longer maintain his supreme standard. He said, *The irony of football is that you learn most of its secrets only after you cannot perform them any more.* Today Blanchflower, twice voted Footballer of the Year by the Football Writers' Association, writes a widely-read column in the *Sunday Express,* a job he

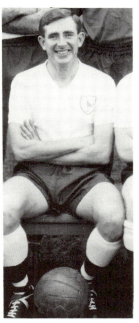

Danny Blanchflower in his days as Tottenham Hotspur captain.

has been doing these past twenty years. It says much of the man when he tells you that he tore up a contract with the *Observer* because they wanted to interfere with his articles. A BBC contract was also shredded for similar reasons: *People who didn't know what they were talking about were telling me what to say, which meant that I didn't know what I was talking about either.* Only the fact that *Sunday Express* editor John Junor promised him no interference persuaded him to sign for that newspaper.

Today he sees no bright colours in the game. He said, *Every colour is grey, coaching is grey, and all too often the coach is a fellow who couldn't play himself. In my day we played primarily for fun. Football was a party, a celebration and that is what it should be. When a coach comes along and tries to change things he is pilloried. Look at Graham Taylor who has returned to the game of chase. Watford rouse crowds, excite them. They may even anger some people, but they never bore them. One journalist,* who writes better than he thinks, said that Watford will put the game in Britain back ten years. If only they could. We would have bigger attendances, no million-pound transfers with wages to match, and fewer debts.

Blanchflower, who managed Northern Ireland for a spell, spent ten months as manager of Chelsea, from December 1978 to September 1979, and he recalls his first week at Stamford Bridge when a teenage player came into his office and demanded a move. I told him, 'Son, I don't even know your name, so move yourself – from my office'. You see, he'd heard stories of players being transferred and receiving large sums of money. Another player I wanted to sign asked me for £25,000 tax free. I wouldn't be a party that, but I know it goes on. There is the story of another player, a former international still playing today in the Second Division, who asked for, and got, £40,000 tax free from a club, and it wasn't one of the so-called super clubs who paid him either. Every business needs discipline and football is no different. The reason why Manchester United were such a great side after the war was because Matt Busby had no money to buy players, so he had to cultivate them from grass roots. Today Manchester United are one of the richest clubs and they don't just try to outplay everyone else; they try to outbuy them. Freedom of contract and the abolition of the maximum wages are the twin evils. Wage ceilings could have been raised considerably without taking the roof off; and freedom of contract was crazy and just added to the problems.

Blanchflower's recollections of the football of his youth brought him to the conclusion that today's game is divided: We went on the same buses, pushed through the same turnstiles, and jostled good-naturedly with opposing supporters because a football ground was a community. Today the game is divided. Football is not about VIP boxes. Sponsorship has caused more problems than it has solved. Sponsors aren't in the game for the good of football, only for what they can get out of it. Now there is talk of big video screens at matches, but you have to ask yourself where it will all end. More technology will see more commercialists creeping into the game, there is a new breed of carpetbagger in football. What will it do for the soul of football? Football mirrors society. The Italian game with its artistry and passion, and its brutality, mirrors the two institutions in that country, the Vatican and the Mafia. Football in Britain is divided because our society is divided. The old communal joy has gone. The man in charge of our wolf cubs team in Belfast was not a coach, but he loved football. On Sunday mornings he would read out the match reports of the previous day's big games. He made football a romance, and above all else, that is what the game should be.

But in the end it is about controlling the money, and about how we treat the losers. When the rewards for success are moderated then winning will not be more important than the game itself. You see, you cannot have a game without a winner and a loser. There are far more losers than winners *and if we say we cannot lose then we have no game. If you cannot lose, then you cannot learn – and if you cannot learn, then you cannot improve.*

TOM FINNEY

The day I went to see Tom Finney was typical of the outsider's picture of industrial Lancashire. Rain sheeted down from a sky as grey as gunmetal and bounced up hard from uneven pavements. I was early for our appointment and lunched in the small dining area behind the counter of a fish and chip shop, which was the nearest thing to a restaurant that I could find in the Fullwood area of Preston where Finney's successful plumbing, heating and electrical business is situated. In the condensation on the window someone had written the letters 'PNE'. The heat from the fish fryer soon sent the letters running messily down the window, which seemed to adequately sum up the plight of once-proud Preston North End, First Division giants for many years, but at that time hovering perilously cose to the bottom of the Third Division.

The previous Saturday, Preston had entertained Portsmouth. Five thousand people had drifted into Deepdale to watch a goalless draw which helped Portsmouth, themselves one-time First Division giants, a little nearer the Second Division. Thirty years earlier, a match between the two clubs would have attracted six times that number of spectators, for that was the season in which Preston finished runners-up to the league champions Arsenal. The following year Preston lost the FA Cup final to West Bromwich Albion, all of which reminded me that Tom Finney OBE, JP, veteran of nearly 600 first-class games, holder of seventy-six England caps, and now president of the club which he served for a quarter of a century, numbers neither a league championship nor cup winner's medal among his trophies. The man who was the first to be twice voted the Footballer of the Year, has neither of the major club honours. Born in Preston in 1922, he signed for the club in 1937, played — and scored — in all five forward positions, and when he retired in May 1960 over 30,000 people packed Deepdale to see his last appearance in an otherwise meaningless match against already-relegated Luton Town.

Best remembered as a winger (the debate as to whether he or Matthews was the greater still rages and can never be settled except to say that they were both great players with differing styles and Finney was undoubtedly the more complete footballer). Tom Finney also revived a flagging Preston team in 1956-7 when he adopted a deeply-lying centre-forward role, though his fleeting appearances in the England number nine shirt met with only limited success. He was the textbook footballer, with broad shoulders and narrow hips, leaning over the ball with perfect balance. He glided, rather than ran, over the turf and he was so often in total charge of the proceedings that some people accused him of hogging the stage. Such a charge was nonsense, for Finney's instinct was never to waste a ball and he preferred to hold it rather than lose it. He was both artist and artisan, elaborate but never flamboyant. He could play the old wing forward's game of rounding his full-back and laying on the pinpoint centre or ground pass; and the fact that he scored almost 250 league goals is a measure of his phenomenal cutting edge which followed his hard, direct runs at goal from the wing.

Tom Finney, the outside-right, sends yet another defender floundering.

Tom Finney, the successful businessman, magistrate and president of Preston North End.

Today Tom Finney heads the firm which is the result of his father's advice to get a trade before signing professional forms for Preston. Finney completed his six-shilling-a-week apprenticeship while playing as an amateur. It earned him the nickname, in later years, of the 'Preston Plumber', and over eighty people now earn their living from the family firm he began with his brother Joe, who died tragically young. Tom Finney the successful businessman, is still easily recognisable as Tom Finney the footballer of twenty-five years ago. The fair, wavy hair sits further back on his forehead, and his weight may be a few pounds over his playing days of ten and a half stone, but he is still the same Tom Finney, with kind, tolerant features, an alert and friendly man who speaks with the rich voice of an East Lancastrian.

He is in no doubt about what people want to see when they pay to watch a football match: *They want goals, goalmouth incidents and displays of skill by individuals. But I find it hard to believe that there will ever be the same excitement or the same abundance of truly great players as there was in my day. There has been just one golden era since then and that began when Spurs won the double in 1961 and went through to the Manchester United side of George Best, Bobby Charlton and Denis Law, when Best was in his prime for those two or three seasons. There was Jimmy Greaves, too, but since they finished there has been a real scarcity of quality players. True, an occasional example occurs, like Kenny Dalglish, but I wonder if he would have stood out quite so much in our day. I do see an improvement in entertainment in 1983 and there are signs that managers were trying to be more positive, but they still have a long way to go. The game is short of genuine wingers and I'm surprised that more managers haven't looked more closely at the Brazilians and some of the other successful international sides of recent years. They have all used at least one orthodox winger.*

As president of a Third Division club in 1982-3, Finney knew all about the monetary problems gnawing away at football, though he claimed that Preston were perhaps better off than many Third clubs. But as he pointed out, the club was also in one of the most concentrated areas of top-class professional football in the world. Lancashire, birthplace of the paid game, boasts, if that is the correct word, fourteen Football League clubs. The First Division's two most glamorous clubs, Liverpool and Manchester United, are within easy reach of Preston, and in 1982-3 there were also Everton and Manchester City in the top league, and four Lancashire clubs in the Second Division. Said Finney, *With transport to matches now so easy – good motorway links and wholesale car ownership – it is inevitable that Preston people will go to Anfield and Old Trafford. When I visit local schools and youth organisations and ask the boys who they support, they'll tell me Manchester United and Liverpool, and when I ask why they don't watch Preston, they'll tell me that it's a rubbish club in the Third Division.*

Finney had hit upon one of football's problems. Less than twenty years ago it would have been largely unthinkable for a boy to watch any team other than his hometown club. Today supporters owe no allegiance to their home side, especially if, like Preston, that side languishes in the lower reaches of the league. The same desertion is felt by semi-professional non-league clubs who might have numbered several thousands among their supporters a generation ago. Football League clubs like Preston have also suffered because of the removal of the maximum wage. Said Finney, *When we were in the First Division we had six or seven local boys in the side. With a maximum wage there was less reason for them to move because they could earn no more at Manchester United than at Preston North End. With the ceiling removed, and with the club sliding down the league, we were unable to hold on to the players who, if they had stayed, might well have brought about a return to the successful days.*

The only way that a player could move for more money in Finney's playing days was if he went abroad. In 1952 the Italian millionaire president of the Sicilian club, Palermo, offered Finney a stunning financial package, for those days, c ʿa £10,000 signing-on fee, wages of £130 per week for two years, a car, Mediterranean villa, and free travel for the player and his family. Preston refused to let him go and that was the end of the matter, though if Finney had made money his god, then he could have packed his bags and deserted the club. Finney does not know how to be bitter, yet he cannot help but reflect on a system which denied him a rightful wage while playing before massive crowds. He said, *I don't resent today's wages and I think any man should be able to hire his labour for as much as he can get. I was just unfortunate to play in the days when wages were not in line with the crowds we were packing in. It was the clubs who got rich then.* There is more emotion in his voice when he describes how players were treated off the field. International stars could travel first-class if that was how their clubs did things; so Arsenal men returned from England matches in luxury while players from the likes of thrifty Preston occasionally found themselves in the crowded corridors of second-class railway carriages. However all of life's dark moments have a lighter side and Finney laughs when he recalls Tommy Docherty's time at Deepdale. The hard-tackling wing-half went into the manager's office to complain that Finney was earning two pounds a week more than Docherty, winter and summer. *He's a better player than you,* said the manager. *Not in the summer, he's not,* retorted Docherty.

Tom Finney's playing experience was limited almost solely to First Division and international football. As president of Preston North End he now knows more about life at the other end of the scale and he is convinced that Third and Fourth Division clubs must go part-time if they are to survive. He said, *I was never a full-timer in the truest sense because I worked at the business before and after training. Footballers train for only a couple of hours each day and I cannot see why they can't cope with a full-time job and maintain an adequate level of fitness and skill at the lower levels.* He is in the minority of Third and Fourth Division club officials who want to see a return to regionalisation: *It's got to come, bringing less travelling and more local matches. Smaller divisions are also long overdue. For many clubs the season is over in January. Let's have more clubs involved in promotion and relegation battles right to the end of the season.*

Tom Finney is optimistic about football's future. He sees clubs like Preston, and many bigger clubs too, going right back to the parks and streets in search of raw talent. The big cities will throw up more coloured players and almost all clubs will spend more on youth policies and less on buying established stars. Whether clubs like Preston will then be able to retain their own talent and fight their way back up the ladder, or whether they will still be tempted away by a handful of still-rich clubs in a super league, is something which even Tom Finney, the man who Bill Shankly called *the greatest ever* is unable to answer.

TREVOR BROOKING

The 1982 World Cup should have been the highlight of Trevor Brooking's career. Instead it lasted for just twenty-seven minutes of intense frustration and ended with England being eliminated from the quarter-finals in Real Madrid's magnificent Santiago Bernabeu stadium. Brooking's international career had begun in 1974, and after waiting eight years for the chance to play in what should be the pinnacle of any footballer's career, a groin injury sustained in the game against Scotland at Hampden Park in the month before the World Cup finals robbed him of his glory. Only when England were in desperate straits, in the quarter-final match against the host nation, did Brooking and Kevin Keegan, himself relegated to the sidelines through injury, find themselves pitched into the battle. The rest is history. Each man missed a clear-cut scoring opportunity and England failed to gain the victory which would have put them into the last four. Brooking and Keegan had to swallow the bitter pill that they would never again play in the World Cup. Years of preparation and waiting had culminated in less than half an hour of intense, agonising frustration.

For Brooking, injury and frustration were to be constant companions for the next twelve months and it was not until the very end of 1982-3 that he was able to return to the West Ham United first team, the club whose claret and blue he had worn since leaving Ilford County High School in 1965. Trevor Brooking is cast in the mould of the classic English sporting hero, tall, dark and strikingly good-looking, clean-cut and intelligent, a gentleman in a harsh game which has become increasingly competitive and certainly less enjoyable for those who play and those who watch. He made his league debut in 1967, his full England debut seven years later, and won FA Cup winner's medals in 1975 and 1980, heading the winning goal in the latter final. It was in 1975-6 that I registered my most vivid memory of him when he scored a brilliant goal against Derby at the Baseball Ground, and five months later I watched him display brilliance of a different kind when creating a goal for Keith Robson in the European Cup-Winners' Cup semi final against Eintracht Frankfurt at Upton Park.

I met him for the first time at the Savoy Hotel in London where managers, players and journalists were gathered to pay tribute to his former West Ham and England manager Ron Greenwood. Brooking exploded the myth that Greenwood was too technical for his players to understand. According to Brooking, Greenwood had told his players over and over again that football was a simple game, made complicated only by the people in it. Blackboards and model pitches were never used; moves were worked out with real people on real grass, sometimes at walking pace, but never by diagrams. Brooking felt that Greenwood was a better international manager than club boss, because he sometimes struggled to handle the day-to-day problems at club level. At either level he had had one philosophy: to enjoy the game.

Brooking said, *I've been lucky to play with a club like West Ham and I probably wouldn't have enjoyed my football so much elsewhere. Under Ron Greenwood and John Lyall players have always been encouraged to express skill and style and it is a fine reflection on the directors that these men have been allowed to manage in their own way, even when things have been going badly. Another club would have had a dozen managers in the time these two have been at Upton Park. The atmosphere created by the directors has helped because too many managers at other clubs have been afraid to entertain and have erred on the side of caution. I can't blame them because fear of losing has made the game very negative, but the merry-go-round of managers can have done the game no good at all. Ron's great strength has been working with attacking players whereas John, while encouraging attacking soccer, also demands greater defensive consistency. But the philosophies are the same. Too many managers are on one-year contracts and they haven't time to breathe. They get short-term results with short-term measures. It does the club, and the game, harm in the long term and managers should be given time to finish their job.* Brooking's own philosophy is to enjoy the game just as much as he did when he was a schoolboy: *You have to think positively and if you tell yourself that you're going to have a good match, then you most likely will. There is more pressure today, true, but I think the awarding of three points for a win is a good thing. It makes sides attack more away from home, especially at the end of the season when promotion and relegation are in the air. You used to be happy with a draw at home – there was still that buzz in the dressing room – but now the place is like a morgue if you drop two points at your own ground. It has certainly opened the game up.*

Brooking enjoys the lifestyle of a wealthy stockbroker, in a large

Trevor Brooking is one of soccer's few remaining genuine sporting heroes, intelligent, good-looking and a player of international class.

thirties house situated in a quiet cul-de-sac in a small Essex town. There are five bedrooms, three bathrooms and three reception rooms, the result of extensive redesigning, and a large secluded garden with a swimming pool. It is the sort of haven to which a man with Brooking's commitments needs to be able to bury himself along with his Finnish-born wife and his two children. Brooking's parents are from the East End and his father was a Metropolitan policeman for twenty-six years, retiring with the rank of sergeant to become a school attendance officer. Brooking and his elder brother, Tony, played for hours after school and in the holidays, working with a plastic football on the grounds of the South East Essex Technical College after first scaling the spiked fence to avoid the caretaker. In later years, after doing his grammar school homework, Brooking would be out in the garden of his parents' home, again working with that ball. It is a feature of schoolboy life that is missing today.

There is no doubt that certain standards have dropped, and the reason is that youngsters don't spend as much time as we did on developing their individual skills. I do not believe that there should be any eleven-a-side football for children under eleven. Far better to have small-sided games where the boys are involved in actually touching the ball, and less worried about team organisation. They should be encouraged to develop control, and that individual flair is not being allowed to come to the fore in schools and junior football. Admittedly there are sponsorship schemes which encourage boys to work hard, but there are so many different diversions today. When I was a boy I spent almost all my leisure time working with the ball, setting myself little challenges. I would be out in the garden, tapping that ball against the wall, trapping it, heading it, trying to make it do things. We only had an old black and white television, today there's colour TV and video games and a host of other sports vying with football for boys' attention.

Brooking's father was what was known as a 'tough-tackling' centre-half in a local police team and he had his two sons practising with both feet, working hard on the 'bad' foot. Even at his primary school Brooking was perfecting the art which won him forty-seven England caps: *I used to run along the pavement, kicking a tennis ball against the garden fences and controlling the rebounds. I am confident that this early work is the reason why I have always been considered a skilful player. You do not see boys playing football in the street today.*

Brooking was ten years old when his father took him to see his first match at Upton Park. They stood on the North Bank in the days when fathers took their sons to football in an atmosphere of comradeship, and when policemen watched the match, not the spectators. When the crowds were particularly big, small boys would be passed down over the heads of the spectators to the front for a safer, better view. Brooking is doubtful whether he would allow a boy to stand there today and he feels that until we recreate a more disciplined society, trouble at football matches will continue. He said, *I do not believe in corporal punishment in principle, but the cane must make a return in schools, of that I am convinced after witnessing the behaviour of boys I have taken on coaching courses in the East End. I could hardly believe some of the standards of behaviour and there appears to be no respect for teachers who have an almost impossible task in some schools. Those youngsters who cause trouble at football matches would have a shock if they were exposed to the discipline of a professional football club. It is ironic that the game upon which they attach their lawlessness should be one of the few institutions which still demands old-fashioned standards of behaviour from its participants.*

Brooking was in his thirty-fifth year when we talked. Injury had made his immediate playing future somewhat vague, and in any case he had no plans to stay in the game once his playing days were over. His current contract with West Ham ended in the summer of 1983 and while he was considering another year in the First Division, he had no plans to stay in the game as a manager. He considers the life too insecure and besides, he has a number of business interests, any one of which would be welcomed by a player whose career is over. He said, *Any involvement I may have with football will most likely be with coaching schoolboys. If I could produce a professional from that then it could be the most rewarding task of all.*

BRENDON BATSON

When Brendon Batson made his Football League debut for Arsenal in 1972 he was still something of a rarity. Batson's rise through the ranks had been conventional enough, and after being spotted in schools football at the age of thirteen, he had worked his way up until Bertie Mee gave him his first taste of league soccer in the season after Arsenal won the double. What set Batson apart from the overwhelming majority of professional footballers at that time was his colour. Today coloured players are a welcome feature of the game and they have played at full international level, but at the beginning of the last decade coloured players were still rare enough to be noticed for their skin rather than their ability. It may be argued that there is no need to mention the fact that Batson is of West Indian origin, but the point to be made is that the emergence of coloured players has been a significant feature of the game over the past ten years. There have been coloured players in football since before World War II, but not until Clyde Best made his mark with West Ham in 1969 did a coloured player establish himself in the public's eye. By then there was regular televised football.

Batson came to England from Grenada when he was nine years old and the family went to live in Essex. Until he started school in England he had never seen a football match and it was the sight of boys leaving school half an hour early to attend football coaching that launched him on a career which took him to First Division and England 'B' soccer. He said, *I thought if it got you out of school early, then I'd join in, and that is how I got interested. The old Arsenal player George Male spotted me and I signed for them, though it didn't mean as much to me as it did to other boys because I hadn't grown up with the club's name ringing in my ears. It didn't take me long to realise that Arsenal was special, however. It must be one of the few clubs where you have to walk up steps to get in, and Bertie Mee used to take us apprentices to dine in the best restaurants in London, just to let us know that we were with a very special club.*

Batson did not suffer the pangs of homesickness which have sent more than one young player scuttling back to more familiar surroundings. He said, *I was lucky because I could still live at home, but it is a problem and if you conducted a survey, I bet you'd find that of all professional sportsmen, footballers get married the youngest. It is important to have that firm base and security away from the game, and, most of all, someone to talk to when things aren't going so well.*

He played a handful of games before moving to Cambridge United in 1974. There was absolutely no pressure placed upon him, but the youngster felt that he needed regular first-team football. Cambridge had just been relegated, but by the time Batson moved again, following the United manager Ron Atkinson to West Bromwich Albion in 1978, he had helped them back to the Third Division and well on the way to the Second. Batson said, *Atkinson is thoroughly professional and I knew that under him I would go places. That's not to say that I ever thought he'd take me with him when he moved, just that his style of management at Cambridge left me in no doubt that my game would improve and my prospects would be that much better for having worked under him. Joining him at the Hawthorns was an unexpected bonus.* Atkinson moved to Manchester United and left Batson behind, but he did not forget his pupil when Queen's Park Rangers knocked West Brom out of the FA Cup semi-final in 1982. *That was the worst moment of my life,* said Batson, *you feel as though you have let everyone down. Ron phoned me the following morning and said, 'You may think that it's the worst round to get knocked out in, but remember, it's better than going out to Leatherhead in the first round.' That was exactly what had happened when I was at Cambridge.*

Today Batson lives with his wife and two children on the outskirts of Walsall, some six miles from the West Bromwich ground. He had not played football since October 1982 because of a knee injury and after two operations he was looking towards a summer of rehabilitation and a resumption of his First Division career in 1983-4. It had been an intensely frustrating time and Batson would not go to watch his team if it was not a club rule. He said, *I hate watching and I've asked not to be included in pre-match team meetings. I appreciate the gesture but I cannot sit there and not be part of it. I know that the other lads are tensed up and I would rather leave them alone. I'm just in the way.*

Brendon Batson surveys the knee injury which kept him out of soccer for most of 1982-3.

Batson is a highly intelligent, articulate footballer. He is an executive committee member of the Professional Footballers' Association and feels that his fellow players are presented in a distorted manner by the media: *People don't give players enough credit for thinking like responsible adults. Of course we know and care that the game is at a crisis point. At my own club we are aware when season tickets go on sale for next season and we have the same responsibilities as anyone else at the club, probably more. It affects our attitudes to pay claims, and we know that we must do better on the pitch to encourage more people to back us for another year.*

It is on the pitch that the responsibility cannot be escaped. Said Batson, *Of course, when you are presented with a situation where a split-second judgement is called for, then all the instincts and years of training and playing come into force. But over ninety minutes, the times a player touches the ball is relatively small and during lulls and periods of relaxation, when the ball is at the other end of the pitch, you are constantly thinking about the pressures and the significance of that particular match. During the FA Cup semi-final I could see our chances of reaching Wembley ticking away on that big Highbury clock.*

The status of players in society is 'diabolical' according to Batson, though one suspects he meant the opinion which people have of them rather than their financial status. He said, *Footballers have simply reflected the change of the times and yet we have been maligned by the press and the public. One of the greatest criticisms levelled at us is that we fought, and won, freedom of contract, yet where else would it be acceptable for one group of people to tell another group that they cannot leave to better themselves? Although players will have to adjust to the changing face of the game, it must always be accepted that they have the right to ask for bigger salaries and better conditions. If the directors do not want to give us these things, then so be it. But we must have the right to ask.*

Paid directors would be a good thing for the game because they could be sacked, like managers and players, if they did not do their job properly. Too many of them are in the game for the wrong reason at the moment. It's partly a social ladder for them, partly business. Many of them are in the selling game and if they can offer clients a seat in the directors' box and a drink in the boardroom, then it is all part of the selling technique. I think it is beginning to dawn on the public that the players aren't solely to blame for the game's problems. We've taken too much unfair stick in the past from directors who have got things wrong and then put up a smokescreen by blaming greedy footballers. That is not to say that there are not many good directors who work hard for the game and their club. But boards must take their fair share of the blame for the state of football.

Muhammad Ali is Batson's great hero, a sportsman who has done much for the self-esteem of black people, and there is no doubt that being black does have its problems for professional footballers. Batson grimaced at the thought of the crude, vile abuse which he has suffered at places like Leeds and West Ham. *When I first came into the professional game it was mostly good-natured banter between the crowd and the player. But in recent years it has become really malicious. Leeds and West Ham are terrible places to visit, though I must say that it doesn't bother me so much now and I just get on with the game.* I wondered if he had any problems with opposing players: *You know, you're the first person who has ever asked me that. I haven't really thought about it before, but, yes, in the early days there was a fair amount of aggro. But it just seemed to die out and I cannot remember the last time that an opposing player abused me over my colour.*

The increase in the number of footballers of Negro origin is now an accepted part of the game, but although local parks abound with just as many Asian boys playing football, none has yet made his mark in the Football League. Batson said, *It is all to do with culture. West Indian parents always wanted their youngsters to go into the professions – medicine, law and so on – but they woke up to the fact that their sons could be successful in other ways, such as football and cricket. Until Asian parents change their attitude of mind, then their sons will not be encouraged into the game. They want the professions, too, but their culture decrees that they won't get into football as readily and I find them the hardest people to get to know.*

Brendon Batson is certainly not a difficult man to get to know. He talks easily, and thinks hard about the game which gives him his living: *The game of football takes a lot of knocks, but it is better now than it ever was and I am convinced that players are fitter and better equipped. Years ago you had good, average and bad footballers, with one or two great players. Now you have great, very good and good players. The problem is that the spectators' expectations often exceed reality. We play for very high stakes and we do our jobs properly. There is no room for the irresponsible player who may cost you a game, and perhaps thousands of pounds, if it happens to be the one which would have sent you into the cup final or into Europe.*

For Brendon Batson there are too many myths in football, not least the 'professional foul'. He said, *Football is a contact sport, a game of ascendancy, one player over another. The amount of times that you see a player dragged down when he is clean through are minimal in the context of a game. So-called gamesmanship is a myth too. In any sport, cricket, soccer, snooker, darts, whatever you like, players are aiming for an advantage. It's a strange thing about referees that they see the minor infringements in a ruck of players, but they never see the tackle which could break your leg. But football isn't a dirty game overall. We are all professionals earning a living and the vast majority have too much respect for their fellow pros to try to cripple them. The clampdown was a good idea implemented in the wrong way. Take forty-six Football League games any Saturday and you will have forty-six different ways of refereeing.*

Batson was about to spend the summer in Cambridge, working hard to be ready for the 1983-4 season, and the thought of getting back into the blue and white shirt of West Bromwich Albion, coupled with the support of his wife and family, had been his crutch through the season. He nodded to his international caps, hanging proudly on the wall beside other medals and awards, many of them from the supporters' club at West Brom, saying, *Those caps and medals have been the bonuses of my career. But most of all I wanted to be a professional footballer and that I have achieved. Anything else is the icing on the cake. I only hope that I have a few more slices left.*

PHIL BROWN

There could have been few more depressing places in football than the Victoria Ground, West Hartlepool, on the wet, cold morning of May Day Holiday 1983. Hartlepool United were at home to Colchester United in a Fourth Division match vital to both clubs; to Hartlepool because they were in the re-election zone and almost certain to go cap-in-hand to the Football League's annual meeting for the thirteenth time in their history; to Colchester because they lay just outside the top four in the table and therefore had a chance of promotion. But if there was a compelling nature to this match, it escaped the football supporters of the area. Just 804 people, the lowest attendance that Hartlepool United had every attracted, even in their mostly bleak history, turned up to watch. The pitch was in a terrible condition after hours of heavy rain and the game would almost certainly have been postponed, but for the fact that the visiting side had made the long journey from Essex and had stayed overnight. In the grim financial restraints of the Fourth Division, nothing short of an earthquake would have prevented the game being played.

Hartlepool lost the match 4-1 and thus sank further into the dread, dead band of the re-election zone. Earlier in the season, a glance at the league table would have shown their position right enough; now, with two matches left to play, the national newspapers had drawn a line above the twenty-first club in the table. Anyone below that line after the final match was played would be forced to beg for readmittance to the Football League, and in recent years, though league clubs are still renowned for looking after their own, there has been slightly more chance of being ejected, as several clubs can testify. After their defeat by Colchester, Hartlepool United stood in twenty-second place, with Crewe and Hereford, themselves voted to membership at the expense of Barrow in 1972, below them. It was a depressing day, even by the standards of Hartlepool's long-suffering and ever-dwindling band of supporters.

Playing in the Hartlepool defence that day was Phil Brown, a footballer who celebrated his twenty-fourth birthday later that month and who was already the veteran of over one hundred Fourth Division matches. The overwhelming majority of football supporters in Britain had never heard of Brown. He was no one's Kevin Keegan or Trevor Brooking, just an honest toiler who admitted that his greatest moment so far had been playing in front of 16,807 spectators at Leeds Road, Huddersfield, in May 1980 on the night that the Yorkshire club clinched the Division Four championship with a 1-0 win. That was his first season of league football and he was still a part-time footballer, following his trade as an electrician by day and training with Hartlepool in the evenings. Eventually he won himself a full-time contract and became a veteran of such dreary football battlegrounds as Rochdale, Halifax and Tranmere, a world away from the bright lights and deafening roars of Anfield and Old Trafford. This was, however, his first taste of the struggle to survive re-election. In his first season Hartlepool had finished just outside the bottom four, then as high as ninth, missing promotion by six points, and then fourteenth in 1981-2. Now he was learning how to cope with the shadow of humiliation as not even a thousand people considered his club's fight for survival worth supporting.

We spoke on the morning after the Colchester match. He had allowed himself the luxury of a lie-in at his parents' home in South Shields where he was living until his marriage six weeks later. He was still hurting from the memory of the previous day. He said, *It's terrible to play at home these days. There are so few people in the ground that you can hear every insult that's hurled at you, in fact I reckon I can recognise most of the crowd. I wouldn't call them supporters, not real supporters. They only come to hurl abuse and it gets to the younger players especially. We must be the only team in the Football League who would rather play away from home. On other grounds you can build up quite a rapport with the opposing supporters. At Hartlepool it's plain bloody murder.*

Brown's one consolation was that he did not live in Hartlepool and did not have to walk about the town. He was spotted playing for a team called St Hilda's in the Jarrow and District League and he was, and still is, a Sunderland supporter. He had never seen Hartlepool play until he signed for them after one of the club's directors, who lived in South Shields, saw him in local soccer, and he admitted that football at the windswept Victoria Ground was a spartan experience, even when the team was doing reasonably well. Anyone who has ever stood there to watch a match will know the spiteful wind blowing in from the North Sea. From a distance, and especially in the dark, the back of the main stand looks like a warehouse. The official entrance is an anonymous door set in a long corrugated iron fence, and the referee's changing room door had the word 'Referee' chalked on it the last time I heard. During World War I, a German Zepplin pilot found himself over West Hartlepool with a full bomb-load and ablaze following a mid-air battle with a Royal Flying Corps pilot. As he headed to the coast and safety, the German dropped his bombs over the town. Two of them scored direct hits on the main stand at the Victoria Ground and demolished the structure. For years after the war Hartlepool United

Phil Brown of
Hartlepool United spent
1982-3 battling against
re-election and the abuse
of home supporters.

bombarded the German government with demands for £2,500 compensation, but the only tangible reply they received came during World War II in the shape of another bomb dropped by the Luftwaffe. A temporary stand, built after the first bombing, was still in use fifty years later, and the secretary is said to have tried three times to burn it down, on each occasion being discovered in the act by the police. In the early seventies when a new road scheme meant that part of the ground had to be rebuilt, his dreams were realised.

All this illustrates the nature of football at Hartlepool. According to Brown the visitors' dressing room always causes complaints. Footballers the world over are noted for their desire, immediately after a match, to sink into a hot bath with their fellow players. There is nothing peculiar in this, just the simple need to wallow and relax with the fellows who have fought alongside you. In the Hartlepool away team dressing room the bath is so small that only two at a time can be accommodated and visiting teams have to queue up, thus destroying the bonhomie of it all. The home dressing room is better, said Brown, who admitted that they had a gas-fire.

The training facilities for Hartlepool's players had taken a turn for the better since the club had been offered the twice-weekly use of the ground where Northern League club Billingham Synthonia play. Otherwise they took traffic cones and set them down on grassland earmarked for a trading estate. They travelled to away grounds and back in a day when the opposition was within 250 miles of Hartlepool, but they always enjoyed the steak-and-toast pre-match meal favoured by almost all football clubs over the years. On the way back from matches such luxuries were quickly dispensed with and hungry stomachs were eased with fish and chips, bought from some local establishment pleasantly surprised by the sudden appearance of a footballer demanding, 'Cod and chips twelve times please.'

There were sixteen full-time professionals at Hartlepool by the end of 1982-3, two apprentice professionals having been dismissed when their time was up. The former Tottenham and Derby player John Duncan was manager after being unceremoniously thrown out of his job at Scunthorpe, and a measure of how civilised they are at Hartlepool was the fact that Billy Horner, manager since November 1976, had agreed to step down to first team coach to accommodate the younger man. First team coach George Smith had in turn stepped down to look after the reserve side.

Phil Brown could see a time when all Third and Fourth Division footballers were part-timers, with the possible exception of clubs like Sheffield United who found themselves, they hoped, only temporarily embarrassed. He said, *It's definitely got to come. I didn't find any particular problems when I was a part-timer and I used to come off nights and play. The only difficulty might be getting time off to travel overnight to away games. At Hartlepool we already have part-timers and now we train in the evenings which is the only time we can get together to work on set-pieces like free-kicks and corners. The only problem from a playing point of view is that it tends to bring the full-timers down to the part-timers' standard and not the other way round.*

Phil Brown wanted to stay in the game, and he heard that Peter Taylor and Roy McFarland had watched him earlier in the year with a view to taking him to Derby County where one of his friends, Bobby Davison who grew up on the same South Shields estate, was playing, but his more immediate worry was a recent players' strike for which he felt he was unfairly shouldering the responsibility. *The club owed money on a tax bill and we weren't paid for three weeks. I am the club's PFA representative and I was asked to find out from the secretary of the player's union, Gordon Taylor, if we could refuse to train unless we were paid. He said that not only could we do that, but that we could refuse to play our league matches. We threatened not to play against Halifax unless the money was forthcoming. It got television publicity and the money was found, but I think the chairman feels I'm a troublemaker. I was naive and I should have taken a couple of lads in with me to spread the burden. But they elected me to represent them and I never thought that the club would see it any other way. Now I've got to see the chairman and I don't know what the future will be when my contract expires.*

In the meantime Brown continued with the job of trying to help Hartlepool stave off the threat of re-election — they failed — and hoping that Derby County or somebody else would take him away from the biting winds and abusive spectators at the Victoria Ground. For every allegedly overpaid star in Pierre Cardin shirt and Gucci shoes, there must be a few dozen footballers like Phil Brown whose highlight to date has been a Fourth Division match at Huddersfield, a footballer who, on his own admission, holds no special place in the community.

The Managers

The chairman has assured me that my job is safe, said Charlton Athletic manager Ken Craggs the day before he was fired, thus giving credence to the old football joke that a vote of confidence from the directors is the kiss of death for a manager. Craggs was yet another managerial casualty of the 1982-3 season, a man out of a job in what must surely be the most insecure profession in sport. Since World War II more than one thousand football managers have parted company from their clubs, almost all of them dismissed because of lack of success, although abject failure alone has not always been the reason why directors have suddenly felt the need to dispose of their playing boss. The controversial Scotsman Tommy Docherty was summarily dismissed as manager of Manchester United when it was discovered that he was having an affair with the wife of a member of his coaching staff; and Dave Sexton, his successor, was levered out of Old Trafford, after steering United to the FA Cup final and the First Division championship in successive seasons, because the following season he could manage only eighth place in the table: good enough for many clubs but not for Manchester United.

The overriding problem about being a football manager is that insecurity is the game's very essence. The fact that teams can rise high after a season of mediocrity, or can fall steeply less than a year after sweeping all before them, gives the game much of its drama. An emerging talent, a dash of luck, a new understanding, an inexplicable increase in the will to do well, all these things can bring a hitherto ordinary combination to the threshold of success; similarly, injuries to a couple of key players, a run of bad luck at the start of a campaign when the ball refuses to run for you, or the simple evaporation of resolve can turn a winning team into one struggling for survival at the foot of its division; and the man who was hailed as the messiah the previous May, may well find himself out of a job by Christmas. The football manager is a lonely animal, not a member of the team and certainly not a member of the governing elite of his club, the directors (notwithstanding the move towards paid directors which led Fulham's Malcolm Macdonald to become both manager and director).

The manager is the professional appointed by the amateurs, the butchers, bakers and builders who run the Football League clubs. He is answerable to men who may never have kicked a ball in their lives; he is answerable to the club's supporters at large, and indeed, directors are first and foremost football fans, people whose view of the game is taken from a totally different perspective to that of the manager.

What makes a good manager? If the answer to that question was known, then presumably more than a thousand of them would not have been sacked since 1946. Certainly it is no passport to First Division titles and cup finals to have been a great player. Sir Matt Busby, Bill Shankly, Don Revie, Sir Alf Ramsey, Bill Nicholson and Brian Clough were all internationals and they made highly successful managers; but Billy Wright and Bobby Charlton were each capped more than one hundred times for England and neither could master the art of football management. On the other hand, Keith Burkinshaw has succeeded with Tottenham Hotspur and yet his career was spent with Workington and Scunthorpe United, discounting one game for Liverpool. Graham Taylor took Watford to runners-up position in the First Division after playing with Grimsby and Lincoln; and Lawrie McMenemy keeps Southampton in the First Division, yet never played a first-class game of football in his life. So a great performer does not necessarily make a good teacher, while it is possible to successfully impart one's knowledge without possessing the highest degree of playing skill. The two factors which the successful manager must have are the ability to communicate and the ability to dominate. He must communicate his ideas to his players, and he must dominate them, not necessarily by thumping the table, but certainly he must be the boss. The styles of Brian Clough and Peter Taylor have intrigued many people. When they were together at Derby and Nottingham Forest they displayed a combined genius which hoisted both of those clubs from relative obscurity to the league title. It has, however, been difficult for the outsider to assess the part each plays. Willie Young, who played under their combined management at Forest before Taylor temporarily retired, said, *With Cloughie you saw people almost jump to attention when he came in the dressing room. Peter was different. He burned a lot of nervous energy, but he was more approachable.*

The manager must deal with many day-to-day aspects of the club not always directly related to the match at the weekend. There are players' contracts, transfer deals, and, if he is not very careful, the danger of being ensnared in the internal politics of the club. The manager must try to remain aloof from all such internecine wranglings, but it is a lonely road to tread. Some managers remain with a club for many years, though that has as much to do with the philosophies of those clubs as with the manager's own record. Liverpool is the classic example of a club offering its manager time and security, though (undoubtedly because of it) they have been successful at the same time. Ipswich Town and West Ham United have stuck by their managers when things have not gone so well, while other clubs have offloaded the team boss at the first hint of a crisis. Styles, of course, have varied greatly and perhaps the greatest indictment of the game's environment is the comment that a man is 'too much of a gentleman to be a good manager', implying that a degree of ruthlessness is required to succeed in the manager's chair. Of course, there are a great many gentlemen who have succeeded. There are, too, more than a few of the other kind. When the *Daily Express* ran a series of articles about great managers in 1982-3, the author David Miller said, *Having talked to almost every successful manager since the war and watched their teams all I know is that there is no blueprint. There have been as many successful bullies and extroverts as there have been quiet thinkers and tacticians. Nor does success exclude the morally dishonest from the ranks of the virtuous.*

The interviews which follow in this book draw on the experiences of managers from across the board including those who have known the heights of winning the First Division championship and the FA Cup, and those who have known the frustrations of maintaining a successful team in the lower divisions without the open cheque book ever at their disposal. Some of them were successful players, some of them were modest performers. The only thing they have in common is that they have not been drawn from the ranks of the morally dishonest.

TONY BARTON

The sight of the European Cup standing ignominiously by a wastepaper basket on the floor of the receptionist's office at Villa Park said it all. Ten months earlier, that same trophy had been the focus of everyone's attention. A goal by Peter Withe had been enough to beat the West German champions, Bayern Munich, in Rotterdam and keep Europe's premier club prize in England for the sixth year in succession. Now Villa were out of the competition, beaten by the Italians of Juventus, and the thirty-inch high cup stood ignored amid the boxes of paper clips, paper and other office equipment, awaiting collection. Soon it would be the focal point of thousands of different supporters, in another city, another country. Aston Villa, meanwhile, were more concerned with a First Division place good enough to win them entry into the following season's UEFA Cup. Proud though they might still be about their European Cup triumph, it was now just a pleasant memory and meant nothing to Villa's current preoccupation with qualifying for Europe once more. There is nothing so ephemeral in football as the victors who have themselves been vanquished. Yesterday's cup winners are just that. Only the future matters to managers; they cannot be certain of surviving for even one day on past glories.

Aston Villa's manager had just celebrated his first twelve months in the job when I met him in the greenhouse which is the manager's office at Villa Park. Though it was cold outside, the early Spring sunshine beat through the large glass windows and brought the reflection from Tony Barton that when people talked about the manager having the hottest seat in football, they probably had his office in mind. He was also celebrating his forty-sixth birthday, which is relatively old to be marking your first year as a manager. Most of today's Football League managers took up their first appointment at a much earlier age.

Tony Barton was presented with the challenge of taking over a First Division team, and with it his first manager's job, when, as Villa's assistant manager, he stepped up in the wake of Ron Saunders who resigned in February 1982. On 1 April, the softly-spoken caretaker-manager had his appointment confirmed, and the man who enjoyed a modest playing career with Fulham, Nottingham Forest and Portsmouth, found himself elevated to one of the most coveted jobs in British football, for Aston Villa Football Club is one of the game's pillars. Villa Park is one of football's stately homes and the club's pedigree runs rich with the blue blood of one of soccer's aristocrats. When Barton took over the league champions they were fourth from the bottom of the First Division and faced a difficult European Cup quarter-final tie against the Russian champions, Dynamo Kiev. By the end of the season Barton had guided them to eleventh place in the table and, of course, to triumph in Rotterdam. Thus, in two seasons, Aston Villa had become the champion club of England, then the champions of Europe. Yet the following season saw a significant drop in both season ticket sales and attendances.

Barton was at a loss to explain why his success had not met with greater support, never mind the puzzle that less people wanted to see the team which had just proved itself to be the best club side in Europe. He said, *We were on the crest of a wave at the end of last season and I felt that this would surely be reflected in season ticket sales for 1982-3. The fact that it was not is a puzzle and, so far as I can work out, there can be only two possible explanations. Either we are suffering from the general decline in attendances, or we presented our fans with an anti-climatic situation. Whatever we did the following season, even if we won the league title or the European Cup again, we could not do better.* Barton also knew that if a winning team could not draw crowds to Villa Park, then no team anywhere had the right to expect that success would be followed by capacity crowds. When the roving Tommy Docherty pitched his tent there he said, *You could get ten thousand to watch the shirts drying on a clothes line at Villa Park.* Certainly it is a club with what those in the game call 'crowd potential', a big city club steeped in tradition and to which local folk feel a close and special affinity.

But even people with a deep affection for their local football club have to watch their pockets, and the West Midlands, once a thriving industrial region, has been hit harder than most places by the recession. Unemployment and short-time working have meant smaller incomes and tighter family budgets. So as far as football supporters are concerned the economies are directed at the less attractive matches. Barton said, *Visits by Liverpool and Manchester United will always attract large attendances, and so will our local derby matches with Birmingham City. But people with less money to spend*

Tony Barton, a quietly-spoken unassuming man who guided Aston Villa to European Cup victory.

become more selective and if they buy a season ticket, well that commits them to watching less glamorous teams. The answer is to pay at the turnstiles to see the big clubs, and to give teams like Notts County, Luton and Norwich a miss.

Yet this selective nature has perhaps made clubs realise that now, more than ever before, they must entertain. Simply to win is no longer a guarantee that the turnstiles will click merrily away, and Barton had long since seen the need for his team to play attractive football. *A manager's first priority is to win, of that there is no doubt. But he must also entertain. A winning side will not necessarily attract crowds if it is boring; an entertaining side will certainly not pack them in if it is not successful. But a side which wins* **and** *entertains ... well if crowds do not come in then, then the game really is doomed.* The much-maligned Watford team drew no condemnation from Aston Villa's manager: *We've played them three times in 1982-3 and each game has been a good game. We beat them 3-1 and 4-1, and they beat us 2-1, and on each occasion they allowed us to play. The reason we succeeded overall was that we were able to shut down their wingers and also win the aerial battle with their two front men. But they never let us alone in any of the games and I admire Graham Taylor for making the very best use of his resources. He has proved that you can succeed and entertain if the organisation and attitude is correct. The crowds who saw us play against Watford saw three exciting, end-to-end games. We have had other classics this season too. We encourage players to do the simple things and we do not stifle them. Liverpool's game is based on simplicity – need I say more?*

Barton is supported at Villa Park by an assistant manager, reserve team coach, youth coach, physiotherapist, kit manager, youth development officer and a chief scout who controls a country-wide network of talent scouts similar to that of most top clubs. Barton tends also to look closer to home, an area often neglected by other clubs. He said, *When I came here as a coach I found that we had fourteen scouts all around the country. Today that number is down to nine – another economy cut – but we look harder at our own area. Too many clubs are intently watching other parts of Britain to the detriment of their own neighbourhood. That was something I corrected and our system has thrown up players like Gary Shaw who was born in Birmingham.*

It would be difficult to imagine two more dissimilar men than the quietly-spoken Barton and the man he replaced. *I'm not a hard man like Ron Saunders was painted. Some people like to bang the table at team meetings and that's quite all right if it works for them. But I am a quiet sort of a person and I prefer to chat to players individually and gee them up that way. Everybody is different, managers and players, and no two people react exactly the same. The secret of this game is to get as much out of your players as you can, make them play to their absolute potential. I don't try to place too much emphasis on the opposition, either. We have them watched so that we know what they like to do at set-pieces. But if I gave my players an in-depth assessment of Liverpool, then I'd frighten them to death..*

Four days before our talk, Aston Villa had played Birmingham City in a First Division match vital to both clubs. Villa had emerged victorious and in the post-match press conference, one sports journalist asked Barton if Ron Saunders had shaken his hand and congratulated him. It was, after all, Saunders's return to Villa Park as a manager, fourteen months after his resignation which had led to his assistant stepping into his shoes. *I told them that I hadn't seen Ron after the game, nothing more than that. Yet the following day's newspapers carried headlines like 'Saunders Snubs Barton!' It was all a lot of nonsense and, of course, it did my relationship with Ron no good at all, although he's been in the game long enough to take that sort of report with a large pinch of salt.*

Newspapers, particularly the national dailies, are constantly putting their sportswriters under extreme pressure to produce the sort of headlines which suggested that Ron Saunders had stormed off in a churlish huff after his team was beaten by his former club. They are also used by managers anxious to unsettle players who they wish to buy from other clubs. Said Barton, *There are two managers in particular who spring readily to mind. They will telephone you and ask if so-and-so is available for transfer. When you tell them that he is not for sale and refuse them permission to talk to him, the managers will then call a reporter who they know well, and tell him that they want to sign the player, and they name him, from Aston Villa, but that Tony Barton won't sell him. The player reads this and so the approach has been made. It's illegal but there is absolutely nothing one can do about it.*

Tony Barton was not bitter about such newspaper involvement, for he is not that kind of a person. He was more saddened than angry, and far too busy plotting his next move back towards European football. *Playing in Europe is so totally different from the everyday league matches. In our early encounters we tried to score early on. We soon realised that patience is the biggest virtue you can possess when playing abroad. The Europeans play with a sweeper, while we don't use one in British football, and after all I've said about playing attractive football, it is a fact that you have to err on the side of caution when playing an away leg of a European tie.*

A super league, not containing European clubs, however, will probably result from football's current ills, according to Tony Barton. *We must have a smaller First Division but we must not make the same mistake as they have in Scotland where their Premier Division is so small that they have to play each other four times. I cannot imagine people wanting to see the same team twice in a season, unless it happened to be Liverpool, or perhaps Manchester United. But we will have to do something to avert disaster. The writing has been on the wall for some years now.*

GRAHAM TURNER

It was on a trip through the grim back streets of Liverpool on a cold, wet Sunday in January 1983 that Graham Turner finally convinced himself of how lucky he was to be the manager of Shrewsbury Town. On the face of it, the small-town club which plays at the Gay Meadow on the bank of the River Severn, has little to offer a football fan. But as the Shrewsbury team bus moved cautiously through the greasy streets on the way to Everton's Goodison Park and an FA Cup match, Turner could not help but reflect that life in rural Shropshire had much more to offer than that of industrial, run-down Merseyside. Not that an ambitious young manager like Turner does not have thoughts of managing one of England's great clubs. He would not be true to himself or to his profession if he did not occasionally cast a covetous glance at some of the bigger jobs. It was simply that the quality of his life, and that of his family, means as much to Graham Turner as does the need to rise to the top of his profession, and after ten years by the Severn he had decided that *Shrewsbury is a smashing place to live.*

What is more, Turner has combined thrifty housekeeping and brilliant man management with a sense of realism, and he has done what most people in football thought was impossible, kept Shrewsbury Town riding high in the Second Division. At a time when the financial plight of football occupies as many column inches in the newspapers as does the action on the field, the example of 'what Graham Turner is doing at Shrewsbury' is the one most quoted by directors of small, debt-ridden clubs anxious to instil into their own managers, before it is too late, the fact that clubs can compete without breaking the bank in the transfer market.

Turner knows the difficulties only too well. *Football is a game based in industrial Britain. Out here we are in farming country which means that the people are not historically followers of professional football and they do not have the passion for the game which has been passed down in other towns and cities. Coupled with that there is the simple mathematical fact that we are in a relatively sparsely populated area, so we will never attract the crowds of 20,000 and more, even if we were in the First Division.*

Turner had been at Gay Meadow for ten years when we spoke, yet his initial interview for a move to Shrewsbury as a player lasted only two minutes. That was all it took for him to consider the offer made to him by the then manager, Maurice Evans, before casting a quick glance around the little ground where a winter wind seemed to invade every corner, and catching the next train back to Chester after turning down Evans. Two days later he changed his mind: *The only reason I moved was because I'd been five years in the Fourth Division with Chester and I wanted to move up. I wasn't particularly happy with the wages at Shrewsbury, especially since they were paying a club record £30,000 for me, and the same month, January 1973, they received £90,000 from Manchester United for Jim Holton. But I've never made money my god and I can look back now and know that I made the correct decision. I've had ten gloriously happy years at Shrewsbury.*

As a player — and in 1983 he was still turning out, mostly as a substitute but occasionally playing a whole match — Turner was one of those 'grafters', a hard-working, unspectacular midfield player, one of football's very necessary artisans. As a manager he has kept to his principles, and his style is one of uncompromising reality, a man who

126

knows and accepts the position of the club he steers. Yet there is nothing uncompromising about the off-duty Turner, or about the club which he describes as having a *close-knit family atmosphere.*

He said, *Stability is the name of the game at Shrewsbury. I took over as player-manager in December 1978 and I am only the third holder of the manager's job in the last decade. A year after I signed as a player we were relegated and Maurice Evans left. Alan Durban took over with Richie Barker as his assistant and they took us straight back up.* By the time Shrewsbury were next poised to unpop the champagne corks, Turner was in charge. It was May 1979 and Shrewsbury needed to win their last game to win the Third Division title, or to draw to be promoted. *It was a fabulous night,* said Turner, *there were over 14,000 people in the ground to see us beat Exeter and go up as champions..*

Since then Shrewsbury have been involved in relegation battles each season until 1982-3. In 1981-2 they finished fifth from bottom of the table and Turner's reaction to that near-disaster was so refreshing. He

Graham Turner, the ambitious young manager who has done what many people regard as a soccer miracle by keeping Shrewsbury Town in Division Two on a shoestring budget.

told me, *I thought that this season we would try and attack a bit more. After all, we couldn't do much worse than last season. It seems to have worked and results have been encouraging. At any other club I would almost certainly have been sacked because too many directors are too ready to dispose of the manager if things go wrong. The secret of Shrewsbury's success is that the directors are patient, they have enjoyed the club's status in the Second Division, and they have worked hard to help keep us there. The result has been that you never hear any bad publicity about Shrewsbury Town and that is now helping us to attract young players who might otherwise have gone to bigger clubs. We cannot afford to wine and dine the parents like some of the big clubs, but when they sit in my office and have a cup of tea and a sandwich, they realise that we are honest, homely, and there is a greater chance for their son to break through into first team football.*

Turner knows that the fostering of local players is his one salvation, the one chance he has of netting a star, albeit one who has yet to win his spurs: *We cannot afford to go out and pay even £25,000 for a player, so we look to the youth. In 1982-3 we have seen a Shropshire lad called Wayne Williams, a right-back, force his way into the first team; and another youngster, Nigel Pearson, a centre-half who we signed from Derbyshire non-League football, also made great strides in Second Division football.* Shrewsbury's first team options rested with sixteen full-time players, together with six apprentice professionals, two of them being on the Government Youth Opportunities Scheme. *That is the way it has to be,* said Turner, *because with gates of only four thousand we have no room to speculate. Supporters will sometimes ask why we don't sign such-and-such a player, perhaps an established star who is past his best and is on a free transfer. The reason he is on a free is probably because his club cannot afford his wages. It may seem like we'd be getting a player for nothing, but if we paid him the money he wanted, then we would ruin the whole pay structure of Shrewsbury Town.*

Turner's position at Gay Meadow was that of manager, coach, trainer and player. In the 1982 close season, when his assistant Graham Hawkins went to manage Wolverhampton Wanderers, the board told Turner that he could either appoint a new man, or do both jobs himself and sign another player. Naturally he chose the latter. The first four games of the season were lost, but that did not surprise him. *I had to cut the wage bill in the summer and released twelve players. We started the season with only fourteen and the upheaval meant that the season came too soon and that the team was not right. But the spirit at the club is tremendous and I knew that if we worked hard we would get it straightened out. I just accept the financial situation. Of course there are players who I would like to sign, but we just could not afford their wages.*

Turner, more than anyone, knows the cold wind of financial deprivation in football and he is convinced that even many Second Division players will have to go part-time. *We have looked at the possibility closely here at Gay Meadow. The one problem is, of course, that with over three million people out of work, you have still got to find a part-time footballer a job outside the game. Of course, I think that clubs like Sheffield United, even though they drop down into the lower divisions, will always be able to support full-time professionals because they are a big city club. Regionalisation may also have to come, but I should hate to see the end of clubs like Crewe Alexandra and Tranmere Rovers. They are just as important to the overall structure of football as anyone else.*

Shrewsbury Town's young manager differed from many of his colleagues in one vision he had of football's future: *I am sure that summer football, perhaps played on Friday evenings, should be tried. We played at Leicester this season and halfway through the first half I noticed that the water in the trainer's bucket had frozen over. You can do all you can to improve stadia, but at the end of the day most people still have to sit outside, and there is no attraction to watch even a top match if the temperature is 10 degrees below freezing.*

Graham Turner is rarely in the spotlight, which tends to flash over, rather than settle on Gay Meadow. But he has one last ambition to fulfil before he hangs up his boots: *If we got promoted – and that would be the achievement of the century for a small club like this – then I would have to be substitute and put myself on just once, say for twenty minutes. Then I could sit back and say, 'Well, I played in the First Division'.*

Lean, fair-haired and in his mid-thirties, Graham Turner is one of the new breed of younger managers who may well make his mark in the First Division, though it will not be with Shrewsbury Town. He has an open, honest face and refuses to be distanced from the grass roots of the club. Even his office is built to face immediately on to the forecourt and car park of Gay Meadow and, unlike almost all other managers, who lock themselves away in the bowels of their grounds, Graham Turner can look out of his office window and see the comings and goings of the fans. But this delight in little Shrewsbury, and the grim memory of Liverpool's back streets, does not blind him to the fact that he has almost certainly gone as far as he can with Shrewsbury Town. He confessed: *I am an ambitious person and I want to manage the First Division champions and then go on to win the European Cup.* One sensed that simmering below that relaxed exterior, at ease with life in rural Shropshire, was the frustration which must come with working on a shoestring budget. Turner has already proved himself to be a fine manager of a club with limited resources, an example to anyone who claims that success must be purchased in football. One could only imagine what heights he might achieve with a cheque book.

MALCOLM MACDONALD

Not long before he was appointed manager of Fulham down on the banks of the Thames, Malcolm Macdonald was at a First Division match where he heard a visiting coach compliment the coach of one of

129

the competing clubs on the quality of his team's rotationals. It was a remark which caused Macdonald a great deal of bewilderment. Although his own career had spanned a dozen years of league football, in which time he had scored 191 goals in 372 games (counting three appearances as a youthful substitute for Fulham in his first season), won fourteen full England caps and played in three Wembley cup finals, Malcolm Macdonald had never seen anything in a game of football which he considered could remotely justify the description 'rotational'. Driving back down the motorway towards London that night, Macdonald mused on what he had heard and quickly an impression of that game formed in his mind. He said, *I realised that the players had drifted through the game, unsure of what they were supposed to do. That began a thought process which led me to the conclusion that if you can simplify a player's life, then you allow him the freedom to go out on to the pitch and express his individual strengths and talents imaginatively. That is my basic philosophy now and I have expanded it to fit the needs of Fulham Football Club.*

We met as Fulham were striving to win promotion from the Second Division and Macdonald, the first paid director of an English Football League club, told me of two other basics of his philosophy which had been passed on to him by men he admired. The first came when he was scoring goals for Newcastle and it was given to him by a man who is still remembered as a goalscoring legend on Tyneside, the great Jackie Milburn. He told Macdonald, *Remember that if you get the ball with one minute to play, you have to have saved up enough energy to run, perhaps from the halfway line, and ride a tackle or two before shooting for what might be the winning goal. You will have to have saved up some energy, should you be presented with that situation.*

The second piece of golden advice came from Macdonald's chairman at Fulham, the straight-talking Ernie Clay, who told Macdonald, *We are a corner shop and we can't afford to compete with the supermarkets like Manchester United and Liverpool, so we'll have to find a new way of trading if we want to stay in business **and** get into the First Division.* Clay told Macdonald that he could manage the club in his own way, *as long as it doesn't cost us any money. It won't,* said Macdonald and he was true to his word. After injury ended his playing career at Arsenal in 1979, the man they called Supermac joined Fulham as the commercial executive at Craven Cottage. In November 1980 he became manager and on 18 May 1982 a goalless draw at home to promotion rivals Lincoln City ensured Fulham's return to the Second Division. With the exception of one free transfer player in the shape of West Ham's Ray Houghton, the same players were good enough to be pushing hard for promotion to the First Division twelve months later. When Macdonald took over at Fulham the club were fifth from the bottom of the Third Division and he transformed the team with the help of his assistants Ray Harford and Terry Mancini.

In his playing days Macdonald was a swashbuckling goalscorer, a

130

player who oozed confidence, and he generates that same confidence as a manager. It is one of the many positive sides to his character and it has done much to lift the side which took Fulham from the Third Division into a position where it was capable of challenging for a place in the First. The lack of money at the club had made Macdonald opt for nurturing raw talent rather than hoping to buy success with proven stars, and in any case, Macdonald cannot see the point of spending money when he can build from readily available material. He sees big spending as the manager's ego trip — probably the chairman's too — and yet he was himself a well-paid star who moved for significant sums of money. In 1976 he came to Arsenal from Newcastle for a record fee, for the London club, of £333,333, and he was easily the club's highest-paid player with a weekly wage in the region of £380. Does that give him the right to criticise those managers who have in the past paid out lavish transfer fees and signed up players on lucrative contracts?

I have never blamed the players for asking for as much money as they can get. I was worth every penny of the money which Arsenal paid me. I scored plenty of goals and their attendances increased because of it. What I am saying is that too many managers have gone to their boards and asked for money to buy the 'last link' in what they assure them will be a winning team. All too often the club has not had the success it was promised in return for this latest sacrifice, and instead it has been left with a financial headache.

It is this financial disarray which has led Macdonald to believe that there will be some kind of super league, based as much on money as on playing ability. He said, *It will come because the poor cannot mix with the rich. There will be a situation where clubs will have to submit themselves to a kind of means test to prove just where they can afford to compete. The Football League will have to decide through its auditors just what a club can afford to pay in wages. Like water the game will find its own level. Manchester United may be able to afford to pay players £1,000 per week, but Manchester United cannot take everyone and players will have to accept that if they are at Manchester United then they will get Manchester United wages; but if they are at Fulham, then they will get Fulham wages, even if that club is in the First Division and doing well. Players will have to understand that clubs will have to take everything into consideration, attendances, crowd potential, commercial activities, before settling on a wage structure. If that happens then it will see the standard of football improve. A degree or two of improvement in the First Division will be a vital factor because ultimately it is Liverpool who can sell the idea to people to go and watch Reading. If the game at the top is right, then there is a great deal of hope for the rest. At the moment the game is about paupers and millionaires, and football cannot put its stock – the players – into the books. Spectators, too, will have to accept that it will cost more to watch football at Fulham because we get smaller crowds, so our charge per head must increase to compensate for that.*

Malcolm Macdonald, the colourful centre-forward who brought laughter to the game when he took over as manager of Fulham.

Improvement on the field is already being seen, according to Macdonald, who felt that there was a greater emphasis on forward movement and goalscoring in 1983. *I do not want to decry the old players, but standards of fitness and ability have gone up dramatically and the great player isn't so outstanding these days. There is still room for improvement however and players don't work hard enough on individual skills in the same way as the Continentals and the South Americans.*

Macdonald drew on his cigar and spelled out the bad news for those old football reactionaries among us who yearn for the days of two wide wingers and a 'good old-fashioned' centre-forward in the Nat Lofthouse mould who would be there to outleap defences and head home the pinpoint crosses sent over by the men wearing the numbers seven and eleven shirts: *It is the easiest system in the world to mark against and because defences are so well organised today, you will never see that system return. Even Greece found it easy to blot out England's wingers in the 1983 international at Wembley.*

The good news is that attacking football does not begin and end with two wingers and a bustling centre-forward. Macdonald said, *At Fulham we play with four midfielders. One is a forward defender and the others are slightly withdrawn forwards and the whole thing is done on acute running. There is plenty of scope for attractive attacking football with other systems besides the old 'WM' formation.* At Fulham, Macdonald has divided the field into three zones and he explained the function of this system: *In the first third – that's our defending area – we tell the players to get the ball away at all costs. In the middle third, say from the edge of our penalty area to ten yards into their half, we want possession. In that final third we have got to be prepared to lose the ball in an attempt to do something positive with it. Coaches will tell you that possession is ten-tenths of the law, but what they often fail to realise is that the exciting, creative things are only achieved by what is attempted at the risk of losing that possession.*

The coaches have got much to answer for, says the man who scored nearly 200 league goals purely through natural flair and instinct, not through slavish adherence to the coaching book. *Coaches have got too complicated over the years and there is a simple reason for that. Basically there are perhaps 200 coaching jobs in football and there are five, perhaps ten times that number trying to get in, so they have to justify their own existences. The more complicated a coach can sound at an interview, the more impressed the directors of the club to whom he is applying are likely to be. The problem is that coaches are in their thirties and older, and they start talking science to young players who haven't the faintest idea what they are on about. The majority of footballers want to be inventive, it is only natural to try and create, but they often have that inventiveness knocked out of them by coaches.*

At Fulham the young players train alongside the senior professionals, unlike many clubs where the first team squad are an elite who practise alone. Macdonald feels that this is of benefit to established players and young apprentices alike. The junior players learn much from the seniors, and the enthusiasm of the teenagers rubs off on the first teamers. Macdonald is anxious that all his players should appreciate each other and he said, *They are each treated according to the needs of their job and their temperament. For instance, they may feel that one player is lazy, but we have to show them that he has qualities which are vital to their game and to the team effort.*

Now that the bottom has apparently fallen out of the transfer market (*The bank managers have seen to that, says* Macdonald) and the wage structure may follow suit, the Macdonald way at Fulham may soon be the only way for dozens of clubs, even clubs fighting alongside Liverpool and Manchester United in the First Division. Still in his early thirties, Malcolm Macdonald believes that the ultimate weapon with which to fight soccer's ills is laughter. *I will do everything I can to give to football what it needs most – entertainment. If the side are enjoying the game then the enjoyment will spread to the crowd. Be happy, work hard with your youngsters until they are ready for the jobs you have prepared them for, and above all let them have the freedom to express themselves.*

DAVE SEXTON

Dave Sexton tends to keep such a low profile that one is often inclined to forget that he boasts a record of managerial achievement which must be the envy of many more colourful members of his profession, the sort whose faces are instantly recognisable to millions of television viewers. Those managers appear on panels of experts to digest and analyse top matches, and they are eagerly sought after by television commentators and newspaper reporters because they are always ready with the quotable quote. Yet, give or take the odd exception, the one thing which they all have in common is that they do not appear to have won very much, unlike the quiet Sexton who can point to several major achievements in his eighteen years as a manager. There was the FA Cup final victory with Chelsea in 1970, and the European Cup-Winners' Cup triumph the next year. Then there was the Football League Cup final, again with Chelsea, in 1972, and the guidance of Queen's Park Rangers to within one point of Liverpool's 1976 First Division title. More recently he took Manchester United to the FA Cup final in 1979, and to First Division runners-up position the following season. So, although he is unlikely to be seen alongside people who make a profession out of being a celebrity as well as a football manager, Dave Sexton is better qualified than many to give his opinions.

His efforts, which took Manchester United to the FA Cup final and the league championship in successive years, were rewarded with dismissal in 1981 when United finished eighth in the table, too low a position for the thoroughbreds of Old Trafford to accept. He was out of work for only a few days before Coventry City made him an offer and the man who Denis Law described as *one of the most successful failures of all time* was suddenly back where he likes it best, out on the pitch working with the players. He said, *At United I was more of a manager because we had a chief coach in Tommy Cavanagh and you don't appoint a man to that position and then do all the work yourself. But at Coventry I became more involved in coaching again.*

The answer to the question was already obvious, but the way in which he answered it spoke volumes for the character of Dave Sexton. Did he enjoy his work at Old Trafford better, or was his role at Coventry more pleasing? Sexton's face broke into an involuntary beam which radiated sheer pleasure and more than a little excitement: *Oh, here,* he said gently, nodding towards the football pitches on Coventry's luxurious eighteen-acre training centre set in splendidly landscaped grounds a few miles from the city centre. He needed to say no more, for it was obvious that Sexton the manager is happiest when he is Sexton the coach.

That is not to say that he was not tremendously proud to be Manchester United's manager, just that he was removed from the things about football which he enjoyed the most. It is not to say, either, that he is in any way bitter about being dismissed after two major near-triumphs in four years. He said, *There is always special pressure on the manager of Manchester United and, just as it is a manager's right to find*

Dave Sexton outside Coventry's plush training complex. A few days later Sexton had been sacked and the future of the training centre was also in doubt.

someone else to replace a player who isn't doing quite enough, so it is the directors' privilege to find a manager who they think can do better. To go to Wembley and lose, and then finish second to Liverpool, might be considered good enough at most clubs, but you have to understand the special place that Manchester United hold in British football to know that second place isn't good enough for them. They are a great club and treated me very fairly. I am pleased for their success in reaching two cup finals in 1983, especially when three youngsters in the side were introduced by me. I remember signing Norman Whiteside as an apprentice and knowing that he would make a big mark. I signed Kevin Moran and had the same feeling about him, and I had the satisfaction of giving Gary Bailey his first team debut. No, being manager of Manchester United was a privilege.

The measure of esteem with which Manchester United are held in the game can be measured from the fact that Sexton bears them no ill feeling despite being sacked after a run of seven successive victories and only one defeat in his last ten matches as their guiding light. It is also a measure of the understanding nature of Sexton, whose reputation while he was at Old Trafford, of having little time for the supporters or the media, is made a nonsense during an interview with him when he shows a degree of tolerance for other people, not prominent in many a manager's make-up.

He played as a goal-scoring inside-forward with Luton Town, West Ham United, Leyton (as they then were) Orient, Brighton and Crystal Palace before a knee injury ended his career at the age of thirty. He won only two honours as a player, both relatively minor ones, when he was selected for Third Division South against the Third Division North, and for an FA team against the Royal Air Force. He then embarked upon his managerial career at Orient, and later at Chelsea, Queen's Park Rangers and Manchester United. There was speculation of a move to Arsenal around the time we met, with at least one national newspaper canvassing his move to Highbury if and when Don Howe assumed a full-time role with Bobby Robson's England. Sexton's record at Coventry, where he took charge in May 1981, had been one of consolidation. It was a task to which he warmed immediately, looking after and improving a squad of talented but raw youngsters. By a stroke of irony his new club's first opponents were Manchester United and a capacity all-sitting 20,050 saw the young Sky Blues beat the mighty Reds 2-1 at Highfield Road. Later that season Coventry won 1-0 at Old Trafford and at the end of 1982, Sexton's youngsters, guided by the former England captain Gerry Francis, crushed United's Bank of England team 3-0. For a time it looked likely that Sexton would steer the club then headed by Jimmy Hill into Europe, despite lowly gates, but a poor run of results ended that dream and by the beginning of April 1983 it was United who were gaining revenge with a 3-0 win at Old Trafford.

For Sexton there has got to be intense rivalry and romance in football, and for that reason he sees no future for super leagues and amalgamations between clubs to form a small but powerful elite with the rest nowhere. *One of the driving forces of football is that my street wants to beat your street,* he said as he recalled the days he stood on the terraces at White Hart Lane in the 1940s and watched Eddie Baily and company steer Tottenham Hotspur to glory. *There has got to be local rivalry and we cannot destroy that and try to force upon football supporters totally artificial situations. Clubs have grown from local tradition and they are the product of perhaps a century of local pride and folklore. It is not possible to supplant that with new organisations which have no roots beyond the need for economy.*

For Sexton, local rivalry still means Tottenham against Arsenal, and while these two famous old clubs would undoubtedly be among the main contenders, along with Liverpool and Manchester United, for any kind of super league and would therefore not be involved in a merger, the principle is the same wherever one looks, according to the trim, alert Londoner with the piercing blue eyes. Spurs and Arsenal, Reading and Oxford, the numbers opposed to a merger may vary considerably from club to club, but the intensity of passion remains the same throughout. The existence of Reading FC is just as important to the Reading supporter as is the identity of Tottenham Hotspur to the Spurs man. That does not rule out ground-sharing which Sexton feels might make sense in the game's current economic climate.

He is also opposed to a super league comprising an elite to which there is no admittance, nor indeed from which there is no automatic dismissal. He said, *To deny the chance for clubs such as Watford and Swansea to climb from the Fourth to the First Division is to kill almost all the romance in football. We may as well restrict the FA Cup to the First Division because it would be a similar policy. The success of small clubs is the very life blood of competition, the David against Goliath, the prospect unexpected is essential.*

He does not subscribe to the view that football was at one time all about goals and dashing performances and thrill-a-second soccer which had the crowds on their toes for ninety pulsating minutes of every match: *The quality of football must take some of the blame for the game's present problems, and there have been far too many negative aspects and too much safety-first play in recent years. But there were just as many dull games when I played and although there has been an over-cautious approach over the past decade, we have to get it into perspective. The charge that players are frightened is not one to which I subscribe, either. A good manager knows when he's got a good player and he won't stifle that player. Young players are accused of not having the basic skills and yet I have been pleasantly surprised by some of the things I have seen. Kids imitate and one of the things you'll see nowadays is youngsters passing the ball with the outside of their foot. They've seen Cruyff and Pele on the television and they copy them. It is something you wouldn't have seen in my day.*

Sexton is happy with the future of English football and he was pleased with the form of the England under-21 side when he had charge of it. He said, *There are players like Gary Mabbutt, Gary Bailey and Sammy Lee who look set for long and illustrious careers in this game. I was delighted when Bobby Robson was appointed England's manager. He is a good man and when he has been able to change things around to the way in which he wants them, then we will see good days for the national team. Don't forget it takes time and it is unfair to expect him to walk in and succeed overnight. Notwithstanding the financial problems, the game of football has in many ways never been in a better state. There are more people playing the game than ever before and that has to lead to brighter, better days if the people at the top can get the professional game's problems sorted out.*

They could start, according to Dave Sexton, by scrapping the home and away legs in the early stages of the Milk Cup. He said, *Home and away legs are necessary in European competition, but to impose it on a domestic cup is to invite defensive tactics and to give people too much football. Let us have more of the old instant-death approach, let us encourage the thousands of people who play football every week, and let us foster local pride and tradition. All these factors are from where the game obtains its life and soul.* With that he made his apologies and left to study a video recording of a recent match, underlining perfectly that even in football tradition and romance have to live alongside technology.

Footnote: In May 1983 Dave Sexton was dismissed by Coventry City. Bobby Robson stepped in and made Sexton his assistant for the Home Internationals and England's tour to Australia that summer, a position which later developed into something more permanent.

RICHIE BARKER

If suggestions such as free professional football for everyone, funded by the local rating system, or wider goals to encourage high-scoring matches, sould like the wild ramblings of someone who knows little about the game, then nothing could be further from the truth when those thoughts are spoken by Richie Barker, the man who took unfashionable Stoke City through to the fringes of the battle for a European qualifying place in 1983. Indeed, the thoughts of manager Barker are exactly those one would expect from his kind of man, sharp, objective and highly original. He speaks, not in the jargon of the gold-braceleted 'quotes-brigade' who number significantly in his profession, but in straightforward English devoid of coaching mystique and cliche, and he is all the more quotable for that.

The fact that Barker came into league football as a player quite late in life (he was in his late twenties when Brian Clough and Peter Taylor plucked him from the backwater of then Southern League Burton Albion and signed him for Derby) probably has as much to do with his uncomplicated view of football as anything. He was earning good money as an architectural draftsman which, coupled with his wage from non-league football, made him better paid than many First Division players when Clough and Taylor took him to the Baseball Ground where he helped in the first part of that pair's Derby miracle, promotion from the Second Division in 1969. Taylor knew of Barker from his own days as manager of Burton Albion and although it is rare for a player to make his league debut when he is nearer thirty than twenty, the unique management team that was Clough and Taylor had no fears about introducing Richie Barker to league soccer. At first he was still a part-timer and reasoned that, if things did not work out, then he could always revert to non-league football. But Barker found it much easier to get on the merry-go-round than to step off it.

He said, *I became a full-time professional and when the time came for me to move on, I found it wasn't so easy to say, 'OK, I'll go back to Burton*

138

Albion'. Derby now knew that they could get a fee for me and the pressure to move within league football was greater than I had imagined. I went to Notts County and then to Peterborough before I finished playing, and by then I was a football person, not just a chap who had a regular job and played for fun at weekends. Once you are caught up in the atmosphere of the full-time professional game it is immensely difficult to turn your back on it.

Barker had played in almost 200 games for his three league clubs and scored over fifty goals when he retired and he became manager of Stoke City in the close season of 1981 following spells as manager of Shrewsbury Town and assistant manager of Wolverhampton Wanderers. From the time he took over at the Victoria Ground until the transfer deadline of 1983, a period of two years, Barker's financial dealings and his production of a side good enough to challenge for Europe after finishing in eighteenth place the previous season, won him universal respect. He sold players to the value of well over one and a half million pounds, and rebuilt a side which played attractive football for less than half that figure. The players who left the Victoria Ground largely struggled at their new clubs, none more than Lee Chapman who went to Arsenal, while Barker moulded a new side around veterans like Mickey Thomas, Sammy McIlroy, Dave Watson and the exciting black winger Mark Chamberlain. Thus, the Stoke City manager proved himself to be one of the game's most astute thinkers, and also one of the most refreshing, for that period outside the full-time game was a vital one for him. Given that most professional players join their full-time club on leaving school, Barker had ten years of working in industry and playing football mostly for fun. He did not find himself in the goldfish bowl world of full-time professional football until after his basic ideas on life in general and football in particular had been formed. Too many football people know only of football. Barker's experience has given him a broader outlook and a deeper perception of the game's place in society.

His office under the main stand which runs along Boothen Road is a busy place and I can think of more than one manager who would have flown into a rage when someone interrupted our conversation to return a morning newspaper. Richie Barker apparently runs an easy, relaxed ship, built more on trust and respect than fear. When you ask him what he learned from Clough and Taylor, two men known for their iron discipline and unlikely to have encouraged such an interruption however trivial, Barker simply smiles and says, *They worked well together, bounced off each other, which is what a good team does. But my style isn't particularly abrasive. It can't be because players are people and people are so different. There are players – one springs readily to mind at this club – who you wouldn't see again if you bawled them out. No, some have to be bullied and some need to be coaxed.*

Although Richie Barker's 1983 Stoke City side won new admirers with its attractive brand of football, Barker was under no illusions

Richie Barker came into full-time profesional football later than most. He wants to see a return to the clean-up campaign which he feels referees let slide in the second half of 1982-3.

about what mattered most to the club's hardcore supporters. *I don't think that any manager has ever had a directive from his directors to go out and entertain. You get absolutely nothing for being entertaining, just three points for winning and a point for a draw. To entertain and succeed consistently is virtually impossible in the toughest league in the world. A First Division team can afford to entertain and win if it is playing in the Southern League, but it can't go out and put pleasing the crowd before anything else when it goes to Anfield or Old Trafford. A classic example was our FA Cup fourth round tie at Liverpool in February 1983 when we lost 2-0. When we went back for the league game the following month we tried to be more attractive, to take the game to the opposition, and what happened? Liverpool put five goals past us. In terms of success we would have been better employed to defend and perhaps lose only 1-0, because at the end of the season those extra goals we conceded might have made the difference between qualifying for Europe and finishing just outside the top four or five. So it isn't just about winning and losing, its about degrees of success and failure too.*

For Barker there is one simple problem in football: *The game can never quite make up its mind whether it is an entertainment or a business. It is unlike any other form of the entertainment industry in that people don't just come to see pleasing things. They come to see success. You can go to a theatre and be entertained by a good play and there is no sense of failure providing that the cast has done its job well. But professional football demands that we succeed first and please second.*

It is the elimination of errors which has made the game less entertaining, according to Barker. The evening before we met, his reserve side had entertained Blackpool reserves at the Victoria Ground. *It was a filthy night, pouring with rain, and the game should not really have been played because the pitch was in a terrible state. But Blackpool could not afford to come back and so we played. We won 6-0 and the pitch was so bad that there were many errors, all of which made this one of the most entertaining games that I had seen in a long time. This is why I would not like to see artificial turf in general use because it takes away all the variables. We should also investigate the possibility of making the goals wider because it is goals which people want to see, so why not make them more plentiful?*

The instructions given to referees at the beginning of 1982-3 helped the flow of the game, or at least it would have done if the momentum had been allowed to continue. People want to see one-on-one situations and that is when you get a real buzz in the crowd. The instruction to severely penalise a defender if he brought down a goal-bound player in full flight was a laudable one. But too often the big decisions in football are not black and white, and the individual referees' interpretations of the laws have spoilt the game. Other innovations haven't really worked. Three points for a win has made the leagues much tighter for far longer, notwithstanding Liverpool who had practically won the First Division by Christmas 1982, but the extra point has not necessarily produced a lot more goals, which is what people want.

Though Barker felt that not enough top-quality players had worked hard enough across the country, thereby creating a lack of success in the internationals he would not accept that the players were earning too much money and that mediocrity was well-rewarded. He said, *There are around 250 players competing in our First Division each Saturday. Compare that with the tens of thousands of footballers in England and I do not think that you can make out an agrument for those First Division players being mediocre. What is more, they are entitled to be well-paid because they support, not only what happens on the pitch each Saturday, but a whole football industry.*

It was at this point that Richie Barker introduced his most imaginative theory: *It is an accepted fact that when a local team is doing well, productivity in local factories is increased. Also, towns and cities which would otherwise never be in the news are regularly brought to national prominence. How many times do you hear of Accrington now that Stanley are dead? Would you know where Wigan is if it wasn't for Wigan Athletic – and the pier perhaps? Cities and towns without a Football League club pay tens of thousands of pounds to advertise themselves to industry and commerce. League football puts places on the map, so why shouldn't local industry support the club? I will take that a stage further. Why should football not be on the rates, an amenity like swimming baths and libraries? Let the councils finance the clubs and admit the townspeople for free. When you consider the millions which are spent each year, it would take a relatively small amount to support a football club.*

These are imaginative, bold words from Richie Barker, though he, as much as anyone, knows they are likely to remain just words. It would be politically suicidal for most councils to prop up their local soccer clubs, though the idea has a great deal to commend it to further debate. Barker, too, knows the problems in trying to make his young players more adventurous. He said, *We need footballers who will make decisions, just like Watford who will ensure that the coaching manuals are rewritten. It is difficult to get young players to go forward. Stan Cullis told me that when he was at Wolves and the winger found his full-back pushing upfield, he didn't worry about him because it was the defence's job to take care of him. So why should a winger chase back after a full-back today? Surely, the full-back will not go wandering up the field if he realises that the winger isn't going to go with him? If the winger is given that freedom, then he should use it.*

*I tell my players to take chances and they say, 'Yes, but what happens if we lose the ball?' That is negative thinking and I say to them, 'Yes, but what happens if we keep it?' They have this expression about **playing** and say, 'But boss, we don't **play**'. What they mean is that they want to stroke the ball about instead of eliminating defenders with good, direct passes. Yet when they are a goal down with a few minutes to play they are pumping the ball downfield. So if they think that will get them a goal in the last five minutes when they are desperate, why do they not think it will get them a goal in the first five minutes? Eighty per cent of goals come from moves of four or less passes. Why make the game hard when it can be simple?*

Richie Barker thinks in clear terms. To him football should be a black and white game, and that in turn will introduce bright new colours. One thing that the Barker way will never do is to paint football grey.

TERRY NEILL

Football, said Terry Neill, *is a marvellous game for keeping your feet planted firmly on the ground.* A few days earlier, Neill, manager of Arsenal, had been reminded of that fact, if such an experienced warhorse needed reminding, when his side took the lead in the FA Cup semi-final against Manchester United at Villa Park, and then proceeded to lose one player with an injury and the match 2-1. Presumably only those who have actually experienced getting to within ninety minutes of Wembley and then losing, can possibly imagine the numbing shock. Players, managers and supporters never look at the possibility of defeat, everything is geared to winning and a day at the FA Cup final. For Neill, cup disappointment usually came in the final itself — he had taken Arsenal to three successive Wembley games and been on the losing side twice — but now twice within a matter of weeks he had tasted this particularly bitter pill. In the semifinal of the Milk Cup his side had also been beaten by Manchester United.

It was in character for Terry Neill, former manager of the Northern Ireland national team, to view those twin body blows philosophically. He is a thoughtful Irishman and one not given to public displays of great emotion, preferring to leave that kind of thing to the more extrovert of his profession. He first joined Arsenal as a raw seventeen-year-old from Bangor and worked his way through the ranks. His playing career coincided with one of the less successful eras at Highbury and his one medal was won for being substitute in the side which lost the 1968 Football League Cup final to Leeds. In contrast his international career began in April 1961 and he won fifty-nine full caps. Probably his greatest international experience was to score the only goal in his country's memorable win over England at Wembley in May 1972. By then he had left Arsenal, for £40,000, to join Hull City as player-manager. Neill had played 242 league games for Arsenal and he appeared 103 times for the Tigers of Hull, keeping them in the Second Division. In September 1974, Tottenham Hotspur were looking for a man to replace Bill Nicholson, and it was to Neill they turned.

Fifteen years earlier Nicholson had led Spurs to the double and his was a big chair to fill. Neill's spell as manager at White Hart Lane was not particularly successful and in June 1976 he moved across North London and back to the club which had introduced him to English soccer. At Highbury he was stepping into an even more daunting position, following in the footsteps of Chapman, Allison and Whittaker, and of Mee who had taken Arsenal to the double in 1971. Neill took the Gunners to three successive FA Cup finals and in 1980 felt the pain of losing two cup finals within five days when Trevor Brooking's Wembley winner was followed by a defeat on penalties in the Cup-Winners' Cup.

Neill said very little at the time, but if he preferred to keep his own counsel this did not mean that he was not acutely aware of the price which many people placed on what they saw as failure. He told me, *The repercussions of not winning a major trophy are felt right throughout the club. The manager, players, directors and supporters are all touched by it. The players are afraid of losing, and the spectators rarely have that old idealistic view of football which said that the game is more important than the result. Of course, winning is desperately important, but if spectators were more willing to accept the efforts of the opposition, then things would be easier. But they cannot tolerate defeat and the fact that, on the day, we might have been beaten by a better team. There have been rare exceptions at Highbury. One of them was earlier in 1982-3 when we were beaten by Moscow Spartak. Our crowd rose to their feet and applauded the Russians off the pitch, but that sort of thing is rare indeed these days.*

Terry Neill, the Arsenal player who became manager at Highbury.

Neill's playing career was one which largely spanned the days of the old values, and while not compromising his principles, he has been forced to adapt his views to understand what success means to other people. *It is all part of social change and today we make wealth and position the most important yardstick of a man's success. Our definition of a winner is a man with a Rolls-Royce and a large country house. We rarely question the man's integrity, indeed we accept that he may well be a little bit suspect, that he probably is a bit shady. Otherwise, we ask ourselves: how has he achieved his position? The media glorify the bad loser, too, and we look at John McEnroe, for instance, and say to ourselves, well that's how it must be. But, of course, it mostly certainly need not be like that. The day after the 1983 semi-final at Villa Park, I ran in the London Marathon and it occurred to me that it must be just about the only sporting event in the world in which taking part is still more important than winning.*

For all the pressures on a manager to succeed, they do not abandon the desire to entertain the public. For the first time in our conversation Neill's voice was less than relaxed when I put to him the popular suggestion that coaches and managers put fear into players' hearts. He said, *I'll accept that players can get frightened and I've already said as much. But I take umbrage when people suggest that managers and coaches stifle players. If there are such men about then I don't know any.*

All the people I know want to encourage players to be creative. To suggest otherwise is wrong and yet it is now one of the biggest fallacies in the game. We are continually looking at the need to entertain.

There was no doubt in Neill's mind that such myths often begin life in the columns of national newspapers: *The media are the cause of many developments in football. They create stars and then when they tire of them they knock them down. They criticise star status, yet they invented it. The other day, just before the FA Cup semi-final, one reporter asked me, 'Will your big stars be fit?' What did he mean? He had, by a slip of the tongue, labelled some of the senior players thus. But it was his label, not mine. No, it is the media who create the star status, not the managers or the players. It is the same people who build up managers into larger-than-life figures and then complain that managers have become too prominent I agree, and I say to pressmen, well OK, don't ring me up for a quote if you think I am getting too important. I will quite happily fade into the background. I never ring up the press, they call me. In the same way they had a hand in pushing transfer fees up. The first million-pound transfer was encouraged by the newspapers speculating on that development. Let's face it, a million pounds looks better in a headline than £900,000. I full appreciate the reporters' problems. They are under pressure from editors to produce headline stories, but I wish we could see more stories about the good games and the great goals, and less about personalities and off-the-field happenings.*

Terry Neill saw the coming of the super league as inevitable, though not through any urgent desire of football's rulers to alter the structure. He said, *In this country we have a track record of being affected by change, rather than effecting change. Therefore I can never see the game's overlords rushing out to make any significant changes to it. But they will have to yield to events which will make those changes inevitable. For some years now we have had a super league of about ten clubs contained within the twenty-two club First Division. The wealthiest clubs will almost certainly continue to draw farther and farther away from the rest until one day there will be such a gulf between the rich and the poor that the official super league will be there in all but name, and then it will just need the rubber stamp.*

Unlike many former players, Neill could not support the argument that football was better in the good old days: *Time mellows the memory and there were a lot more bad games when I was playing than there are today. This season I have seen a lot of very good football matches which were both entertaining and exciting. It is easy to dismiss today's game as a load of rubbish compared with that of previous eras, but it just is not true. Football is better organised and more competitive than it has ever been. Maybe there are fewer absolutely top-flight players, but the overall standard is better, and there is now that unquenchable thirst for success which was not nearly so prevalent in previous times. Standards are measured much more harshly and if there is a worry, it is in the lack of skill shown by youngsters still at school. At Arsenal we have started running six-a-side matches for schoolboys so that they can become more involved.*

Assuming the mantle of the manager at Highbury meant much to Neill. He said, *I am sometimes reluctant to talk about this club because it is the one so many people love to hate. There is the tradition of Arsenal being the aristocrats of football. But, yes, there is something so very special about the place. The people who modernised the stadium in the thirties were visionaries and even today it is still functionally the best around.* There is, too, the Arsenal tradition, dating back to Chapman and before, of not breaking the bank to sign players. Of course they spent £1.25 million on Clive Allen's transfer from Queen's Park Rangers in June 1980. But does this really count, since two months later — and before he had kicked a ball in a league match — Allen was on his way to Crystal Palace for approximately the same figure. Said Neill, *I don't think there is a policy not to pay big fees at Arsenal, just to pay only sensible fees and not to get into debt by shelling out money you cannot afford. That would seem to me to be the only way to run any business and it is a credit to the directors of Arsenal Football Club that this is the way they have always run things.*

Terry Neill's position as Arsenal manager also said much for the policy of consistency, which is apparently the watchword at Arsenal Stadium. He was only the seventh Arsenal manager since World War II, and had been in office for seven years, though in the week we spoke there was some kind of supporters' splinter group demanding explanations for a season without a major honour. It was exactly the sort of development with which Neill had opened our conversation; evidence that the label of failure is not reserved just for the relegated clubs, but for anyone who does not steer his side to the league championship, one of the two cups, or a place in the UEFA Cup. It was a development which also helped Terry Neill to keep his feet firmly on the ground.

He was confident of one thing, that football has a future. He said, *Football will survive because of its very simplicity. You do not need many props with which to play the game; you do not even need eleven players on each side and we witnessed in the six-a-side at the National Exhibition Centre that the game of football can be just as exciting, just as entertaining at whatever level it is pitched. If people could adjust their sights slightly and come to appreciate the game as a whole, if they could accept that there has to be losers as well as winners, then the game stands an even better chance of improvement. Of course, winning is vital and I am not asking people not to care whether their team does well or not, for without the desire to win the game really is dead. But if we can stand back and take a broader view of football, then we all stand to gain something.*

13 The Money and the Directors

Only those approaching middle-age or older will remember Accrington Stanley. Stanley was one of the famous names in football, albeit a club which had never risen to the heights. There was an Accrington team in the original Football League and I can recall vividly the day when Stanley held Derby County to a draw at the Baseball Ground in March 1957 as Derby pushed hard for promotion from the Third Division North. Accrington Stanley finished third that year, behind Derby and Hartlepool, but five years almost to the day after I watched them battle for a 2-2 draw against that season's champions, they went out of business. It was a surprise to say the very least. Accrington had finished second, third, third and second in the four seasons beginning with 1954-5. The pitch had been levelled, crowds had been around the 10,000 mark during that period, and the capacity of Peel Park was eventually increased to 24,000. Then things began to go wrong. Runners-up place in 1957-8 assured them of a place in the new Third Division, but in 1960 they were relegated after finishing bottom. Eighteenth place in the Fourth Division in 1960-1 added to their problems and attendances were now around the 2,000 mark. By the end of 1961 rumours were rife that the club was in deep trouble and the following March a statement showed that Accrington owed £62,000. A letter of resignation was sent to the Football League, followed by another rescinding the first, but the league noted only the initial communication and Accrington withdrew.

Stanley's demise was due to problems which were to become all too familiar to league clubs in later seasons, but at that time the possibility of a Football League team collapsing in mid-season, or indeed at any time, was largely unthinkable. True, Stanley had always had their troubles, and even the original team of 1888 had to leave the league in 1893 after losing First Division status and being unable to accept an invitation to join the newly-expanded Second Division because of mounting debts. But Stanley, who were founder members of the Third Division North in 1921, had managed well enough in recent years and it was a shock when they went.

Behind the club's demise lay more than just the fact that they were now badly supported. It was a self-inflicted blow which finally killed them off. Already crippled with debt as the club was, the directors took the astonishing decision to buy the grandstand from the Aldershot

Tattoo at a cost of £14,000. That delivered the mortal blow, and in recent years many clubs' difficulties have lain, not simply in dwindling attendances and receipts, but in gross mismanagement of their financial affairs. Football clubs have paid out large sums of money which they did not have, mainly on players (through transfer fees and wages) who more often than not did little or nothing to justify the expense and did not recoup the outlay through increased success and greater receipts. There have also been examples of clubs spending hundreds of thousands of pounds on prestigious new stands which have then remained largely empty, there simply to mock the men who had them built.

It is one of the most remarkable things about professional football that Accrington Stanley is the only club in most people's memory to have closed down. Stanley did it when football was in a far healthier state generally, so it is doubly surprising that in the climate of the eighties, with football having lost half its audience since the war and with many businesses having gone bankrupt, there has been not one case of a Football League club following suit. Of course, football clubs have one significant factor going for them which the rest of commerce and industry does not: ready cash. Clubs' incomes benefit greatly from the fact that cash is received through the turnstiles, and season ticket sales actually bring the money in advance. Yet in 1983 probably only a dozen of the ninety-two Football League clubs ran at a profit, and more than a few of those managed to make the balance sheet appear healthier only by including income which came from outside the game. Arsenal were a classic example in 1981-2 when, on a turnover of more than £2 million, they managed a small profit of £56,000, due only to selling off some houses which the club owned, for just over £97,000, plus the benefit of exceptionally high interest rates on bank deposits. Arsenal's income from football was around £2 million, made up of £1.5 million in gate receipts and £500,000 from commercial deals and ground advertising. Running costs were over £2.25 million. The shortfall was made up by non-football items.

Of the other few clubs who found themselves in the black, most had the transfer market to thank. West Bromwich Albion's accounts to 31 May 1982 showed that they would have made a loss of some £53,000 had it not been for selling Bryan Robson and Remi Moses to Manchester United. West Brom's income was £1,756,738. The club's expenditure was £1,809,770, of which £951,881 was for salaries, wages and bonuses. The resulting loss of £53,032 was converted into a profit of £585,218 by the success of the transfer market. The club also spent heavily on a new stand and other equipment (£1,203,797) which raised the value of their fixed assets in the balance sheet to £2,984,273. And although current assets were £383,858 against current liabilities of £1,473,486 West Brom managed to show a surplus of assets. The reason was that Manchester United had paid them over £2 million for the two players, Robson and Moses. By the same token, Manchester

Trevor Francis was the one example of a million-pound player who proved
value for money. Here Francis dives to head the winning goal for
Nottingham Forest in the 1979 European Cup final in Munich.

United's huge trading loss of £2.2 million was due almost entirely to
these lavish transfer deals. Liverpool, through good housekeeping
which included trimming the playing staff at the end of 1982-3 and
shelving a £2.5 million plan to redevelop part of the Anfield ground,
had made economies of around £150,000 a year and were hoping to get
that figure up to £200,000. They also managed to pay for their players
as they bought them, but were owed half a million pounds in transfer
fees by other clubs. Their general secretary Peter Robinson said, *If
those clubs went out of business, then it would seriously affect our own
position.*

Yet by 1982-3 the bottom had fallen out of the transfer market. By
the time the transfer deadline (the date after which no player may be
signed and then played in a match affecting promotion or relegation)
of 24 March 1983 was reached, total transfer deals that season had
amounted to £8 million. The previous season the figure had been £26
million, while in the peak year of 1979-80, more than £43 million
changed hands. That measure of transfer dealing, which began with
Nottingham Forest paying over a million pounds for Birmingham's
Trevor Francis in February 1979, and culminated in the transfer of
Robson to Manchester United in October 1981 as the most expensive
seven-figure player, has done much to place football in its present
precarious state. The classis example of a club spending huge
sums of money in the transfer market and having nothing to show for it

except debt and misery is Manchester City. In the nine years ending with the final game of 1982-3, Manchester City had spent £8.5 million on players. For that outlay they have just one League Cup final win to show, and they are playing Second Division football in 1983-4. Managers Malcolm Allison and John Bond, under the chairmanship of Peter Swales, spent huge sums of money. Allison's net loss on the transfer market was reckoned to be some £3 million, Bond's around £1 million. Million-pound players included Trevor Francis (later sold because the club could not afford his wages, reported to be £2,000 per week), Steve Daley (released for a huge loss) and Kevin Reeves (transferred at a fraction of his seven-figure fee). City paid Preston North End £765,000 in July 1979 for the relatively inexperienced Mick Robinson and twelve months later sold him to Brighton for £400,000, and yet when they did win a trophy — the League Cup in 1976 — eight of their team on duty at Wembley that day had been produced by the club's youth policy. The Maine Road club presented an eccentric picture in 1983 for many reasons, but undoubtedly the most eccentric feature of all had been their dealings in the transfer market over the previous decade.

Francis's reported salary, and one can only relay the figure reported by newspapers, was another demonstration of the kind of money which is circulated in the game. The last person to be blamed for Trevor Francis earning a small fortune each week is Trevor Francis. Indeed, Francis said that he was amazed by the offer, but the fact remained that such wages, and those of some other players, rocked the financial structure of Manchester City so much that Francis had to be sold to Italian football at a reported loss of around half a million pounds. Wages continue to be the biggest expense at every club and even Liverpool made a loss in 1981-2. It amounted to £154,798 and more than half of the club's expenditure was taken up by players' wages and bonuses. Yet it is the breakdown of the transfer system, rather than astronomical wages bills alone which has brought many clubs to crisis point. Until recently any club faced with an unacceptable loss simply sold one or two players to balance the books. Indeed, the economic strategies of most Third and Fourth Division clubs were based on selling players to First and Second Division clubs. By 1983 those days appeared to be over. The star players could not command the huge fees of the previous few years and those coming up from the lower leagues found themselves 'marked down' accordingly. Similarly, with many players finding themselves unemployed at the end of the season — though in 1983 the figure was not as great as had been anticipated — clubs could be more selective, often signing the player they wanted without having to pay a transfer fee at all. The drawback to picking up players for nothing is often their wages. Players bought neck of their club. Although the value of a player is not shown in the balance sheet, they nevertheless form part of the club's financial thinking. A player bought for, say, £600,000, might have been sold later and a great deal of the money recouped. But with transfer fees falling dramatically this is not now always possible; and there are many cases where a club is stuck with a player who they cannot dismiss because of his contract, but whose high salary no other club wants to pay, even if the selling club wants to give him away.

A classic example was the plight of Birmingham City who had to put on the transfer list two international full-backs, David Langan of the Republic of Ireland, and Mark Dennis, of England under-21s, because the club could not afford wage rises due in their contracts for 1983-4. These two players, and club captain Kevin Broadhurst, were each due to receive more than £100 per week in salary increases and loyalty bonuses under the terms of contracts agreed three years earlier. Birmingham, who had narrowly escaped relegation in 1983, asked the three to accept a wage freeze, but apparently only Broadhurst agreed. Ron Saunders, the Birmingham manager said that he did not want to let Langan and Dennis go *but the economic situation here leaves me no option.* The alternative to retaining the players and paying them the agreed rise was to offer them free transfers when their current contracts expired on 31 July, thus enabling them to negotiate good signing-on fees from other clubs — providing clubs with such money could be found.

A *Sunday Times* survey showed that in 1981-2 some £40 million was received at the turnstiles for Football League matches, with a further £10 million coming from cup games. On the commercial side the ninety-two clubs raised between them another £25 million. Of that, television contributed £2.3 million, and the football pools £4 million, though when one considers that the pools turnover was £452 million (of which £184 million went to the government in betting duty), it is hardly surprising that the clubs would like a larger slice of the pools income which, without those clubs and their matches, would not exist. Altogether then, football took in around £75 million that season, and yet the game is deeply in the red. At the last estimate the clubs owed a total of £40 million to the banks and a further £20 million to other creditors and if one asks the great majority of football club directors to explain just how this has come to pass, the answers will include all the usual reasons such as changing social patterns, hooliganism, too much televised football, and the rest.

There is just one observation to make on such responses: these may be reasons why fewer people go to watch football; they do not explain how and why football clubs have allowed their expenditure to run riot in the face of falling income, the downward pattern of which has been clear for many years. The reason why football clubs are in such an awful financial situation is quite simple: with very few exceptions most clubs have been run by businessmen who are also football fans and who hang up their bowler hats on entering the boardroom, and don football scarves and take up rattles. They have ceased to apply the business principles which have made them wealthy and they have spent money which the club does not have. Talk to anyone but directors and the general opinion is that the men in the boardroom are satisfying their own ego. Most, it is accepted, have a genuine love of football, but their own vanity has seen to it that many clubs are deeply in trouble. Stuart Webb, himself a director of Derby County and a man considered to possess one of the most brilliant commercially-orientated minds in the game, was secretary at the Baseball Ground in the seventies. He said, *I've sat by and watched directors behave like excited children with a new toy when a manager has suggested the signing of a big-name player. The financial logic of the signing goes out of the window. They can't wait to write the cheque and impress their friends and business acquaintances.*

It has long been accepted that the institution of the football club director is the sport's most obvious paradox, where the amateur governs the professional. Only in the eighties has the paid director been permitted and only now are there men in the boardroom whose first professional duty is to the club, and they are still a tiny minority. The amateur directors are not in the game for the money which can be made out of it directly, because the dividend which each club may pay its shareholders is minimal, and in any case most clubs make a loss, not a profit. The benefits for such a director lie in status. Most of them head local firms and there can be little doubt that their positions as directors bring in business. Most of them have been childhood supporters, pushing their way on to crowded terraces. Now they have changed the terraces for the mahogany boardrooms where the framed sepia photographs of yesterday's heroes gaze down solemnly on the haze of cigar smoke and the glint of gin and tonic glasses. The old-style director, of which there are still plenty, will have acquired his shares through his family or through some influential friend. Then begins the in-fighting and more than a few boards have their cliques, rival factions bidding to assume total control. Of course, there are the boards which present united fronts and mean it. Liverpool, Ipswich Town, West Ham United and Manchester United are such contented clubs, while the boardroom battles at Aston Villa and Derby County have, over recent years, made more headlines than their teams.

The director will have to have committed money to the club and so a degree of wealth is essential before he can be elected (there are exceptions like Webb at Derby whose committment is not financial but whose exceptional flair at raising funds through commercial activities makes him a major contributor to the club's finances). Mostly the directors offer loan guarantees to the bank, until recently in the comfortable belief that no bank would alienate the local population by withdrawing its support for the club. In the last few years that belief has been exposed as wishful thinking. Chelsea first came under pressure from Barclays in 1976, and again in 1981, Bristol City, Derby, Wolves . . . the list of clubs whose bank manager's indulgence has finally reached breaking point is almost endless. So far, no-one has followed Accrington Stanley into oblivion and the clubs appear to cry 'wolf' and then carry on with some new-found benefactor at the helm.

One option available to clubs facing extinction seems to be to call in the brokers' men. In June 1983 Bradford City were reported to be ready to liquidate their old company and set up a new one. Apparently, Bradford's debts were such that the players' pay cheques had bounced and there were other people owed money too, including Customs and Excise for VAT. Bradford's move looked likely to save them, although just what non-league Maidstone United, unsuccessful applicants to the Fourth Division the same month, made of it all was not clear. There must have been some anger that they had been denied the opportunity to progress, while a member club in deep financial difficulties had been able to survive in this way.

Not many clubs can now count on directors dipping into their own pockets. Elton John put £1.3 million of his own money into Watford and has been rewarded for his investment by seeing his team storm to second place in the First Division, but there is no one to match him. A new breed of director has emerged, a younger man not at all in the image of the bowler-hatted mill owner of football's past. It is also not always possible to ascertain who actually owns a club these days and for the first time other companies have become intertwined with the limited company which is the club. A classic example concerned Charlton Athletic, the Second Division club owned for fifty years by the Gliksten family until in 1982 when it was bought by a foreign company and had as its chairman a 28-year-old businessman called Mark Huyler who owned no Charlton shares. In 1982 the Glikstens sold their shares in the ailing club to a subsidiary of Marman A.G., a company registered in Switzerland and dealing in grain, coal and spices, though with little trade with Britain. A subsidiary, Marman Sports Ltd, nominally hold the Charlton shares: Huyler was, at the time of writing, a director of the subsidiary, but just who owns the parent company and therefore Charlton Athletic remained a mystery. Huyler was quoted in the *Sunday Times* as saying that the Marman A.G. shares were owned by *an American chap and some others*. Charlton Athletic certainly appeared to be dear to Huyler's heart, but why a Swiss-registered company with little trade with Britain should want to assume control of a tired old English football club is difficult to understand. The new regime did, however, apply some of the 'expertise' showed by other clubs when they signed the Danish international and twice former European Footballer of the Year Allan Simonsen. Simonsen's transfer fee from Barcelona was £325,000, to be paid in instalments, and his weekly wage reported to be around £1,500. When Simonsen's appearance failed to increase gates at The Valley sufficiently in 1983, the Dane had to be released with the comment from Huyler, *The viability of the deal was non-existent.*

In the summer of 1983 Charlton were yet another club reported to be facing extinction and a name by now familiar to ailing football clubs was connected with them. Anton Johnson, chairman of Rotherham United and the man the media had dubbed 'The King of Clubs', looked likely to be masterminding yet another financial deal to save a dying soccer club. Johnson was known to have involvements in several other clubs besides Rotherham and the connections of the millionaire Essex businessman were the subject of discussions at the Football League, which largely forbids one man being involved with more than one club. Johnson's motives appear to be innocent. He is a self-confessed soccer addict whose interest in the game extends as far as watching his local Sunday morning side. Had it not been for him it is quite possible that in 1983 at least one club would have followed the path of Accrington Stanley.

Just what motivates men to own a football club is not, however, always as clear today as it was a few years ago. Then it could be explained away by accepting that the directors were moved by a love of football, a desire to increase their own status, and coupled with that, the hope that business would spin off from their connection with the club, particularly if they happened to be the chairman. Today there is a feeling among some that motives are not always as pure as they at first appear. Most football grounds are situated in highly industrial areas and the land alone is valuable. So the question has been asked: if a club does go out of business, who stands to benefit? The club's only real asset would be its ground, but what use would a football ground be to a town without a football club? The only value would presumably be in the value of the land. So a man who owned a football club would be left with a prime piece of land. Only time will tell whether the suspicions of people like Danny Blanchflower, who sees a danger in the sudden interest which property dealers and the like appear to be showing in the unsound institutions which are football clubs, are justified.

Recently the Football Association increased the dividend payable to shareholders of a football club from 10 to 15 per cent, but, of course, the likelihood of a club making a huge profit and then declaring a healthy dividend is remote. Purchase of such shares has always been an act of support for that club, or perhaps an attempt to gain control, rather than a business investment. Nevertheless, as more clubs look towards additional methods of trading and maximising the hitherto massive under-usage of their grounds, so investment in football club shares in the future may take its place alongside investment in other commodities. Shares have normally been held by a tight-knit circle of people. In 1983 Tottenham Hotspur broke the mould by offering shares on the Stock Exchange, though the shares on offer were those of a holding company and not of the football club itself.

Professional clubs outside the Football League are also facing financial difficulties, but there is little sign that they are suffering to the same extent as the full-time professional clubs. The major league outside the Football League is the Alliance Premier, followed by three of approximately similar standing — Northern Premier, Southern and Isthmian — then the triangle broadens considerably down to local leagues at the very base. Glen Kirton, of the Football Association, said, *There is no indication that non-league clubs are suffering from anything like the same problems as those clubs in the Football League. To a great extent they do not depend on the paying public and rely largely on commercial enterprises such as lotteries. When income from such sources dwindles, then part-time professional clubs are in a much better position to use fewer paid players, or, more likely, pay less to those they retain. Although part-time clubs have, inevitably, suffered from the recession, their problems are far less grave than those of the big clubs. This side of the game is still relatively healthy and there are still plenty of part-time professional players in football.*

Football directors themselves are a fascinating breed of men and I present three of them. Gilbert Blades was the man who wanted to run his Third Division club on lines which he saw were realistic, taking into account that club's position. He saw no hope of increasing the club's income by any significant amount, so he attempted to cut expenditure instead. His policy was rejected by the manager, players and supporters and he resigned after one of the most controversial episodes in football history. Don Robinson assumed control of a Fourth Division club and helped it into the Third Division because he was fired by the belief that any club could be run as a wider part of the entertainment industry. He saw the club's potential and set about presenting it to the public in a way which earned him the cold shoulder when he walked into the boardrooms at other grounds; many directors did not like the Robinson way. Martin Spencer was the man who was asked by one of football's most famous clubs to rescue it from extinction. Spencer succeeded in saving the club, not once but twice, the second time by working out the kind of new deal which may well be the face of football finance in the future. The three men have widely differing backgrounds and personalities and although their methods and philosophies are poles apart, they appeared united in their wish to keep their respective clubs alive.

GILBERT BLADES

In the weeks folowing his resignation as chairman of Lincoln City in March 1983, Gilbert Blades received calls from football club directors from around the country. Their message was always the same: *What has happened to you is a warning to us all.* Blades and his sympathisers had one common fear: that money-madness and player power, which they see as having spread through the game like a cancer in the past decade, are twin evils which will account for more directors, and even the existence of clubs themselves, unless sanity is restored.

I first met Blades in 1977 when we found ourselves in the same hotel while abroad for an England World Cup qualifying match. A solicitor, Blades was at that time a director of Lincoln City, a Conservative politician with that dry sense of humour which seems to blossom in the Lincolnshire fens and wolds. He was enjoying his football and his first full season as a director in 1975-6 had coincided with Graham Taylor steering the club to promotion from Division Four, scoring 111 goals and amassing seventy-four points in the days of just two points for a win. Just as important to Blades was the fact that the club had made a profit of £44,000 and that gate receipts exceeded the wage bill. *It's the only way to run a football club,* he told me one evening. The next time

Gilbert Blades, the chairman whose attempts to run his club on a tight budget were thwarted by manager, players and fans.

we met was in the wake of his resignation as Lincoln chairman, an event which made the headlines of the national newspapers which is unusual for the affairs of a Third Division club. Blades took over in May 1982 after Lincoln had been pipped for promotion by Fulham in the final match of the season. The team began the following season by pushing hard for promotion and their manager Colin Murphy wanted money to buy the players he felt would ensure Second Division football. There had already been a row over the players' bonuses — Blades felt that the club could ill-afford them — and when a run of bad results checked the team's charge for promotion, Murphy held a widely-publicised conference on the eve of an important match and told the players that Blades and his fellow directors would not back him financially.

The move was designed to exert pressure on the board and it had perhaps more than the desired effect. Some supporters, angry that Blades would not support Murphy's team-building plans and seeing Blades as a man who would cost the club promotion by his insistence that there was no money available, took it upon themselves to launch a vicious campaign against the chairman. He was subjected to anonymous death threats, his property was daubed with paint, and he and his family were subjected to obscene chanting as they watched a home game. It was the final straw and Blades, along with the rest of the board, resigned. One week after leaving the club he could muster enough humour to tell me, *It wasn't so much the death threats or the vandalism, but when you sit with your family in the directors' box and hear a couple of thousand people chanting 'Gilbert Blades is a wanker', then you feel that it's about time to go.'*

For anyone to claim that Blades does not still have Lincoln City at heart, or that he did not want promotion, is not to know the man. He said, *When I took over as chairman from Dennis Houlston, a local potato farmer who stepped back when I resigned, I was appalled by the financial state of the club. We owed money to just about everyone, including the taxman and the VAT people, and it was touch and go whether we had to liquidate the club. The profit and loss account for the year ended 30 June 1982 showed a nett loss of over a quarter of a million pounds. More significantly, our wage bill was £358,792 out of a total expenditure of £620,893. Our income from gate receipts was only £163,206 which was raised to £241,255 with the Football League levy, cup pool and so on. The club's commercial activities were a joke and we lost £40,000 in two days when a Dolly Parton concert was attended by only 300 people. If it hadn't been for our assets Lincoln City would have been guilty of fraudulent trading.*

It was the biggest of those assets, the Sincil Bank ground, which saved the day: *We sold the ground to the council for a quarter of a million, which just about paid off the debts. Then we set about plugging the leaks, including halting the supply of free tickets to a hundred off-duty policemen, players' families and their friends. I didn't see why, if you were an off-duty copper, or happened to live next door to a footballer, you should expect to get in free every week. It was far from popular, but the move meant that finances improved considerably in that area.*

There was also the business of the players' bonuses. The club's professionals were more than a little dismayed when Blades told them that the bonuses would have to be cut by 43 per cent because there was just no money to pay them. The players were protected by their contracts and eventually agreed to a reduction of 8 per cent, though Blades said, *It took a weekend in Majorca to settle the dust.* The dust had certainly been blown about liberally and players were openly critical of Blades when television cameras visited the ground. Blades said he bore no grudges: *Players like anyone else should be free to speak their minds, so long as they don't mind being criticised too. But I think it was disloyal of Murphy to call that meeting just before an important game. He was always asking for money and I was always telling him that we hadn't any. He argued that if he took Lincoln into the Second Division, then the gates would improve, but he seemed to think that Sincil Bank was in the middle of Liverpool or Manchester. Go fifteen miles outside of this city and all you'll see are sheep and cows. The support just isn't there.*

Within a short time of resuming the chairmanship Dennis Houlston was promising money for new players but Blades just sighed and asked, *Where is he going to get the money from? If the club gets into massive debt again then it will be the end because there will be no ground to sell next time. What people don't seem to realise is that you have to run a club according to its resources. We knew the extent of the income so we had to cut down on expenditure. People who think otherwise live in cloud-cuckoo land. The past has been a fool's paradise with lotteries keeping a lot of clubs afloat and postponing the fatal day. But all that is over. I asked Murphy a dozen times why he couldn't accept Lincoln's position and set his sights accordingly just as Graham Turner has done at Shrewsbury. Managers are all ex-players and they almost always take the players' side. At Lincoln it was one continual battle and the PFA have ensured that players' contracts are watertight and this, coupled with weak directors allowing managers to dictate finances, has led to the present mess. It's a fact that many directors are in it for the ego trip. I didn't come into it for that. I wanted Lincoln City Football Club to survive.*

A lot of managers can't grasp a balance sheet and Murphy told me that money must be available at Lincoln because in December 1980 he'd sold a player, Mick Harford, to Newcastle for £180,000. What he couldn't understand was that the youth programme which produced that one player had cost us £200,000. So we'd lost £20,000 in real terms. The collapse of the transfer market is the final red light for little clubs like Lincoln. At one time you could survive by selling the occasional player to a First Division club, but not any more. Wages have got to be based on gate receipts because it's wages, not travelling, which are the drain. There is no future for regionalisation of the lower divisions, but a part-time playing staff has a much greater appeal. The golden days when clubs made so much money that they spent it rather than pay tax are over. Players will have to realise that the perks available when the gravy train was rolling are no longer there. Many directors have told me that they see the Lincoln situation as a warning. Clubs must be run on commonsense financial lines and no one, especially not players and managers, must be allowed to override that philosophy.

DON ROBINSON

Don Robinson, the chairman of Hull City, noticed a distinct drop in the temperature when he visited boardrooms on away grounds in 1982-3. Home club directors tended to look the other way and Robinson was rarely offered more than one drink, being given the distinct impression that the sooner he was off the premises the easier everyone would be able to breathe. Robinson was guilty of no social atrocity and he is the sort of man who you would be happy to introduce into any circle. His 'crime' in the eyes of football's establishment was to impose an unorthodox brand of boardroom leadership upon the Humberside club which could remember the days when the turnstiles at Boothferry Park clicked merrily as they admitted upwards of 50,000 people, but which in 1981-2 had rarely accommodated one-tenth of that number.

Robinson took over the chairmanship of a club which had finished eighth in the Fourth Division and which had earlier looked highly unlikely to complete the season because it was faced with crippling debts. He replaced Christopher Needler and so ended the dynasty which had pumped so much money into Hull City since the end of World War II. Harold Needler, the self-confessed soccer fanatic who made a fortune in the quarry business, started it and turned a sad ailing

Hull City chairman Don Robinson hands out champagne to supporters. Robinson's fresh approach to reviving an ailing soccer club won him few friends in rival boardrooms.

club into one which attracted huge gates in the late forties. The club's old ground at Anlaby Road had been virtually destroyed by bombing and for £10,500 Needler, two brothers and a few friends acquired the club's debts and the new ground at Boothferry Park. A public appeal raised £50,000, the board put in another £50,000. The arrival of Raich Carter fired even greater enthusiasm and Hull City took the Third Division North title in 1948-9, playing before regular 40,000-plus crowds at home and breaking attendance records away from Boothferry Park. Since then Hull's progress has been sketchy, alternating between the Second and Third Divisions until in 1981 they slipped down the Fourth and with it the threat of total oblivion. Gates dropped to an all-time low and in February 1982 Christopher Needler, who had recently given the club an interest-free loan of £325,000 and a bank guarantee of a further £225,000 was told by his advisors that it would be unwise for him to continue his support on such a scale. One week later manager Mike Smith, the former Welsh national team boss, and his assistant Cyril Lea, together with the club's commercial manager were dismissed.

Hull City were in the kind of financial mess which was becoming rife throughout the professional game. There seemed no hope and yet along came football's equivalent of a fairy godmother in the shape of Don Robinson, former chairman of non-league club Scarborough. To those not involved or interested in football it seems little short of incredible that a successful businessman like Robinson should want to take over the debts of a lame, some might say dead, duck like Hull City at the end of the 1981-2 season. Yet such men continually emerge to bail out dying clubs. Often the motivation is a simple love of the game, for all directors are football fans at heart; it has also been alleged that the opportunity to swell the ego has moved rich men to assume control of football clubs. With Robinson there appears to have been a third and perhaps much more important factor which propelled him towards Hull City: the burning belief that, if things were done properly, the club could not only survive but prosper.

Don Robinson's background is in the entertainment industry.

In Scarborough he owns attractions which include an amusement park, theatre and marine world. His job is, as he puts it, *to get people into seats.* As chairman of Scarborough he had turned a loss into a profit, and it said much for his style that in June 1982 he appointed Colin Appleton as manager of Hull City; Appleton had once been sacked by Robinson as manager of Scarborough. Appleton did his stuff on the field and after one more season of Fourth Division football, Hull were promoted. Robinson, meanwhile, had made an equally significant impact in his off-the-field dealings. A debt of around one million pounds had been paid off, three-quarters of it by reaching an agreement with one creditor to accept loan stock redeemable over a number of years, the rest by selling an area in front of the ground to a supermarket chain while the club still owned the ground itself. Robinson was then looking at increasing the Hull City share issue, though he was quick to underline that his was the controlling finger. Most of all he impressed upon one that he was going to run the club as a business venture *because I know it can be done.*

He said, *I succeeded at Scarborough and I always knew that the same methods could be used successfully at a Football League club. I tried to buy Halifax Town but was unable to do so. Now I have control at Hull I am able to show that if a club is run on proper lines, and we accept that it is part of the wider entertainment industry, then the sky is the limit.* One of Robinson's first moves was to go out and meet the fans, not only at the Boothferry Ground and its surrounds (Hull City have their very own railway halt) but at away grounds too. Massed bands of Tigers supporters on the terraces at York and Halifax were confronted by the chairman's proffered hand. He said, *Too many football clubs have remained aloof from their supporters. Shareholders and fans have a right to be able to talk to directors and we hold open forums where people can come along and point the finger if they wish. Players have to be told that they are part of the community and that they must get around the works and schools to meet the fans.* It is a philosphy which Robinson extends to the more troublesome element: *I go out and meet the yobbos, take them around the ground and then into the boardroom for a drink. Communication is the key word and I am turning Boothferry Park into a stadium for the people.*

Thanks to the Humber Bridge we have a catchment area of some one and a half million people within easy reach of our ground, but we cannot expect to succeed simply by running Hull City as a football club because those days are over. Society has changed but football has remained static. We have plans for a Hollywood Bowl type of arena in the ground so that we can stage pop concerts. The gymnasium is now an indoor sports arena seating 3,000 people and attractions like the Haarlem Globetrotters, big international tennis, even a circus behind the main stand will be regular features of Hull City's ground from now on. Everyone will have to take a broader look at football's place in society. The Hull players were farsighted enough to agree to my suggestion that wages should be tied to attendance figures. *As gate receipts have increased, so have the players' wages. It is the only sensible way to run things, pay by results and then everyone profits from success.* Hull City were one of the first club's to market their own soft drink and Tiger Cola raised £20,000 in its first year. But there are some boardrooms where Don Robinson is lucky to be offered any kind of drink. *Some club directors have tried to make me feel very uncomfortable because they don't like someone new coming in and applying original ideas to the game's problems. It's sad, not for me but for their clubs and for football. Sooner or later they will have to accept that this is the way things have to be done if football is to survive. And if they leave it too late they may not have a club to run.*

MARTIN SPENCER

Martin Spencer was a football fan out of habit. Until 1967 he had a season ticket for Highbury and watched Arsenal regularly until he realised that the game was offering him less and less in the way of entertainment. He let his season ticket lapse and in the next nine years watched only one professional match. As he said, *Once you go away from football it's my experience that very few people go back.* In fact Martin Spencer did go back, though not because he was suddenly fired with a new enthusiasm for the game. It was in his capacity as an insolvency expert that he found himself at Chelsea's Stamford Bridge one day in May 1976, called in by the then chairman Brian Mears to be confronted by what he later described as one of the most appalling examples of mismanagement he had ever seen. It was a meeting which led Chelsea to some kind of recovery and Spencer to a place on the board and the position of chief executive, though only after weeks and months of painstaking negotiations to salvage one of football's most famous clubs. In 1983 Spencer was still associated with Chelsea. The chartered accountant who works from a practice just off London's Harley Street told me of the day he discovered just in what sort of a financial mess Chelsea found themselves.

I went to Stamford Bridge that day, not imagining for one minute the situation which I would find. The club had liabilities of £4 million and the only real asset was the stadium which was then valued at £2 million. The bank's patience had, not unnaturally, run out and there was really no way in which the company could continue to trade. In almost any other circumstance liquidation would have been the most obvious answer, but I felt right from the beginning that it would be wrong to liquidate an institution like Chelsea

Martin Spencer was the first of a new breed of soccer administor, the salaried chief executive.

161

Football Club. I prepared a sixty-page report which was scathing in its criticism of how the club had been run, but I also suggested that we should ask the creditors to stand aside. Perhaps if the team did well, then there might be a chance. The club was losing £12-15,000 a week, bank interest alone was £400,000 per annum, but eventually we won a twelve-months moratorium. After that, if the team failed us, we would agree to call it a day.

Chelsea could do no worse and the alternative was to close down the club there and then. One of the first things which Spencer did was to increase manager Eddie McCreadie's salary from £7,500 per annum to £9,000 *because you didn't pay a manager that kind of money in those days.* McCreadie was good value for his rise. He lifted an ordinary side to greater heights and within twelve months Chelsea were playing First Division football. The effect on the club's financial state was immediate. Money rolled in from greatly increased attendances and the Christmas fixture against Fulham attracted over 55,000. Although there was a threat to wind the club up due to non-payment of PAYE contributions, by the end of the season all the government creditors had been paid off, and Chelsea made a nett profit of £410,000 which cleared the bank interest. Perhaps most important of all, the club's creditors received an initial payment of ten pence in the pound. Spencer's good housekeeping which included rigid spending controls and working to a budget even down to the petty cash, cutting back on behind-the-scenes staff, and ceasing to use an expensive training ground meant that the awful slide into financial ruin had been checked. But how had Chelsea managed to get themselves into that position in the first place? Spencer explained that it was a combination of circumstances all of which surrounded the building of a prestigious new stand. *When the team were doing well in the early seventies the directors looked at the old stand and decided to build a new one. It was the correct commercial decision, but they got the financing of it badly wrong. Then everything went wrong, the team began to slide and the stand became a giant millstone around the club's neck.*

Spencer halted the club's runaway financial slide and fifteen months after first walking into Stamford Bridge in inspect the books he was invited to become a director. On 1 July 1978 the other members of the Chelsea board appointed him chief executive — the first salaried position of that kind in the Football League. Spencer said, *I was tired of the internal politics of the accountancy practice with which I was then involved. Other accountants whom I knew said that I should be certified. Well, it certainly wasn't an insane decision, but I quickly realised that I had exchanged one group of politics for another. There was just as much back-stabbing going on and after nine months in the job full-time, I went back into a practice and continued my role as a director with responsibility for the financial and administrative running of the club, on a part-time basis, going in perhaps a day and a half each week.*

Chelsea's creditors finally accepted a once-and-for-all payment of forty pence in the pound and the club's debts slowly came down. But so did the team and in 1979 Chelsea finished bottom of Division One and were relegated. Gates, and therefore income, dwindled and towards the end of 1981 Barclays Bank again put pressure on a club which owed it a considerable sum of money and which was not far short of being unable to pay the players' wages. *The bank said, in effect, that if the directors didn't put in any more money, then neither would they.* Once more Chelsea appeared to be facing extinction, this time caught up in the general recession in football as well as still being dogged by their own financial folly of the early seventies and by the downward fortunes of the team. Then along came another of those fairy godmothers which football clubs seem to turn up in their darkest moments. Ken Bates had been in soccer for well over a decade. He was a former chairman of Oldham Athletic, and later vice-chairman of Wigan Athletic where he was still the majority shareholder, although his holding had been up for sale for some time. He was also a wealthy property dealer. Bates was contacted and a financial deal was worked out as Chelsea underwent a total change of ownership. The ground and the debt (of around £1.5 million) was placed with a holding company called SB Property Company and Bates took over the club itself, including some £300,000 of running creditors, and now paid enough rent to the holding company to cover the loan interest due to Barclay Bank.

Chelsea's Stamford Bridge is a yawning stadium with precious few supporters to fill it. Now it is owned by a holding company who lease it to the club in return for enough money to pay the bank interest on a massive debt.

Thus Chelsea Football Club's immediate future was assured once more, though the long-term future of such an arrangement cannot be judged at the moment. Certainly the club's situation and image does little to help its continued survival. Martin Spencer raised the cost of admission by some 25 to 30 per cent when he came to the club *because football has always underpriced itself* and he received only two letters of complaint. But situated as it is in the decaying area of the Fulham Road with its population of old people, immigrants and transitory bed-sit younger people, Chelsea has no real identity with the locality. Therefore support through the turnstiles and the club's commercial activities suffer. In any case, said Spencer, lotteries had created a false impression when they were first introduced and they were now largely a thing of the past, at least so far as Chelsea were concerned. The club's media image had been blighted by hooligans (Spencer said that there was a National Front element among the yobs) and this meant that there was no club sponsorship because no commercial undertaking wanted to be associated with a club whose fans had become famous for wrecking the oppositions' grounds.

Spencer saw all the accepted reasons why football in general has been hit by recession and, hardly surprising for a chartered accountant, he wanted all clubs to be run on a basis which equated wages with gate receipts. He also mused that if he earned his money from Chelsea to the extent of ridding the club of any financial problems, then his would be a declining job: *If I do the job 100 per cent successfully, one morning I'll wake up and find that Chelsea don't need me any more.* That prospect was not one that he considered too seriously, not because he doubted for one minute his own professional expertise, but because much of football had gone *too far downhill to recover properly.*

Footnote: In August 1983 one football club was offered a unique loan, not by directors, but by management. Peter Taylor and his three-man managerial team supported the signing of Bradford City's Bobby Campbell for Derby County with an interest-free loan of £10,000.

The Union

Entering Manchester's Corn Exchange Buildings in search of the office of the Professional Footballers Association is like stepping into a time-warp. The interior of the building itself can have changed little since it was opened in the nineteenth century, the lifts are of the old wire-cage type which typified so many public buildings of the era, and at each entrance there is a suitably liveried attendent to direct visitors searching for a particular office within the myriad rooms. The corridors have also been left largely untouched by twentieth-century refurbishings, and at the door of the PFA office — room 124 of the great building — one braces oneself, half expecting to meet Billy Meredith himself.

Meredith, the great Manchester City, Manchester United and Wales winger, was the man who chaired the inaugural meeting of the PFA at the Imperial Hotel, Manchester, in December 1907, though it was then known as the Football Players' and Trainers' Union. A players' union had been first attempted in 1893 when the Wolves goalkeeper W. C. Rose, circularised the captains of First Division clubs suggesting that a union be formed 'to protect professional interest'. It was five years before that union was established, but the National Union of Association Players soon became defunct. In 1907 the forerunner of the PFA was formed and recognised by the FA, but when it affiliated to the Federation of Trades Unions, the FA and the Football League refused to accept such an alliance because they feared that a strike in another trade might result in footballers being called out in support. The players threatened to strike anyway if they were not recognised, and the chairman and secretary were suspended by the FA. Eventually the matter was resolved, though not before several players had gone without wages for fourteen weeks. A conference was held in Birmingham in August 1909 which led to the players getting their wages and the union being recognised. The battle between the union and the FA in the years leading up to World War I, while not one solely of class, was certainly based on the struggle between working-class footballers, and the game's rulers and club 'owners' equally intent on protecting their interests.

Back at the door of the PFA office in 1983, it was Gordon Taylor who greeted me, veteran of over 500 league games with Bolton, Birmingham, Blackburn and Bury, former chairman of the union and, since November 1981, its full-time secretary and treasurer in succession to Cliff Lloyd OBE. It was Lloyd who, with Jimmy Hill, steered the PFA on course for the abolition of the maximum wage in 1961. Taylor serves a union which has a management committee of eight members, elected annually by club delegates, and which looks after the interests of some 3,000 professional players, comprising Football League full-timers, apprentices and a number of part-time non-league players from such competitions as the Alliance, Southern and Northern Premier Leagues. The PFA, to quote its own publicity handout, *promotes and protects the interests of the members in negotiations with the governing football authorities... with a view to the abolition of all restrictions which affect the social and financial position of all players and to safeguard their rights at all times.* Legal and financial advisors, a benevolent fund, accident insurance fund, further education and vocational training society, and, in joint-trusteeship with the Football League, a players cash benefit scheme, are all encompassed by the union, as is a company called PFA (Enterprises) Limited, which protects and promotes players' commercial interests.

All this is administered from the Corn Exchange office, a small but bright set of rooms not at all like the building in which it is situated, staffed by Taylor, three female employees and the union's educational officer. During our talk, the telephone on Taylor's desk rang frequently and each time at the other end was a player anxious for some advice which was freely dispensed by Taylor: *No, look, don't do anything silly. You've still got a year of your contract to run, and you'll qualify for a testimonial match at the end of next season. Sit tight and get that over with, and then you'll probably pick up a club in the Third Division.* Though he did not say as much, Taylor appeared to be tiring of professional footballers who wanted to take on their clubs single-handed.

Certainly there was no sign of a militant union which represented footballers intent on bleeding the game dry. Taylor said, *I take no exception to clubs offering players less wages, but if they do then they can't make players stay. That is what is called having it both ways and there's not a cat in hell's chance that we would accept it.* He was referring to what many directors now see as the game's twin evils, the removal of the maximum wage and the introduction of freedom of contract. The wage ceiling was removed in 1961; freedom of contract, where a player at the end of his contract is free to move to another club of his own choice, was a later development. Taylor explained, *Under the old system a player was tied to a club for life unless they agreed to transfer him. It was like the Middle Ages where an employer could sell a workman like a chattel.* In 1963, the old retain and transfer system which clubs saw as the very cornerstone of the professional game, was successfully challenged in the High Court. Mr Justice Wilberforce delivered judgement that the system was an unreasonable restraint of trade, though it would be almost twenty years before players could move

166

PFA secretary Gordon Taylor surveys the Manchester rain and no doubt reflects on the future of the game which has seen hundreds of players thrown out of work in the last few years.

freely at the end of their contracts. The latest change in the system allowed a player to move to the club of his choice, and if the buying and selling clubs cannot agree on the transfer fee, then it is settled by an independent tribunal. Taylor said that the PFA had tried to introduce a system of setting transfer fees by taking into account a number of factors such as the player's age, experience, gross wages from football during the previous season, and the status of the buying and selling clubs. *This would have resulted in a controlled transfer market, but the clubs didn't want it and the result was that transfer fees went through the roof. Now the bottom has fallen out of the transfer market, clubs are left with players whose wages are liabilities, and whose transfer fees they cannot recoup, even in part. But clubs should not jib at freedom of contract because it happens in any other walk of life.*

The removal of the maximum wage in 1961 came about only after the league clubs refused to raise the maximum from £20 to £25 per week. Taylor said, *In the first place we didn't ask them to remove the ceiling, just to raise it, but they refused and that led to the PFA pushing for its abolition.* Taylor resented the accusation that it was the abolition of the maximum wage, and the subsequent astronomical salaries which pushed so many clubs to the brink of bankruptcy: *I was particularly annoyed when Wigan said they were on the point of folding and there were reports that it was the players who had milked the club. At Wigan they had been getting bonuses of £5 for a draw and £20 for a win, which is nothing special. When they were promoted in 1982 the entire playing staff shared £5,000 between them, again hardly likely to bankrupt the club.* Taylor produced a table of First Division players' guaranteed earnings at January 1981. It was headed by two players who were each paid over £60,000 per annum followed by five on over £50,000, eleven over £40,000, thirty-eight on £30,000, 118 on £20,000, ninety-six on £15,000, 102 on £10,000, 143 on over £5,000 and 143 on less than £5,000. *You see, there are a small handful on really big money – but there are a hell of a lot below even the national weekly wage.*

Taylor gave evidence to the Chester Committee and he told me of his plans for the future of football: *We believe it would be dangerous to accelerate change and undermine the tradition of ninety-two full-time Football League clubs, a system which has stood the test of time, albeit precariously. Our league is the strongest in the world and it provides the main body of international players for five countries. Foreigners who come here acknowledge that our system is stronger than anywhere else. Any attempt to introduce a super league for some and part-time football for others would betray the magnificent job done by lower league clubs who have provided First Division clubs with their stars over the years. But, although I'm a sentimentalist and love the game, I can see that some clubs may eventually go to the wall. Every industry has suffered and football is no exception. That's why we have drafted a contract especially for league part-timers because that's the only way some clubs will survive.*

For the same reason I'm not against clubs merging and it may be that sixty or seventy clubs could produce a viable league with a slightly reduced First Division, a regional Fourth Division and an end-of-season national play-off system between the bottom clubs and those in the Alliance League. The less congested First Division programme would give clubs more room in the European competitions and would also mean that players would be more readily available for training with the international squads.

There is too much soccer on television and that might be cured by having one live match per week. There should also be continued pressure on the Government to introduce a Football Levy Board, and a standing committee involving representatives of football, Home Office, local authorities and the Sports Council to establish mutually beneficial links between football and the community. That would help to overcome the kind of problems faced by clubs such as Manchester United, Watford, Luton, Shrewsbury and Hereford who have all run into trouble over planning permission and re-negotiation of leases in 1982-3. The same body could look closely at possible cures for football hooliganism.

Above all the union feels that the Football League should maintain strong financial control over the viability of member clubs and their ability to honour contracts with players and creditors. The league should maintain close control over the assets and liabilities of clubs, and the sale of grounds and takeovers which may eventually result in private individuals or companies benefiting rather than the Football League as a whole. It is true to say that there are now people in the game who are there for the wrong reasons, so far as football is concerned. Strict checks ought to be made on all financial arrangements, and ground facilities and relationships between clubs and spectators should also be of paramount importance. Players, too, will have to play their part in promoting the good things in the game. It is not about 'them and us'. We are all anxious to see that professional soccer survives another hundred years.

15

The Violence

On a glorious and golden autumn afternoon in 1977 I sat outside a cafe in the city of Luxembourg and watched in shame as young men bedecked in Union Flags terrorised the gentle people of the Grand Duchy. Those young men who numbered themselves among the supporters of England (who were playing a vital World Cup qualifying match in Luxembourg that evening) rampaged through the streets of that beautiful old city. They stormed into cafes, smashed beer glasses, overturned tables and openly urinated against shop windows. The local police kept out of their way, for they were tiny in number and powerless to act, and at the modest municipal stadium that evening some England followers caused a further £18,000 worth of damage. At the airport the following day, the girl behind the desk handed me back my British passport and said coldly, *We hope that you English never come back.*

Football violence had manifested itself once more, and the fear of being injured in a football riot is offered as one of the main reasons why attendances have dwindled over the past twenty years. In truth, the terraces at Football League grounds do not run with blood every Saturday afternoon and the chances of being injured in such a 'riot' are minimal indeed, especially if the spectator knows his way about the ground. Those likely to cause trouble will normally congregate in certain sections of the stadium, though in 1983 there was a worrying development at some clubs where the hooligans were not confined to their traditional stamping grounds, the terraces, but had made their way into the stands. Nevertheless, under normal circumstances football grounds are still fairly safe places to visit and perhaps the reason why hooliganism is one of the causes of lower attendances is twofold; first because sensational press reporting often creates a false impression that **every** football match is blighted in this way; second because, while there may be no actual fighting, the aggressive nature and obscene chanting of rival groups of fans does create an atmosphere far removed from the general bonhomie which prevailed in the past.

The charge that newspapers over-sensationalise crowd trouble is a difficult one to argue. There is a school of thought which says that such trouble should be ignored, because to do otherwise is to glorify the troublemakers and risk copy-cat riots. In the summer of 1981, riots by young people, and others, in the Toxteth area of Liverpool were widely reported on television and in the newspapers. Riots which then followed in other English cities and towns were undoubtedly caused partially by people wishing to emulate the Toxteth riots. They had nothing to do with football, but the same philosophy concerning the publication of them held true. The problem is that the media is there to report the news and if five-hundred football fans run amok in some small English town, then it has to be reported. However laudable the reasons for censorship might be, to ignore the trouble would be the thin end of a wedge which could well drive hard into other, more significant areas of society. Perhaps newspapers could 'tone down' their reporting of football violence; but the popular tabloids have their own way of presenting things and it would take more than the interests of football to alter that.

Paradoxically, while Liverpool was the scene of the 1981 riots which set off a chain reaction, the Liverpool football supporters are noted for their good behaviour. It has not always been so, however, and in October 1961, the *Daily Mail's* Donald Mosey commented after a game at Derby, *For years now the behaviour of Liverpool and Everton supporters on their way to, from, and at away games has been a disgrace to soccer.* Trouble had flared at the Baseball Ground where Liverpool, then topping the Second Division, were beaten 2-0 in a tough, bruising game. I was standing on the terraces that day and saw hundreds of Liverpool supporters rush from behind one goal to the opposite end at half-time, straight across the pitch. Later in the game, two incidents involving the Derby centre-forward Bill Curry resulted in a handful of Derby supporters invading the pitch to remonstrate with the Liverpool centre-half Ron Yeats, and at the final whistle there were fights between rival supporters on the pitch. Though there had been isolated incidents of football fans invading pitches throughout the history of the game, this was something new to me. Twenty-odd years ago it was still possible to watch a game without seeing a trace of spectator violence. Indeed, such incidents were still rare, despite the reputation which Merseyside fans had then.

The atmosphere of the game was still one of enjoyment and friendly rivalry and happily Liverpool's fans have since managed to move against the trend and are noted for their appreciation of football and their sporting behaviour, helped no doubt by their team's magnificent record and the general atmosphere of goodwill and consistency which is generated by the club. Similarly, Manchester United supporters had a very bad image until their supporters' club set about improving it. The United supporters club cares deeply about the club's name, and by organisation and hard work has repaired a great deal of the damage. Supporters club officials consult with local police responsible for United's away matches and the results have been encouraging.

Sadly, Liverpool and Manchester United have been the exceptions rather than the rule. Football violence has erupted at almost every

Parts of the Blackburn Rovers roofing has been torn down to provide ammunition for rioting fans.

other ground from time to time, even down to non-league grounds. One of the worst examples, in April 1983, was at Blackburn where Burnley supporters, there for a Second Division match, rained missiles down on to the pitch and police were forced to baton-charge a mob when it was feared that two women were trapped in a kiosk. Darts, coins and smoke bombs were hurled from the Darwen end of Ewood Park and pieces of asbestos roofing were torn down to provide further ammunition. The trouble began early in the afternoon when seven Burnley fans were arrested after breaking away from a police escort to the ground and attempting to confront home supporters. Fighting broke out at the ground before the kick-off and at half-time,

Terry Gennoe, the Blackburn goalkeeper, is struck by an empty whisky bottle thrown from a section of the Burnley fans at Ewood Park.

reported the *Lancashire Evening Telegraph;* police were forced to withdraw from the Darwen end after violent clashes with some of Burnley's 3,400 fans. After half-time the Blackburn goalkeeper was struck on the knee by an empty whisky bottle, and when the home team went into the lead, an element of the Burnley supporters went beserk. The occasional missile became a torrent and the referee Mr David Hutchinson took the players off the field for fifteen minutes while some semblence of order was restored. Police who had been waiting under a stand eventually drew their truncheons and went back into the Burnley mob, making several arrests. The police commander, Chief Supt Gerald Billingham, later defended his decision to withdraw: *It was an attempt to defuse the situation because much of the earlier violence had been directed at the police and we withdrew to see if things would improve. Our absence was purely tactical and when it was apparent that it had not eased the trouble, we went back.* Thirty-one arrests were made that day and the then Burnley manager Frank Caspar said over the loudspeaker system, *You are a disgrace to Burnley FC, we do not want you.*

If the good people of Blackburn Rovers were aggrieved at having their Easter Monday game spoilt in such a way, their troubles were as nothing compared to those suffered by Derby County on two consecutive Saturdays in January 1983. Before the start of their Second Division match with Leeds United, a club notorious for its troublesome supporters, seats were thrown down from the Osmaston End stand. They continued to rain down in the final stages of the match and the Leeds fans caused an estimated £20,000-worth of damage. Several people were injured because immediately under the stand was a section of terracing used by home supporters. It was a recipe for disaster though, thankfully, Derby had just removed seating from that terrace which had been used as a family area to encourage mothers and fathers, sons and daughters to the club. Derby countered the accusation that it was gross stupidity to allow Leeds fans to sit over Derby supporters, by claiming that the Leeds club had assured them that only members of United's supporters club, for who the parent club would take responsibility, would sit there. Leeds had been in trouble several times before; three months earlier Kevin Keegan had been struck by a missile at Elland Road and in the same game his Newcastle collegue John Anderson was struck by a missile thrown by a Newcastle fan at a Leeds player. Both sets of supporters were guilty that day — one newspaper report said that 90 per cent of the forty-five arrests were of Newcastle supporters — and two policemen were injured, one with a fractured cheekbone, the other a broken arm. Then Leeds supporters wreaked havoc at Derby.

One week after the Leeds game, Derby entertained Chelsea, another club with notoriously troublesome supporters, in the fourth round of the FA Cup. The previous week Chelsea fans had run amok at Wolverhampton, and Derby feared the worst. Yet until the home side scored the winning goal in the dying stages of the match, things had been relatively peaceful, quite unlike the previous week's match, and Derby officials were congratulating themselves on the lack of disorder. The goal scored by Derby changed all that. Once more down came the seats, ripped from the Osmaston stand, and there was the suspicion that the referee had used a great deal of common sense and ended the game slightly earlier than the ninety minutes. If he did, then it was a decision to be applauded, and it was something on which to dwell in the light of events which were to happen at the Baseball Ground on the final day of the league season.

It was obvious that the Derbyshire police had as much, if not more, experience in dealing with football violence as any other force in Britain. I spent the day with them watching the policing of the last day of the season, against Fulham on 14 May 1983, and what an eventful day it proved. The man in charge of the police operation was Chief Supt Jack Watson, a well-respected and highly experienced police officer and head of the Derby division of the county force. Football matches are graded by the police on an ABC basis and although Fulham fans had no record of causing trouble, the Derby police had upped the grading of the match to 'A', the category which is applied to matches which it is thought might give most trouble. The reason for the maximum response by the police was simple: Fulham needed to win the game to have a chance of promotion to Division One; Derby had to win to ensure that they were not relegated, though both clubs' fates also rested with other results that day.

Watson held a senior officers' briefing at ten-thirty on the morning of the match. Police intelligence showed that a crowd of some 20,000 was expected, with perhaps 3,000 travelling to support Fulham. It had become something of an end-of-the-season tradition for Derby supporters to flood on to the pitch at the final whistle, and Watson knew that his men would be powerless to prevent this. Twenty minutes before kick-off he walked me around the pitch and showed me the fencing on the popular side of the ground where home and away supporters are segregated on the terracing. He said, *The fence is not high enough. My men can stop the occasional pitch invader, but if thousands want to swarm on, then we cannot stop them.* Watson's tactics were to position police horses and dogs immediately in front of the Fulham section of the crowd about ten minutes before the end of the game, not because he anticipated trouble from them, rather to protect them from a notoriously provocative element in the Derby crowd. The home supporters end-of-season 'invasion' was always a good-natured display of exuberance; better to let them get on with it than risk pitched battles between rival fans if Fulham supporters rose to the taunts from home fans.

The police worked in groups of ten constables, each group headed by a sergeant with an inspector in charge of three groups — ie three sergeants and thirty constables. The position of each man was critical and anyone who thinks that, come Saturday afternoon, the police simply round up a few bobbies and head for the football ground is mistaken. In a small room under the Osmaston stand was a police office to where offenders would be taken during the match. They would be charged, photographed with the arresting officer — *If you've got forty arrests you've got to be able to tie each offender with the arresting officer,* said Watson — and then fastened to a chain which went around the wall of a small adjoining room. However, there were to be 'arrest times' and 'non-arrest times ' when it was considered vital for all officers to be in position, and when no one, notwithstanding the committing of a major offence, could be arrested because the procedure which followed was too time consuming. Police dogs were used more for the effect which the sight of a snarling German Shepherd dog has on an offender, than for actually tackling him. Police dogs are trained the bite the nearest thing to them and they can be extremely indiscriminate in a crowd; also, it is not seen to be *politically expedient* to have police with dogs challenging large sections of the British public, however unruly they might be. Police horses are a different matter. Both Watson and the Assistant Chief Constable (Operations) Ron Hadfield valued the horse as a prized weapon against football hooligans. Hadfield said, *They are worth a dozen foot men and they add dignity to the occasion, especially when giving chase to a mob.* Neither man felt it was useful to adopt the popular suggestion that plain clothes officers could melt into the crowd and identify

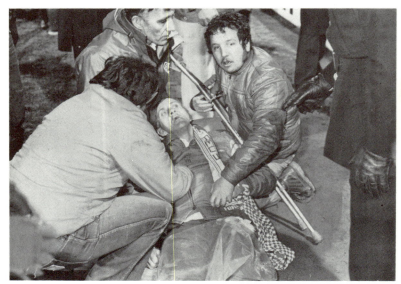

A crippled fan is injured during crowd disturbances after the Derby-Nottingham Forest FA Cup match in January 1983.

174

hooligans. *For a start,* said Hadfield, *a man could say that he didn't know the chap who tried to arrest him was a policeman, and it would also be extremely dangerous for the officer if he was identified as a policeman by a mob of unruly spectators.*

Both Hadfield and Watson are football fans and they care as deeply for the game's image as anyone to whom I spoke. But neither could have anticipated the events of 14 May 1983. The expected pitch invasion by home supporters took place, but an unexpected problem arose when thousands of home supporters crowded the touchline before the end of the game, waiting to run on in the time-honoured fashion. A smaller pitch invasion, which occurred when Derby scored the only goal of the game about fifteen minutes from the end, was cleared. But when fans wedged themselves on to the sidelines with about ten minutes to play, the situation got out of control. One Fulham player was apparently kicked by a spectator as he ran down the wing with the ball, and when the referee blew his whistle to signal offside, everyone thought that the game had ended and thousands ran on to the pitch. The referee, a newsagent from Darwen called Ray Chadwick, had no option but to take the players off, and in the dressing room he revealed that there were still seventy-eight seconds to play. Fulham could not return to the pitch to play out the remaining seconds because one of their players, an eighteen-year-old, had been attacked and beaten by home supporters. Fulham appealed that the game should be replayed — had they won such a replay then they and not Leicester would have been promoted — but the Football League, not surprisingly, refused.

The game raised several important issues. First, there was criticism of the police handling of the situation. From my unique vantage point there was nothing much they could do, given the fact that the fences at the ground were not high enough to prevent a full-scale invasion. Second, there was criticism of the referee who, it was said, should have called the players off earlier instead of battling on. But as he said afterwards, *I was concentrating on the game and when I realised just how many people were on the touchlines, it was too late. To have come off then would have risked a riot.* It is one thing to sit in judgement, but another to be out in the middle of such a hostile environment. Finally, there was Fulham's argument that the league should not allow a team to be chased off the pitch by opposing supporters and then penalise that team for being unable to resume because some of its players had been injured by the crowd. Like most situations in life there was no simple answer. The events of 14 May were due to a combination of circumstances which came together at the wrong time for Fulham. Had they been winning when the game was stopped then it might have been Leicester who wanted a replay.

Excepting the people who attacked the Fulham player that afternoon, the nature of this now-infamous Derby pitch invasion was essentially non-violent, but what about the people who do go to football matches with malice aforethought? Police video film of the Derby-Chelsea game revealed that the vast majority make a lot of noise without actually striking a blow. When the rival factions got on to the pitch they charged each other, but almost always withdrew before blows could be landed. The arrival of the police was greeted almost with relief because there was now no opportunity to take the threats to rival supporters any further. Furthermore, the violence did not seem to be directed at the police, though spitting and obscene chanting at the officers is commonplace. The policeman has to accept that he is going to be spat at, said Assistant Chief Constable Hadfield: *It sounds positively childish when you get to court.* Swearing, too, is difficult to legislate against and Hadfield said, *It is not always possible to identify the offender, often there are several hundred people chanting obscenities, and if you got an offender to court he'd probably have his school uniform on and look so angelic that no magistrate could imagine he was the foul-mouthed yob who was arrested the previous Saturday.*

The same picture applies to the youngster who launches a physical attack on another spectator. Hadfield said, *You get hold of him and he is on a 'high', struggling and kicking like a demented eel. But suddenly he'll go flat and then he presents a pathetic picture. It is almost as though the person who caused the trouble, and the person who has been arrested, as two different people even though they are in the same body. Broadly speaking they fall into the fourteen to twenty age group, though there is a brand of trouble-maker around the thirty-five mark who'll get some drink inside him and then start a fight with opposing supporters of the same age group, probably in the stand.* The myth of all-seater stadia being the answer was exploded by Hadfield: *They are a nightmare for the police and when our officers have had to quell trouble in the stands, they have suffered many injuries, particularly to the shins because it is difficult to get quickly to the trouble spots. Besides, the football hooligan can afford to sit down now and the fact that he cannot stand on the terrace does not deter him. Rather it breeds a football hooligan of slightly higher status.*

The Derbyshire police made use of Dr John Barker, a clinical psychologist and a local football player and coach. He analysed video film of crowd disturbances at the Baseball Ground and drew the conclusion that the police could have done more to establish a rapport with the fans: *From the onset the police adopted a 'them and us' stance. It would have done more good if they had made contact with the crowd.* It should be noted that Chief Supt Watson told me that his officers were now encouraged to communicate with the fans, particularly when escorting them to the ground from railway station and coach park. Dr Barker had also interviewed many hooligans and he felt he had at least part of the answer to why they caused trouble. He said, *Professionalism has done for football what it has done for most things – isolated it from its roots, almost taken it away from its very source of support. The media make a myth of the players and the fans come along and cannot get near them. This creates another 'them and us' situation.*

Football hooliganism is predictable in its patterns. Everyone knows where the trouble will come and youngsters learn the 'football ground game', for the ground is simply serving as a stage. The violence has nothing to do with football, it is simply using the game as an arena and presents the convenient tribal elements. The football hooligans I have seen are largely young people from areas with high unemployment or severe social problems. They take their frustrations to a football ground because it is a superb platform. The arena is an emotion-producing machine where people lose their individuality, where time becomes meaningless and space becomes lost. Sight is replaced by sound, and the sheer rhythmn of that sound pushes up the threshold of excitement. The chanting is inventive and has the same character as the writings on a toilet wall. Chants are used to taunt opposing players and supporters and to affirm one's own superiority. It is all part of a well-orchestrated ritual. There are chant-leaders, but no one is told to take up the chant, it just happens. Then you have the rowdies who will fight if pushed, but would rather just make a display. And there are the nutters, not many in ratio to the rest, but dangerous people who will fight anybody and anywhere. Most of it is born from frustration.

I put it to Dr Barker that life was far harder in the thirties, so why was football violence not a major feature of the game then? Surely the people on the means test and the poor who, unlike the majority of today's unemployed, knew the real meaning of a hungry stomach, had more reason to vent their frustration? He said, *Those people who suffered unemployment and bad housing and other forms of social deprivation in the thirties were far more likely to accept it as their lot in life. There was far less questioning of their roles. Today that has changed and the young people in such areas now feel an intense frustration. They are not content to be bottom of the heap. Within their families there is a 'do as I say' philosophy where authority is allied with physical power. So when they get to football grounds they feel that to assert physical power is to assert authority. People sit in bars and offer cosy explanations, the press describe the violence as 'mindless', and yet nothing anybody does is mindless. There is always a reason for any action. Football violence is a barometer for certain groups of society and the next stage will see it intensify. Football grounds will become more aggressive as violence moves up the age scale.*

It is clear that football violence cannot be isolated as a problem caused by football. In towns and cities there are violent gangs of young people who attach their tribal instincts to schools, areas, even to indoor shopping centres. Nottingham has a kind of gang warfare between the city's Broadmarsh and Victoria shopping centres. Yet, although violence is not caused by football, it is certainly football's problem. The answers lie with society in general, and yet those in the game must make efforts to clean up the image of a sport which has enough self-inflicted problems. The sale of alcohol has been blamed for much crowd violence in England and yet it has not been banned on the majority of grounds. Tom Pendry, then chairman of the All Party Football Committee, claimed in a letter to the *Sunday Times* in March 1983 that banning alcohol would be no solution. He said, *There is little evidence to support the view that the sale of alcohol at matches increases the level of violence. When drinks are not available inside the ground, supporters either arrive 'tanked-up' or else attempt to bring in their own supplies.*

Pendry said that the police officer responsible for policing all sporting events in the Metropolitan Police District, Chief Superintendent David Polkinghorne, preferred to have bars inside the ground *to bring people there rather than attending already half-drunk.* Pendry claimed that one large catering company, which operated on thirty-seven licensed and many unlicensed grounds, had found no correlation between the presence of a bar and hooliganism. He said, *Buying a drink is part of the entertainment of a football match which would be impaired by removing this facility. All clubs rely to an appreciable extent on income generated by the sale of alcohol and other refreshments. At a time of recession clubs cannot afford to lose this sort of revenue.* Pendry's argument did not impress the Scottish Football Association. The SFA assistant secretary Mr Bill Richardson told me that in February 1981 the Criminal Justices (Scotland) Act came into force, prohibiting the sale of alcohol on football grounds and banning supporters taking drink into grounds, or carrying it on coaches and trains designated as football specials. He said, *It has been a great success in preventing crowd trouble. The prime example is the big match between Rangers and Celtic which used to be a traditional New Year's Day fixture, but which had to be moved from the holiday because of continued violence. In 1983 it was possible to move it back to the holiday. Evidence suggests that behaviour has improved dramatically since we banned drink.* In July 1983 it was reported that a secret study involving the Home Office, Football Association, police and British Rail had evolved a plan to clamp down on soccer hooligans. It appeared that the working group were sufficiently impressed by the alcohol ban in Scottish soccer to consider introducing it to the English season in time for the start of 1983-4. Other unspecified measures were reported to be under consideration in what would be *the toughest-ever plans to stop hooligans destroying British soccer.*

Another suggestion offered as a cure for football violence is to ban away supporters and to give all home supporters an identity card. Stuart Webb of Derby County felt it would work. He said, *If we stuck to it, then we'd clean up the game in a season.* Other people saw it as unworkable. Football League secretary Graham Kelly said, *It is more likely to turn people away from the game.* Assistant Chief Constable Hadfield told me, *Gatemen have enough trouble now, without checking everyone's identity card. Our aim is to get people into grounds quickly and that certainly wouldn't help.* Tom Finney, Preston's great star and a magistrate, said that the game would not be helped by such a move: *This is essentially a free country and I can't see how you can prevent people from travelling to football matches. It would create a hostile atmosphere which would do the game no good at all.*

Although football violence is not as rife as many would have us believe, it is nevertheless a problem which does keep people away. The solution lies outside the game, and football can only attempt to stem the tide of lawlessness which rises from time to time. Pre-match entertainment may be one answer, for there are precious few grounds where there is anything to amuse the crowd who may be in the stadium anything up to an hour before kick-off. But most of the trouble happens during and after the match and it is difficult to conceive just what might be done to counter it. Clubs can be made to take stringent precautions, but to hold a club responsible for every single person who throws a coin on to the pitch is unrealistic. Fines on those clubs do little good and the money should be diverted to improving crowd control measures still further. Indeed, that is the line which the FA took over the troubles at Derby in 1983. Crowd violence is an unpleasant face of football which the game can only hope to contain to manageable proportions. It will certainly not go away without a significant social development from outside.

Football and Television

There can be no doubt that television had been one of the most significant and influential development of the twentieth century, shrinking the world to a 'global village', affecting the way we think and act, and altering social patterns which had remained largely unchanged for scores of years. Television has, arguably, imposed upon us new, many would say lower, moral values and standards of behaviour, and the game of football has inevitably been caught up in the television age. Television cameras were at the 1938 FA Cup final when there were 93,357 people in the Empire Stadium to see the game. Under one-tenth of that number saw it live on small black-and-white television sets which received the BBC transmission. After World War II the BBC continued to show the finals live and those houses with a television set in the late forties and early fifties were invaded by friends and neighbours who huddled behind closed curtains watching tiny nine-inch screens. I can remember sitting in such a neighbour's house, one of perhaps twenty people crowded into the tiny front room to watch Stanley Matthews pull the 1953 Cup final out of the fire for Blackpool.

The Football Association also allowed other cup matches to be televised, starting with the 1947 fifth-round tie between Charlton and Blackburn, and international matches and European games — both the early floodlit friendlies and later competitive matches — became a regular feature of television. The Football League, however, were

Arsenal players examine a television camera in 1937.

much more reticent and feared that televised soccer would result in decreased attendances. When the Independent Television Authority was founded in 1955, the new companies quickly saw the potential in soccer, although it was five years before they could persuade the Football League to allow cameras into grounds. In 1960 they reached an agreement, reportedly for £150,000, to screen a number of live Friday evening matches. The first one was Blackpool against Bolton on 10 September 1960, but the crowd was so poor and the game so dreadful that several leading clubs refused to participate and the deal was cancelled.

In August 1964, the BBC reached agreement with the Football League to show an edited fifty-five minute version of a weekly league game. The time was trimmed by ten minutes after the FA protested, and when Liverpool met Arsenal on 22 August 1964, 75,000 people tuned in to see the first *Match of the Day*, then screened on BBC2. From the start of 1966-7, the programme was switched to BBC1 and was now available to all viewers, many of whom could not receive the second BBC channel. This fact, coupled with a temporary boom in football attendances in the wake of England winning the World Cup, saw viewing figures for *Match of the Day* increase dramatically. Since then television has been seen by many as the curse of football. In 1969 the Home International Championship, which had hitherto been spread over the season, was packed into eight days at the end and agreement was reached with both BBC and ITV to screen the matches live. The results were disastrous. Only the traditional England-Scotland game attracted a capacity audience. The most depressing match was at Hampden Park, Glasgow, which the following year housed over 137,000 people for the visit of England; in 1969, when Northern Ireland came to the cavernous stadium on an appalling evening, only 7,834 turned up to watch. The standard of the opposition and the foul weather undoubtedly contributed to such a small attendance figure, but once more live television was seen as the real villain.

Throughout the seventies the television football industry mush-roomed. Players and managers not actively involved in the match being televised that day were enlisted to sit on panels of experts to give their opinions and verdicts on the match; programmes previewing matches began to feature alongside those actually involved with live transmission or edited highlights; and by the end of the decade television was playing a major role in the game. One result was to change the social context of soccer more rapidly than ever before. The game became fashionable to all classes and people who had never been to a football match could now argue the merits and demerits of a particular player, team or match with just as much confidence as those who actually saw the game. Television can distort the pattern of a match, of course, particularly if only edited highlights are shown, for the medium's overriding duty is to entertain, but that has not prevented a whole new breed of armchair critics from adding their voices.

Even to watch an entire game live on television does not prevent the viewer from receiving an incorrect impression, for although camera techniques are far superior to those employed in earlier years, it is still not possible to embrace the whole field of play, nor indeed a significant part of it, in the way in which the spectator at the match can see the game. There is, too, the problem of 'trial by television' when referees' decisions are replayed in slow-motion. It is argued that the referee has to make up his mind in a split-second and does not have the benefit of action replays; yet by far the majority of such replays have shown, time and again, that the referee was correct and 'trial by television' has done more to confirm that match officials are competent, than it has to show them to be wrong. So television has become a major influence on the game and, the argument that a surfeit of televised soccer has resulted in falling attendances notwithstanding, there can be no doubt that the medium has brought football to the attention of millions more people than would otherwise be interested in it. The question to be answered is whether that is a good thing, if, as is constantly alleged, those fans who used to pay at the turnstile are now content to watch from their armchair, and if people have become genuinely tired of soccer because it is so readily available.

The main reason why televised football was a major topic of debate in 1983 was not, however, because those in the game felt that television was robbing them of support. It was all about money. In 1983 the agreement between the Football League and the television companies, which had paid £10 million into football over the previous four seasons (working out at £25,000 per club per season) expired and a new deal had to be worked out. The arguments raged long and loud, but the clear impression given by the clubs was that television could do what it liked with the game *if* enough money was forthcoming. The much. vaunted super league idea owed much to television because the topmost clubs saw a case for retaining the money from television for themselves. After all, BBC and ITV did not pay for the privilege of screening Hereford United and Crewe Alexandra each week. So if the Manchester Uniteds, Liverpools, Spurs and Arsenals were the main attraction, why should those clubs not retain the money themselves? And what better way to do it than to form their own league of super clubs?

By May 1983 it looked likely that a compromise had been reached between television and the Football League. BBC and ITV had at last shifted on their opposition to shirt advertising. Hitherto, although football grounds had advertisements plastered around the pitch perimeters, and despite the fact that racing cars were daubed with advertisements, the TV companies had flatly refused to accept advertisements on footballers' shirts. Indeed, one match recording had to be scrapped in its entirety after it was discovered that one goalkeeper had been wearing a sponsor's name on his jersey, although, major televised sporting events carried the name of sponsors like Benson and Hedges cricket and Embassy snooker. But towards the end of 1982-3, TV agreed to accept shirt logos of not more than sixteen square inches, though they wanted the logos to be four by four, whereas the league clubs favoured eight by two. Television would also offer £5.3 million over two years, and open acceptance of the name of a sponsor who was to give the Football League £3.2 million over three years. The Japanese photographic and office equipment company Canon UK was prepared to use part of its annual £6 million budget for advertising in Britain to sponsor the Football League *if* matches were to be televised.

The Football League's television negotiators had been shorn of much of their debating muscle by the fact that Telejector, a company which had offered to give football £8 million over the next two years in return for being able to show video recordings of matches in pubs and clubs on Monday evenings, had withdrawn their bid. But with shirt advertising, or shirt 'sponsorship' as television preferred to call it, now accepted in principle, and the huge Canon sponsorship hanging on whether cameras were to be admitted in 1983-4, there seemed every reason to believe that agreement would be reached. Then came the disagreement over the number of live matches to be shown. John Bromley, ITV's head of sport, and Jonathon Martin, head of sport at the BBC, both claimed that the idea of showing live matches came from the league *because they wanted a fresher approach.*

Bromley said, *They said that they would take out four matches from the programme each week and we asked them if they could deliver and they said 'Yes'.* The television companies and the league negotiators came up with a plan for seventy live matches, sixty-two second-half and eight full games. But when the forty-four First and Second Division clubs met to consider the plan they rejected it and instead submitted a counter proposal of just four live matches for the season, and they were to be televised live only from half-time onwards. The league president Jack Dunnett explained that it was to be an experiment *and if attendances fall because of it, then the clubs will want to end it.* John Bromley decided that he had had enough: *We've wasted seven months talking to them, no wonder the sport is disintegrating in front of us.*

In fact football had to reach agreement with television and in July 1983, after a few weeks of silence from both sides, it was announced that all but six of the ninety-two clubs had approved a new television deal which included the experimental live televising of ten First Division matches from October 1983. The money available to soccer was £5.2 million in return for a two-year contract. The cutback in live matches was drastic (ten as against the originally proposed sixty-two) and the companies themselves would choose the games with BBC coverage on Friday evenings and ITV on Sunday afternoons. The existing recorded coverage was to continue, though probably not when live soccer was scheduled, shirt advertising permitted to a maximum of sixteen square inches with no letter higher than two inches, and £300,000 set aside each season to compensate clubs whose attendances were affected by live coverage. A four-man sub-committee headed by Graham Kelly would arbitrate on claims. Recorded programmes would begin on the first day of the season as usual and pre-match preview programmes would also be unaltered. A Joint Football League-TV committee would meet every three months to deal with any problems and clubs being featured live would be given at least eight weeks' notice. The leading English clubs would receive the bonus of being able to use shirt advertising in European competitions. UEFA had agreed in 1982-3 that such advertising could be used in their matches but when the British television companies refused, English clubs missed out. Now English clubs in European competition could offer their sponsors the added bonus of exposure on television across Europe. More money from those sponsors was a possibility in the light of this extended coverage. The Football League would also receive £500,000 each year plus profits from the sale of overseas television rights, though it was not immediately apparent just how that would be shared out. The Milk Cup final would also be screened live on a Sunday afternoon for the next four seasons. The ITV companies would cut back on their regional coverage. It is a new concept in televising football and at the time of writing it is impossible to foretell its effect on the game. Whatever else the new-look programme does, however, it will undoubtedly ease the stereotyped diet of small-screen football which had been served up for far too long without any kind of change. Certainly the boom soccer industry of sponsorship and perimeter advertising received a boost.

THE COMMENTATORS

I spoke to two men in the front-line of televised football. Bob Wilson is a former First Division and international player; Brian Moore a director of a Third Division club. Wilson's role with the BBC was one of link man and presenter, with a brief to comment; Moore's position with ITV had seen him grow in status to become one of the most respected and best-liked match commentators in Britain. Between them they offered some thoughts on the future of televised football and on the game in general.

BOB WILSON

Some thirty years ago a young schoolboy stood behind the goal at Chesterfield's Saltergate ground, one of a crowd of perhaps 15,000 for Third Division North soccer, studying the techniques of visiting goalkeepers. In 1983 Chesterfield would have happily settled for one-third of that attendance, relegated as they were in the Fourth Division, and the schoolboy in question was one of the best-known faces on

British television after enjoying a playing career with one of the world's most famous clubs. Bob Wilson, Arsenal's goalkeeper when they won the double in 1971 and a television personality of the eighties, had some forthright views on the game he loved so passionately.

Not surprisingly for the man who hosted BBC's regular Saturday lunchtime programme *Football Focus,* as well as linking *Match of the Day* with Jimmy Hill, Wilson felt that television was unfairly blamed for soccer's current ills. He said, *If there is too much football on television, then I don't really think you can blame the BBC. It can be argued that I'm biased, but where there may have been a problem is with ITV's screening of several different regional matches, which meant that over the country they cover far more games than the BBC do on 'Match of the Day'. So, with Liverpool and Manchester United the leading clubs, it's been quite likely that they'll be on television week after week in some region or other. They could complain of over-exposure, though if clubs do refuse to go on the box, it's more likely to be for tactical reasons – they don't want other managers to have the opportunity of checking them over – rather than because they fear their attendances will be down.*

Bob Wilson, the BBC TV football host, was a goalkeeper with Arsenal and Scotland and speaks with more authority than many commentators.

Football at the very top flight will never be affected by television according to Wilson, who played twice for Scotland before exchanging goalkeeper's gloves for a microphone. *We spoke in the week after the FA Cup fifth round matches of 1983 and Wilson used them as an example of how the medium of television does more good than harm for football. We previewed all eight matches on Football Focus advertising the games and interviewing the managers and players who were each selling their particular match, telling the viewers that theirs was going to be a great cup-tie. The result was not a drop in attendances, but an increase. People will always want to see the big matches. That was proved when Manchester United and Arsenal met in the Milk Cup semi-final at Old Trafford a few days later. The game was effectively dead because United held a two-goal lead from the first leg. In addition it was a bitterly cold night and everyone knew that the highlights would be televised because it was the only cup match that evening. Yet 56,000 turned out. On the same evening England played Wales in a virtually meaningless match at Wembley, with some of the best players unavailable because of the Milk Cup match, and only 24,000 paid to see it. People want to see the real drama, whether it is televised or not.*

What television had done, according to Wilson, was to create a demand for excellence which has meant that the smaller clubs and the less attractive matches lost spectators: *When I was a boy at Chesterfield*

the local club would attract 15,000 or more. Nowadays that just isn't possible for all but a handful of Third Division matches. People are fed on excellence, not just in football but in other sports too, and they want to see only the best. Wilson was hurt when people suggested that television did not always present football in the best possible light: *Of course we have to reflect what is happening in the game, but I eat, drink and sleep football and I'd hate it if people thought that I sat there in front of the cameras and didn't care for the game. I love football, I'm a football person, and I want only for it to succeed.*

Bob Wilson conceded that television producers were sometimes faced with a dilemma when confronted with a dull, boring game which ended in a goalless draw. He said, *In that case we try and pick out what few highlights there are, but we still have to show a fair reflection of the game – and that is the biggest argument against live coverage. Once you've selected a game to show live, then you are stuck with it for better or worse. For instance, if we had chosen to show live coverage of the Burnley against Crystal Palace cup match on 19 February 1983, then we would have finished up with the worst possible advertisement for football because it was such a dreadful game – and we wouldn't have been able to do a thing about it. By selecting two or three games and showing only the highlights, we can then serve the best possible interests of the game.*

Wilson could not understand why the clubs did not realise that there was no more money available from television: *Football must be the only product in Britain which not only refuses free advertising, because that is what programmes like Football Focus give it, but want yet more money. Talking in terms of the 1982-3 figures, people forget that when clubs complain that they get only £25,000 each per season, it is the size of the Football League which is to blame. This is the biggest league in the world and there are more clubs to share the cash. The likes of York City and Aldershot need that £25,000, and if the Manchester Uniteds and Liverpools feel that they are being sold short, then that's the way it is with ninety-two clubs.*

Although the clubs wanted more money, Wilson could see a greater realism from the players: *They will realise that it is better to have a relatively well-paid job in football, than be a theoretical £800-a-week player without a job. When we won the double at Arsenal in 1971, and also reached the last eight of the UEFA Cup, my basic wage was £110-a-week and with bonuses I cleared £17,000 that year. That seems like a lot of money – and it was – but don't forget that we'd just won the First Division title, the FA Cup, and had a good run in Europe. In recent years players have been getting far less than that for winning nothing, and many young players have earned far too much too soon. They have had no chance to settle down and realise life's worth.*

I remember when Johnny Haynes became the first £100-a-week footballer back in the early sixties, I was in Arsenal reserves. Neighbours would say to me, 'Blimey mate, you're doing well, hundred quid a week'. They had to be kidding. In any case, I came into football as a full-timer

186

after I'd played senior amateur football while working as a teacher and I knew what life was about. Believe me when I say that I would have played for Arsenal for nothing, just to play in the First Division. Nowadays the crazy money in football has put players out of work. When I signed for Arsenal they had sixty-three full-time professionals. In 1983 that figure was down to about twenty, so at Highbury alone there are over forty jobs lost over the years. There are a lot of reasons why football is struggling, but I think that too much televised soccer is way down the list. Football needs television because the game has to be kept in the public eye, and we report it more honestly than newspapers who are often only interested in the scandal and the bad features of the game. Television cares about the game and a season of blank screens would serve no useful purpose at all.

reference.

BRIAN MOORE

The reason why Brian Moore is so good, said London Weekend Television producer Ted Ayling, *is that he has the knack of being able to inform people who don't know much about football without insulting the intelligence of those who do.* There is no doubt that although many television commentators manage to get under the viewers' skin by stating the obvious, ITV's Brian Moore has always managed to pitch his commentary at just the right level, helped no doubt by his golden

Brian Moore LWT's Big Match commentator is recognised as one of the best in the country. He is also a director of Gillingham FC.

rule, *If you can't think of anything to say, then shut up.* Popular with viewers, fellow staff and, more significantly, players and managers, Brian Moore has succeeded where many have failed.

Moore's Saturdays in the football season begin with ten minutes on his exercise bicycle, breakfast with wife Betty and then a drive from his Kent home — he is a director of Third Division Gillingham — to the venue of that day's LWT *Big Match.* For a man who makes his living out of televised football, Moore has no reservations about admitting that there might be too much soccer on the small screen. He said, *There could be a case for saying that televised football is overdone. Perhaps we need to slim down midweek games, the earlier round of the Milk Cup for instance. And perhaps we could cover perhaps two instead of three matches at weekends. But regionalised matches are needed by clubs who might not otherwise get the exposure they need to help promote income from ground advertising and sponsorship. Yes, there may be too much televised football, but I think it's a case of some fine tuning rather than wholesale change. The advantage of covering more than one game is that you can juggle them around when it comes to editing the highlights and although we admit to the fact that a game might be a bad one – the Arsenal-Forest match in 1982-3 was an example – our objective is to entertain. The Saturday lunchtime slots wet the appetite, although television does tend to polarise support to the bigger clubs I suppose.*

As a television commentator and the director of a league club, Moore is in a better position than most media pundits to talk about other aspects of the game which affected attendances. He said, *Football as a product is not all that wrong, but there are many other sides to the game which could be improved upon. Of all the letters I receive from fans, the great majority cite hooliganism as the reason why they don't want to come into the grounds. Most of the letters complain about violence and verbal aggression, but that isn't just confined to football grounds. It's the same in the street and on the bus. It's a social problem and the only thing that football can do is to sit tight and wait for the day when people have learned more sense.*

Of all the other suggestions offered about how to get people back into seats and on to the terraces, I can't say that any appeal to me, either in my position as a television commentator or as the director of a small club. The super league is a dead duck. If the clubs went it alone then they would be barred from the FA Cup and from European competition – so that rules out a pirate league – and even if it was something within the structure of the Football League, who would you include? There would presumably be no automatic promotion and relegation, which is the life-blood of league football, and could the small town clubs compete financially, because it wouldn't just be a question of having a good team. Moore's thoughts of regionalisation and part-time soccer for clubs like his were even more emphatic: *It would be an utter disaster to introduce part-time football into the Third and Fourth Divisions. The clubs would lose their mystique and they'd all end up like the Maidstones and the Scarboroughs of*

188

football. Regionalisation wouldn't work either. It would cause more crowd aggravation with more local derbies, so there would be more police expense, more damage, and ultimately smaller crowds because people would stay away for fear of being caught up in the trouble. Gillingham are stuck down in a corner of England and yet we travel to all our away games on the day of the match. It might involve the players in a bit of discomfort, but it saves us up to £500 a time.

Like most Third and Fourth Division directors, Brian Moore felt that sky-high wages, not travelling, was the real problem which was crippling many football clubs: *Wages will have to be rationalised and there will be fewer and fewer top players earning enormous sums of money. Youngsters coming into the game will have their wages fixed at a realistic level and gradually a new pattern of pay structure will emerge. I had every sympathy and admiration for what Gilbert Blades was trying to do at Lincoln and it was a great pity that the manager and the players and supporters did not back him up. Directors must do their best for their clubs and do what Blades was trying to do – ensure that the clubs survive. There has been this time-honoured tradition to leave financial dealings with managers, but they are essentially birds of passage and they largely care only for the present. When they move on they leave behind them the responsibility for the financial mess which their old club might find itself in. The directors then have to pick up the bill, so the sooner directors take a firmer attitude to managers who want to buy expensive players and pay them lucrative salaries, irrespective of the club's financial position, the sooner professional football will solve one of its major problems.*

Note: These comments by Bob Wilson and Brian Moore regarding the format of televised football were made before the decision to experiment with live televised football in 1983-4.

17

The Future –
Soccer in 2000 AD

Professional soccer has reached the end of its first hundred years and within twenty seasons the game will have swung into the twenty-first century, so what might be the face of football in the year 2000 AD? Indeed, will there be a professional game at all? Certainly, if clubs do nothing to check the alarming financial problems bedevilling them, and if attendances continue to fall at the present rate, then there is every prospect that professional football in its present form will have disappeared from the social fabric of Britain. Of course, that is supposing that no one in the game, either at club, league or FA level, is prepared to change at least some aspect of a sick sport; and surely enough people in soccer will have woken up sufficiently soon enough to prevent such a situation. Indeed, the very fact that the subject is now being earnestly debated is evidence, surely, that football's rulers are aware of the dangers besetting their game, whereas in the past the clubs have gone merrily downhill, spending enormous sums of money in the face of declining interest in their sport, apparently oblivious to the fact that they were committing suicide.

Realism in the financial side of the game will have to be the first priority. Already the transfer market has collapsed and it is unlikely that we shall again see players changing hands for seven-figure sums. Wages will presumably follow suit and as young players come into the game their salaries will be fixed at a lower rate than those who benefited from the days of financial recklessness, although in June 1983 Arsenal were reported to be offering the Scottish international Charlie Nicholas, still a relative novice in the game despite scoring over fifty goals for Celtic and Scotland in 1982-3, the staggering weekly wage of £2,400 — a sum which, if invested wisely, will have made the 21-year-old Scot a millionaire by the time his projected four-year contract with the London club expires. Tottenham Hotspur was another club reputed to be ready to pay a staggering amount to one player in 1983-4. It was reported that Spurs' midfield star Glenn Hoddle would collect close to a quarter of a million pounds for a single year's work. Hoddle's contract was at an end and with the Scottish star Nicholas just down the road at Spurs' North London rivals, the White Hart Lane club were apparently prepared to hold on to its own stars at any price. Yet surely such salary arrangements must be the exception rather than the rule for the future.

If clubs trim their expenditure, particularly in regard to wages and transfer fees, to match income, then there is surely great hope for the game of soccer. But economies, though absolutely vital, are only part of the answer. Football must also win back its lost supporters, or perhaps more realistically, check the steady stream of fans who are turning away from the game. It is totally unrealistic to compare the attendance figures of the eighties with those of the forties and early fifties. That was a different age, affected by different social conditions, and one may just as well run comparisons with Victorian or Edwardian soccer. The days of forty million people going through the turnstiles each season will never return, so football must base its plans on the present near twenty million and work at retaining them and on running its finances accordingly. Changing social patterns have meant that today's man has far more alternatives to watching soccer. There are now a wider range of sports open to him to take part in — squash and badminton, for instance, have increased hugely in popularity — and Saturday afternoon television offers neatly packaged sports action without the need to move from one's fireside, a great attraction on a wintry afternoon. People lead much more sophisticated lives in the eighties and the prospect of standing or sitting at a football stadium in below-zero temperatures is not so attractive to the modern fan who lives in a centrally-heated home. His father, who may have been used to trudging to an outside lavatory at the bottom of the garden in the small hours, would have been prepared to endure such hardships. Clubs do not possess the resources to turn nineteenth-century soccer grounds into futuristic stadia. Luton Town will have to move from their present Kenilworth Road ground in the second half of the eighties because of a road scheme, and the Football League has approved a plan for a new £20 million stadium at Milton Keynes. (Luton's plan for a synthetic pitch looks likely to be turned down by the other clubs, many of which are less than convinced of the desirability of the one currently in use at Loftus Road, the home of Queen's Park Rangers.) This move to a brank new stadium has been

Players for the future? England's youngsters take on Spain in the UEFA tournament match at Stoke in May 1983. From their ranks may emerge a star to excite the crowds.

forced upon Luton and generally the prospect of watching soccer in comfortable and warm grounds in the middle of an English winter is one which eludes supporters, simply because a largely bankrupt game cannot afford them. At the beginning and end of the season, when the weather is kinder, the modern supporter may well take his family to the countryside or the sea and the emancipation of the working-class wife has had a profound effect on football attendances. Professional football has many counter-attractions to fight. People who go to football out of sheer habit are a dwindling breed. The cloth cap and muffler brigade of Priestley's *The Good Companions* grow fewer in number each season.

Accepting that the attendance figures will not increase, how then can soccer retain those spectators who have remained loyal to the game? The main complaint from 'the-man-on-the-terrace' is that soccer is less entertaining. The product is not up to scratch. Yet although we have to allow that there are less truly outstanding players, can we really believe that skill has declined? Perhaps the very definition of that description, the *outstanding* player, holds the key to the argument. The great players of yesteryear stood out, not only because they were great players, but because there were so many ordinary players. The eighties see footballers with a higher degree of fitness and organisation, so that the great players do not have the opportunity to shine in the same way as those of other days. Probably there are fewer great artists because players have been instructed first and foremost in the importance of workrate, fitness and organisation and there is no footballer today who is allowed the luxury of playing only a small part in the team game in return for flashes of potentially match-winning brilliance.

At the start of 1982-3 English referees were ordered to clamp down on the so-called professional foul and players who deliberately handled the ball, or pulled down a player in full flight, to prevent what looked like a certain goal could be ordered from the field. So too could a goalkeeper who handled the ball outside his penalty area for the same reason. In the early months of the season the number of sendings-off rose, but towards the end referees seemed less inclined to interpret the instruction to the letter. During the close season of 1983 FIFA, the world governing body, warned the FA that it was displeased with this go-it-alone policy of punishing the cynical foul with dismissal from the field. It seems that the instruction will be abandoned in 1983-4 and thus we will never know if the 'clean-up campaign' would have resulted in more open, attractive soccer in the long term.

Without doubt football has become much more defensive and negative, and the only way to bring back the crowds, or at least keep the present numbers, is to make soccer more entertaining. But what is entertainment? A Fourth Division match between Crewe and York in November 1982 provided me with as much entertainment as anything I saw that season. Skill was at a premium, but because of that, there were plenty of mistakes and goalmouth incidents which offered a level of excitement not seen at many First Division grounds. Of course, the greedy spectator wants his football thrills and spills *and* displays of individual skill. But how can that be achieved when it is generally accepted that the price of failure is so great that not many managers would dare to risk entertaining the public if it meant the possibility of defeat? The answer does not necessarily lie in changing the laws of the game, for there have been few artificial changes which benefited sport. A gradual process of re-education may be the answer, but that would depend on directors offering their managers more time to obtain success. A manager who knows that he has three or four years without the threat of losing his job would be better prepared to go out and play open, attacking football than the man who has a noose around his neck after six months and who can hear the trapdoor bolt sliding open before he has finished his first year. But which will be the first club to promise a manager such guaranteed luxury?

More attractive football can come if managers and players could perform under less pressure. Though there is much to commend the 'Watford way" of four strong front-runners and lots of well-placed long passes up to them, so the creative and delightful skills of the class midfield players can be just as pleasing, providing that they are allowed to be positive and make decisions while worrying less about the consequences of the risk going wrong.

The pleasing aspect of 1982-3 was that there were more goals scored than at any time since 1967-8. The total was 5,627 - a rise of 350 on the previous season - and an improvement of 12.49 per cent over two seasons. Leading the campaign for more goals were Fourth Division champions Wimbledon who were just four goals short of becoming the first team in seven years to score 100 goals in a season. No less than fifty-four clubs could boast that they scored more goals than in 1981-2 and Football League secretary Graham Kelly said, *I felt that football was becoming more attacking in 1982-3 and these figures back up that im-*

Graham Kelly, secretary of the Football League.

pression. Some of the goals must be due to the stricter intepretation of the laws as they affect the so-called professional foul, but the rest must be due to managers and coaches determination to produce more attractive football. Perhaps the most surprising aspect was the fact that Crewe Alexandra, having increased their total attendance figure by 700 despite having to apply for re-election, also managed to score a staggering 82 per cent more goals than in 1981-2. The Third Division produced most goals in 1982-3, with nineteen of the twenty-four teams scoring at least sixty times.

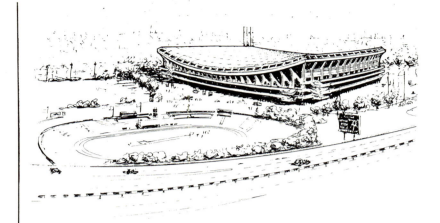

The stadium of the future? Architect Anthony Simms produced detailed plans for a £120 million covered stadium which would seat 60,000 people. The stadium would be totally enclosed under a type of plastic roof and the pitch would be of synthetic grass. It would form part of a wider complex including an athletics stadium and the soccer stadium itself would incorporate squash courts, badminton courts, restaurants and bars. Such a project would be a part-professional soccer stadium, part-public sports centre. No single club could embark upon such a project, but Simms sees a time when perhaps several soccer clubs, other sports clubs and the local authorities might combine to produce such a venue. There might be eight or ten throughout Britain, serving large regional areas such as Lancashire, East Midlands, West Midlands, London, North-East, etc.

Given sound financial thinking and more open football the game would surely prosper, but even then football could do much more to bring itself back to a fully healthy state. The fact that football stadia are used only once a fortnight for nine months of the year, and not at all during the summer months, is an indication of how the clubs are still living in the past. There are signs that things are changing in this direction and at places like Hull City moves are afoot to bring clubs and their grounds into the community. Other clubs must follow this trend in using their grounds for a multitude of other purposes. Not only would this bring in extra revenue, but it would also remind those people visiting the stadium for other purposes — be it a pop concert or a tennis tournament — that there is also a football club. People may become supporters by association with other events. The grounds themselves could be improved, though in many areas there is not the space for great expansion, and better facilities would be a gesture of faith towards long-suffering supporters. The problem of hooliganism is one for society in general, but stadia improvements and pre-match entertainment might help; such a development would certainly do no harm. Properly balanced television coverage and better marketing of soccer would also help to maintain interest and it is now accepted that, while television does not 'ruin' soccer, there has been too much football on the small screen and there is a sound case for reducing it and taking a fresh look at how the game should be presented on TV. It remains to be seen whether the new arrangements concerning a mixture of live matches and edited highlights in 1983-4 will ultimately provide that proper balance.

The reshaping of the season has also been discussed in the past and there is a lobby for summer soccer. The problem is that Britain would be largely out of step with the rest of Western Europe, a fact which would pose problems when clubs competed in the European competitions, and when the World Cup and European Championships came around there would be further confusion. Although the idea of watching soccer on balmy summer evenings is an idyllic notion, the holiday season and counter-attractions of other summer sports would have to be weighed carefully against the number of spectators lost because of cold, wet weather in the traditional football season.

Finally, the restructuring of the Football League is a major topic. The 1983 Chester Report suggested a reduction of two clubs in the First Division (to twenty) and an increase of two in the Second (to twenty-four) with the Third and Fourth Divisions amalgamating into a forty-eight club Third Division. This Third Division would be sub-divided into four groups of twelve who would then play a twenty-two match series in the first half of the season, followed by a repeat of the fixtures in the latter half. The top two in each section would play-off and the top four would go into the Second Division at the expense of four relegated clubs. There would be a similar relegation play-off between the bottom clubs in each section and the team finishing last would be replaced by the Alliance Premier League champions.

When the Football League's annual meeting of 1983 was held, the suggestion to restructure the league was not debated. The annual meeting did agree to allow each club to retain its own gate receipts — previously the away side qualified for a payment of 30p a head for adults and 15p for juniors — which means more money for the better supported clubs and a lot less for those with small attendances. Saturday morning kick-offs were to be allowed if both clubs agreed, the second round of the Milk Cup was to be seeded, and the Milk Cup final probably played on a Sunday; but there was no room for altering the shape of the league itself, nor for changing the system which requires a three-fifths majority before changes to the league can be approved. So football had turned its face away from the most radical of Chester's suggestions.

Whether that refusal will ultimately lead to a breakaway super league is not clear, for that development also depends largely on the direction which television negotiations take. As Football League secretary Graham Kelly told me, *There is little doubt that a so-called super league could evolve if there was enough money available from sponsors. But such a league would be totally committed to sponsorship and it would soon become a hostage to naked commercialism.* It is more likely that clubs will find difficulty in continuing as full-time professional outfits in the Third and Fourth Divisions and if the league does shrink, then it will be as a result of natural wastage. Gordon Taylor, the PFA secretary, might not have been so far wide of the mark when he talked of a Football League of sixty or seventy clubs.

Without the benefit of an accurate crystal ball, it is impossible to say what shape football will take by the turn of the century. All the evidence points to clubs being much more realistic in their financial dealings — the alternative is, after all, extinction — and to football realising that it must provide better entertainment if it is to succeed in halting the loss of spectators. Could it be that by the year 2000 AD we will have our super league, having come about quite naturally from those clubs still able to afford to pay higher-than average wages? Perhaps there may be only a dozen or more clubs in that bracket but Italy's sixteen-club First Division is arguably the most professionalised in the world. The Second Division would still be a class competition; and the Third and Fourth Divisions perhaps relying largely on part-time players in regionalised competitions which also absorb some of the Allience Premier League's clubs. Perhaps the picture will be First Division (sixteen clubs), Second Division (twenty-two), Third Division (twenty-two), with the Fourth Division and the APL splitting into three regionalised sections. This may seem a radical change in 1983-4, but let us not forget that we are talking of twenty seasons hence. Whatever the outcome, it is clear that soccer has reached a crisis. Fortunately there appears to be a way out of that crisis and realism, courage and the willingness to put aside insular interests for the greater good of association football will be vital assets; but the most vital commodity of all is time and the sands are running out. Football has every reason to be optimistic for its future — if it acts now. It can restore sanity and entertainment to what may otherwise become a totally bankrupt game. The future of professional soccer lies squarely in its own hands.

Index

Aberdeen FC, 91
Accrington Stanley, 35, 58, 141, 147-8, 153-4
Aldershot FC, 186
Allcock, Charles W., 26-9, 33, 36
Allan, James, 36
Allen, Clive, 145
Allison, George, 52, 143
Allison, Malcolm, 150
Alonso, Juan, 71
Anderson, John, 172
Anderson, W.J., 33
Appleton, Colin, 172
Ardwick FC, 45
Arnold, Thomas, 22
Arsenal FC, 43, 50-2, 54-5, 58, 61-3, 91, 103, 111, 130-1, 136, 139, 142-3, 145-6, 148, 161, 181, 185-7, 190
Aston Villa, 36-8, 43, 55, 101, 121-5, 152
Atkinson, Ron, 111-12
Attendances, 11, 14, 38, 55, 60-2, 65, 68, 122, 162, 181, 184-5
Ayling, Ted, 187

Bailey, Eddie, 64, 136
Bailey, Gary, 135, 137
Baker, Peter, 78
Bangor City, 143
Barket, Dr John, 176-7
Barker, Richie, 127, 138-42
Barnes, Ken, 75
Barnes, John, 84
Barnsley FC, 68, 101
Barrow FC, 115
Barton, Tony, 121-5
Bastin, Cliff, 52, 93
Bates, Ken, 163
Batson, Brendon, 111-15
Bayern Munich, 121
Best, Clyde, 111
Best, George, 13, 105
Billingham Synthonia FC, 117
Birmingham City, 36, 43, 123-4, 149, 151, 165
Blackburn Olympic, 29, 33-4, 43
Blackburn Rovers, 33, 35, 37, 44, 165, 171-2, 180
Blackpool FC, 62, 64, 95-7, 140, 180-1
Blades, Gilbert, 155-8, 189
Blanchflower, Danny, 68, 99-102, 154
Blissett, Luther, 84, 87
Bolton Wanderers, 32, 37, 43, 55, 60, 165, 181
Bond, John, 150
Bozsik, Josef, 75
Bradford City, 153
Brazilian National Team, 54, 75-6
Brighton & Hove Albion, 136, 150
Bristol City, 10-11, 152
Bristol Rovers, 10

Broadbent, Peter, 83
Broadhurst, Kevin, 151
Bromley, John, 10, 183
Brooking, Trevor, 107-10, 116, 143
Brown, Phil, 115-18
Browne (Notts County), 42
Buchan, Charles, 92
Burgess, Ronnie, 64
Burnley FC, 171-2, 186
Burkinshaw, Keith, 85, 120
Burton Albion, 138
Bury FC, 165
Busby, Sir Matt, 62, 68, 72, 102, 120
Butler, Joe, 51
Byrne, Roger, 72

Callaghan, Nigel, 84
Cambridge United, 111-12
Cambridge University, 48
Cardiff City, 10, 51, 61
Carter, Horatio, 60, 65, 91-6, 98, 159
Caspar, Frank, 172
Cavanagh, Tommy, 134
Chadwick, Ray, 175
Chamberlain, Mark, 139
Chapman, Herbert, 50-2, 67, 75, 143, 145
Chapman, Lee, 139
Charlton Athletic, 60, 119, 153-4, 180
Charlton, Bobby, 15, 105, 120
Chelsea FC, 11, 61, 71, 102, 134, 136, 152, 161-4, 172, 175
Chester Committee, 168
Chester FC, 44, 126
Chesterfield FC, 10, 184
Chester Report, 195
Chester, Sir Norman, 14
Chevallier, J.T.B., 33
Christ Church FC, 43
Clapham Rovers, 29
Clay, Ernie, 130
Clydesdale FC, 32
Clough, Brian, 16-17, 91, 120, 138-9
Coaching, 76, 133-4, 142
Cobbold, W.N., 50
Cochrane, Johnny, 93-4
Colchester United, 115
Common, Alf, 55
Copping, Wilf, 52
Corinthians FC, 52
Cork Athletic, 94
Coventry City, 7-8, 10, 13, 134, 136, 138
Craggs, Ken, 119
Crawford, Ray, 78
Crayston, Jack, 52
Cresswell, Lieutenant, 28
Crewe Alexandra, 43, 115, 129, 182, 192-3
Cruyff, Johann, 137
Crystal Palace, 11, 136, 146, 186
Cullis, Stan, 68, 71, 83, 86, 142
Curry, Bill, 170

197

Daft, Richard, 41
Daley, Steve, 150
Dalglish, Kenny, 105
Darwen FC, 30-1, 33
Davison, Bobby, 118
Dennis, Mark, 151
Derby County, 11, 16-17, 37, 41-2, 44, 60,
  94-6, 108, 118, 120, 138, 147, 152, 170,
  172-6, 178-9
Derbyshire County Cricket Club, 42
Derby, Lord, 40
Directors, The, 147, 150-164, 184, 189
Di Stefano, Alfredo, 71-2
Docherty, Tommy, 106, 119, 122
Doherty, Peter, 60, 65, 94-8
Doncaster Rovers, 95-6
Dougan, Derek, 98
Drake, Ted, 52
Duncan, John, 118
Dunn, Arthur, 34
Dunnett, Jack, 183
Durban, Alan, 127
Dynamo Kiev, 122

Edwards, Duncan, 72
Eintracht Frankfurt, 71, 108
England National Team, 78-9, 181
European Cup, 71, 81, 84, 121
Evans, Maurice, 126-7
Everton FC, 38, 43, 63, 105, 126, 170

FA Cup, 26, 28-31, 33, 36, 38, 40, 42-4, 48,
  51-4, 58, 60, 62-5, 94, 134, 180
Fagan, Joe, 82
Ferrier, Bob, 71
Finance, 9-12, 14, 19, 31, 102, 141, 147-55,
  157, 159-64, 186, 189-90, 195
Finney, Tom, 13, 65, 95, 98, 103-7, 178-9
First Division, 14, 39, 51, 54, 59, 62-3
Football Association, 25-8, 36, 39-42, 47,
  56, 68-9
Football Association Original Members,
  25
Football League, 10-11, 14, 37, 39, 50, 53,
  57, 65, 71
Francis, Gerry, 136
Francis, Trevor, 149-50
Fulham FC, 43, 63, 119, 122, 129-33, 156,
  162, 173, 175

Gambling, 56-8
Gento, Francisco, 71
Gibson, Jimmy, 55
Gillingham FC, 188-9
Gladstone, William, 27
Glasgow Celtic, 178, 190
Glasgow Eastern, 32
Glasgow Rangers, 32, 61-2, 178
Glentoran FC, 101
Gliksten Family, 153
Gorton FC, 45
Goulden, Len, 93
Greaves, Jimmy, 13, 105
Greenhaugh, Earnest, 41

Greenwood, Ron, 108
Grimsby Town, 83, 120
Gunn, William, 41

Hagan, Jimmy, 95, 98
Halifax Town, 116, 160
Hancocks, Johnny, 83-4
Hanot, Gabriel, 71
Hapgood, Eddie, 52
Harford, Mick, 158
Harford, Ray, 130
Hartlepool United, 10, 115-18, 147
Hawkins, Graham, 128
Haynes, Johnny, 186
Henry, Ron, 78
Hereford United, 115, 168, 182
Hibernian FC, 62
Hidegkuti, Nandor, 67, 70, 74-5
Hiley, Peter, 17
Hill, Jimmy, 7, 136, 166, 185
Hoddle, Glen,, 85, 87, 190
Hogg, Quintin, 27
Holton, Jim, 126
Honved FC, 70-2, 84
Horner, Billy, 118
Houghton, Ray, 130
Houlston, Dennis, 157
Howe, Don, 136
Huddersfield Town, 50-1, 95, 116, 118
Hughes, Charles, 86
Hull City, 94, 143, 158-61, 194
Hulme, Joe, 52
Hunter, Jack, 33 .
Hutchinson, David, 172
Huyler, Martin, 153

Ipswich Town, 77-8, 120, 152
Ireland National Team, 42, 69

Jack, David, 52, 55
James, Alex, 52
Jenkins, Ross, 84
Jervis, Frederick, 56
John, Elton, 83, 153
Johnson, Anton, 154
Jones, Bryn, 55
Juventus FC, 121

Keegan, Kevin, 13, 107, 116, 172
Kelly, Graham, 178, 184, 193, 195
Kinnaird, Lord, 28, 33
Kirton, Glen, 155
Kocsis, Sandor, 67, 74
Kopa, Raymond, 71

Lambert, Jack, 52
Langan, David, 151
Lang, James J., 32
Law, Denis, 105, 134
Lea, Cyril, 159
Leadbetter, Jimmy, 78
Lee, Sammy, 137
Leeds United, 85, 94, 98, 114, 143, 172
Leicester City, 44, 93, 129, 175

Leicester Fosse, 44
Lewis, Danny, 51
Leyton Orient, 136
Lincoln City, 26, 83, 120, 130, 155-8, 189
Liverpool FC, 7, 11, 18, 43, 62, 81-3, 86,
  105-6, 120, 122, 124-5, 130, 133-4, 136,
  140-1, 149-50, 152, 170, 181, 185-6
Lloyd, Cliff OBE, 166
Lofthouse, Nat, 65, 132
Logie, Jimmy, 63
Love, Jimmy, 30-1
Luton Town, 36, 103, 123, 136, 168, 191
Lyall, John, 108

Mabbutt, Gary, 137
Mabbutt, Kevin, 11
Macdonald, Malcolm, 119, 129-33
Maidstone United, 153
Male, George, 52, 111
Manchester City, 8, 45, 75, 95-6, 105, 150,
  165
Manchester United, 8-9, 11, 43, 62, 72, 84,
  86, 102, 105-6, 112, 119, 122, 125-6, 130-1,
  133-6, 142, 148-9, 152, 165, 168, 170,
  185-6
Mancini, Terry, 130
Mannion, Wilf, 65, 95
Marindin, Major Francis, 28-9, 33
Marshall, Bobby, 92
Martin, Jonathan, 10, 183
Matthews, Stanley, 13, 60, 64, 95, 98, 103,
  180
McCracken, Billy, 50
McCreadie, Eddie, 162
McEnroe, John, 144
McFarland, Roy, 118
McGregor, William, 37
McIlroy, Sammy, 139
McInroy, Albert, 92
McMenemy, Lawrie, 120
Mee, Bertie, 111, 143
Medley, Les, 64
Mercer, Joe, 63, 68
Meredith, Billy, 165
Middlesbrough FC, 36, 45, 55, 65, 94
Milan AC, 71
Milburn, Jackie, 64, 130
Miller, David, 121
Millwall FC, 36, 43
Moore, Brian, 184, 187-9
Moran, Kevin, 135
Morris, Desmond, 15-16
Moscow Dynamo, 60, 71
Moscow Spartak, 71, 84, 143
Moses Remi, 148
Mosey, Donald, 170
Mullen, Jimmy, 83-4
Muller, Gerd, 81
Munich tragedy, 72
Murphy, Colin, 156-8
Murray, Jimmy, 84

Needler, Christopher, 158-9
Needler, Harold, 158-9

Neil, Andy, 51
Neill, Terry, 142-6
Newcastle East End FC, 45
Newcastle United, 45, 51, 62-4, 130-1, 172
Newcastle West End FC, 45
Nicholas, Charlie, 190
Nicholson, Bill, 101, 120, 143
Northampton Town, 44
Northern Ireland National Team, 96, 100,
  102, 142, 181
Norman, Maurice, 78
Norwich City, 123
Nottingham Forest, 26, 31, 41-2, 57, 91,
  120, 122, 149
Nottinghamshire County Cricket Club, 41
Notts County, 41, 122, 138

Old Carthusians, 29, 34-5
Old Etonians, 29-31, 33, 42
Oldham Athletic, 163
Old Reptonians, 42
Old Westminsters, 35
Orient FC, see also Leyton Orient, 136
Oxford United, 10, 17, 136
Oxford University, 29, 31

Paisley, Bob, 81-2
Palermo FC, 106
Paravicini, P.J. de, 33
Parr, George, 41
Partick Thistle, 55
Parton, Dolly, 157
Pearson, Nigel, 128
'Pele' Edson Arantes do Nascimento, 137
Pendry, Tom, 177
Peterborough United, 138
Phillips, Ted, 78
Police, The, 172-6, 178
Pollard A.F., 39
Portsmouth FC, 45, 62-3, 103, 122
Port Vale, 8
Preston North End, 35-8, 43, 45, 48, 94,
  103-7, 150
Priestley, J.B., 15, 53, 192
Professionalism, 31-6
Professional Footballers' Association, 8,
  113, 118, 165-8, 196
Public Schools, 22
Puskas, Ferenc, 67-8, 72, 74

Queens Park FC, 27, 31, 48
Queens Park Rangers, 7, 44, 112, 134, 136,
  145, 191

Ramsey, Sir Alf, 77-9, 81, 84, 120
Rappan, Karl, 79
Reading FC, 17, 131, 136
Real Madrid, 71-2, 76, 107
Reep, Wing Commander, 83-4, 86
Reeves, Kevin, 150
Revie, Don, 75, 120
Revis (Nottingham Forest), 42
Rial, Hector, 71
Richardson, Bill, 178

Roberts, Herbie, 51-2
Robinson, Don, 155, 158-61
Robinson, Mick, 150
Robinson, Peter, 149
Robson, Bobby, 136-8
Robson, Bryan, 85, 87, 148-9
Robson, Keith, 108
Rochdale FC, 116
Rollin, Jack, 81
Romford FC, 33
Roper, Don, 63
Rooke, Ronnie, 63
Rose, W.C., 165
Rotherham United, 154
Rowe, Arthur, 64, 68, 101
Royal Engineers, 28-9
Ruck, Lieutenant, 28

Santamaria, Jose, 71
Saunders, Ron, 124-5, 151
Scarborough Town, 159-60
Scottish Football Association, 50, 178
Scottish National Team, 42, 48, 69, 181
Scunthorpe United, 118, 120
Second Division, 54, 59, 64
Sexton, Dave, 119, 133-8
Shankley, Bill, 18, 81, 107, 120
Shaw, Gary, 124
Sheffield Football Association, 23, 25-6,
    29, 42
Sheffield United, 40, 43, 118, 128
Sheffield Wednesday, 32, 42
Shrewsbury Town, 125-9, 139, 158, 168
Shrovetide Football, 20-1
Simonsen, Allen, 153
Smith, George, 118
Smith, Mike, 159
Southampton FC, 36, 43, 81, 120
Spencer, Martin, 155, 161-4
Sponsorship, 9, 102, 182-3, 188
Stadia, 60, 194
Stephenson, Roy, 83
St Mirren, 93
Stockport County, 7-10, 43
Stoke City, 37, 43, 60, 62, 138-41
Stokoe, Bob, 93
Sudel, Major William, 36
Sunderland Albion, 36
Sunderland FC, 36, 38, 44, 55, 91-4
Suter, Fergus, 30-1, 33
Swales, Peter, 150
Swansea City, 83, 137
Swedish National Team, 76
Swinburne, Roy, 83

Tactics, 13, 46-50, 52, 79, 81-2, 84-6, 97,
    109, 130, 132-3, 137, 142
Taylor, Ernie, 64
Taylor, Gordon, 8, 118, 165-8, 196
Taylor, Graham, 83-4, 86, 102, 120, 124,
    156

Taylor, Peter, 16-17, 118, 120, 138-9
Taylor, Tommy, 72
Television, 7-10, 180-9, 191, 194-5
Thames Valley Royals, 17
Thomas, Mickey, 139
Thring J.C., 24
Tottenham Hotspur, 36, 45, 64, 78, 85, 91,
    99-100, 105, 120, 136, 143, 154, 190
Townsend, Cyril, 14
Tranmere Rovers, 116, 129
Transfer Fees, 11-12, 55, 126, 131, 145,
    148-51, 153, 191
Turner, Graham, 125-9, 158

Vidal, Rev R.W.S., 29
Vinnai, Gerhard, 18
Violence, 12, 169-79, 194

Wages, 11-12, 40, 62, 131, 148, 150-1, 153,
    157, 162, 164, 166-7, 189-91
Wales National Team, 42, 69, 165
Wanderers, The, FC, 27-9, 40
Watford FC, 82, 84-7, 98, 102, 120, 124,
    137, 142, 153, 168
Watson, Dave, 139
Webb, Stuart, 152, 178
West Bromwich Albion, 35, 37, 103, 111-12,
    115, 148
West German National Team, 79, 81
West Ham United, 43, 51, 55, 107-8, 110-11,
    114, 120, 130, 136, 152
Whiteside, Norman, 135
Whittaker, Tom, 52, 143
Widdowson, Sam, 42
Wigan Athletic, 10, 141, 163, 167, 186
Wilberforce, Mr Justice, 166
Williams, Wayne, 128
Wilson, Bob, 184-7
Wilson, George, 33
Wilshaw, Dennis, 83
Wimbledon FC, 193
Winterbottom, Walter, 68
Withe, Peter, 121
Wolverhampton Wanderers, 7, 10, 37-8,
    43, 55, 63, 70-1, 83-4, 128, 139, 142, 152,
    165, 172
Woolwich Arsenal, 36, 43
Workington FC, 120
World Cup, 11, 58, 65-6, 68-70, 75-6, 79,
    107
Wrexham FC, 48
Wright, Billy, 66-8, 71, 120
Wynne-Morgan, David, 71

Yeats, Ron, 170
Yeovil Town, 62
York City, 160, 186, 192
Young, Willie, 91, 120

Zagalo, Mario, 76